Montagu Burrows

The History of the Foreign Policy of Great Britain

Montagu Burrows

The History of the Foreign Policy of Great Britain

ISBN/EAN: 9783337338633

Printed in Europe, USA, Canada, Australia, Japan

Cover: Foto ©ninafisch / pixelio.de

More available books at **www.hansebooks.com**

THE HISTORY

OF

THE FOREIGN POLICY OF GREAT BRITAIN

BY

MONTAGU BURROWS

CHICHELE PROFESSOR OF MODERN HISTORY IN THE UNIVERSITY
OF OXFORD, AND FELLOW OF ALL SOULS;
CAPTAIN, R.N.; F.S.A., ETC.
"OFFICIER DE L'INSTRUCTION PUBLIQUE," FRANCE

NEW EDITION, REVISED

WILLIAM BLACKWOOD AND SONS
EDINBURGH AND LONDON
MDCCCXCVII

All Rights reserved

PREFACE
TO THE SECOND EDITION

THE favour with which this Course of Lectures has been received has encouraged the author to bring out a Second Edition at a lower price. The principles of British Foreign Policy, the history of which has been traced in these pages, have been most remarkably elucidated by events since the First Edition was published—more than a year ago. It is hoped that in this more accessible form a still wider circle of readers may now take an interest in the subject.

M. B.

September, 1897.

PREFACE

TO THE FIRST EDITION

THE field of English history has been of late so vastly enlarged that it has become necessary to supply the public with numerous supplementary works dealing with its special departments. The present volume, commenced some years ago, attempts to trace one of these continuous threads in the warp of the history, and to draw it out, as far as possible, distinct from the general story of the nation. This, from the nature of the case, can only be an imperfect process. While presupposing on the part of the reader a considerable knowledge of history, it was yet found impossible to elucidate the continuous progress of British policy without reviewing the course and connection of many events which surrounded and shaped that progress, and which lie within the provinces of Domestic or Foreign History. If, then, certain chapters should seem to suggest the more fitting title of a " History of England with special relation to its foreign policy," it cannot be helped. But the method has its advantages. To quote treaties, protocols, and despatches except by way of the briefest reference, to discuss technical rules of the law and comity of nations, would be to invade the frontiers of International Law and Diplomatics. By the general reader the march of Foreign Policy will be more clearly discerned in the light of the history which he knows than in the darkness of the sciences of which he is ignorant.

The main purpose of this work has been to show the continuity, the continuous development, of British Foreign Policy. Now and again distorted, or even reversed, by dynastic interests, by careless diplomacy, by erratic statesmanship, by ecclesiastical dissensions, by foreign rivalry, by stress of circumstance, it has always reverted—as it ever will revert—to the course prescribed by nature and approved by experience. England, this " precious gem set in the silver sea," held a post of vantage unparalleled among the nations. " True to herself " and to her natural destinies, she has endured and prospered. This fortress-isle of Britain, safely intrenched by stormy seas, confronting the broadest face of the Continent, and, later on, almost surrounding it with her fleets, was, and was not, a part of Europe according as she willed. First appearing in the dawn of history as the mysterious Ultima Thule, planted somewhere out in the Western Ocean, she grew to observe more and more closely from her watch-tower the strife of the Continent, and, as her expanding interests dictated, to interfere as a belligerent, an ally, or an arbiter. Yet deeply implicated as she became in the Balance of Power in Europe, she never lost sight of her strong position as an extra-Continental Power,—a position which, as her navy, her commerce, and her colonies grew, expanded into that of a world-wide maritime empire. The development, the oscillation, and the reconciliation of these two principles of national policy form the chief elements of the present work.

On certain points the author has necessarily repeated views already published in his "Commentaries on the History of England." Moreover, a few pages have been transferred from two of the author's books: from "Imperial England," which has long been out of print, and from the "Life of Admiral Lord Hawke," which is about to appear in a cheaper edition, without the introductory matter from which the extracts are made.

CONTENTS.

CHAP.		PAGE
I.	THE PRINCIPLES OF BRITISH FOREIGN POLICY BEFORE AND DURING THE REIGN OF ELIZABETH . . .	1

    Early foundations—The four invasions—An indelible mark—Necessity of a standing Navy and of Continental alliances—Early kings were Continental potentates—English Navy best of the time—The Flemish Alliance—Rise of "Balance of Power"—England the first consolidated State—Cause of the adoption of the system by Henry VII.—Henry VIII. and Elizabeth extend it—For her a necessary policy—Her motives and means of action—The effects of her Foreign Policy.

| II. | BRITISH FOREIGN POLICY UNDER THE STUARTS AND CROMWELL . . . . | 14 |

    The Stuarts reverse Elizabeth's policy—The causes of this reversal—The ideas of Henri IV. and Sully—Balance held by France—Charles I. adopts his father's errors—Cromwell supports France instead of Spain—The Dutch wars—"The Honour of the Flag"—The Barbary Pirates—The restored Stuarts pensioned by France—French attempt to ruin both Dutch and British—Holland ceases to be a Great Power.

| III. | BRITISH FOREIGN POLICY UNDER WILLIAM III. . . | 25 |

    Tudor Balance resumed by William III.—The national service performed by the Whigs—The "Deliverer"—Fine conduct of the English people—Unity of the British Isles recovered—Ireland—Scotland—William secures the Channel—His headship of the Allies—The Partition Treaties and the Mediterranean—Louis XIV. grasps at the Spanish, and then at the British, Empire—And so ruined France—Great Britain accepts the challenge—The state of the Continent at William's death—The Balance loses its dominant religious character—The German States near the Rhine—The Allies of Great Britain—The Balance had proved its usefulness.

IV. BRITISH FOREIGN POLICY IN THE EARLIER PART OF
THE EIGHTEENTH CENTURY 42

Marlborough at the head of the Allies—Tranquillity of Ireland—Union with Scotland—The Dutch portion of the Allies—Success of Marlborough's early campaigns—War of the Spanish Succession—Systematic defence of the Mediterranean—Failure of the Allies in Spain—Capture of Gibraltar—Its importance compared with that of the battle of Blenheim—Effect of capture on France and Spain—George I. undervalued it: the English people never did—Spanish siege of Gibraltar—British control of the Mediterranean—Spain and Great Britain in the West Indies—The British Colonies in America—Their relations to the mother country—Treaties between Great Britain and Spain—Spain exercises the "Right of Search"—A highly complicated history—"Jenkins' ear" no fable.

V. THE EVENTS WHICH LED TO THE WAR WITH SPAIN IN
1739 58

Walpole's peace-policy—Blockade of Porto Bello—Catastrophe of Hosier's fleet—Secret Treaty between France and Spain—France under Cardinal Fleury—Great Britain withdraws from Continental affairs—High spirit of the British Colonists—Walpole takes no notice of the Spanish "Right of Search"—Systematic smuggling—Change from quasi-free to restricted trade—The Assiento—Working of the new system—Hopelessness of improving the system—Incessant insults from Spain—War becomes necessary—The "Patriots" in Parliament—Petitions—Walpole begins to give way—His disgraceful conduct—Attacked on all sides—Address to the Crown—Walpole's final blunders—The statesmen and poets who roused the country—He declares war—Is forced to resign—Burke's statements accounted for—Gloom of the succeeding period—Provocation on the part of France—The war was just and necessary.

VI. BRITISH FOREIGN POLICY DURING THE WARS WHICH
FOUNDED THE EMPIRE—1739–1763 87

Recapitulation of previous history of subject—Ships, colonies, and commerce—Dangers besetting Great Britain and her Colonies—Deplorable state of the Royal Navy—Efficiency of the Navy, the keystone of the national success—The Army could not as yet keep step with the Navy—George II. and Hawke—Alliance with the Low Countries—Hanover and Holland—Melancholy prospects—The Rebellion of 1745—Ireland under Lord Chesterfield—Militia organised at last

—Pitt and George II. at the crisis—Anson and Hawke—
Pitt's failures at first—Prussia and Frederick the Great—
Pitt's relation to the officers in command—A "nation of
shopkeepers"—The Treaties of the period—International
law—British American Colonies first object of attack—Continued during the Peace after 1748—Also upon India, Africa,
and the West Indies—A French America—Nova Scotia—
British outwitted by France and Spain—Who attempt to
close the Mediterranean—British government of her Colonies
—The Seven Years' War and its effects.

VII. BRITISH FOREIGN POLICY FROM THE CLOSE OF THE
SEVEN YEARS' WAR TO THE OPENING OF THE
FRENCH-REVOLUTION WAR—1763-1789 . . . 115

The Peace of Paris in 1763—Changed relations with the
American Colonies — Principles involved — Revolt of the
Colonies — European allies of the Colonists — Views of
George III.—Peace of Versailles in 1783—Effects of the
war—The Armed Neutrality—The rise of Russia—Relations
between Great Britain and Turkey—Plots of the Empress
Catherine and the Emperor Joseph II.—Frederick the Great
interposes—Turkey saved by Pitt—Pitt's Foreign Policy—
Portugal—Position of Britain before the great war—Explicit call to resume the old position in Europe—Modern
attacks on this policy—History coloured by Reform-Bill
politics.

VIII. BRITISH FOREIGN POLICY DURING THE FRENCH-REVOLUTION WAR—1793-1800 136

Pitt's views on the French Revolution—War forced by
the French—Pitt forced to accept—It could not be evaded
—The old Foreign Policy renewed—Naval Supremacy—
Descents on French coasts — Foreign subsidies — British
Credit—Law was king—Efficiency of Navy—French Navy
demoralised—The Armed Neutrality again—Failures in
Holland — Military superiority of France — British army
slowly improved—Pitt's war-policy unfairly treated—Condition of Ireland—Torn by factions—Rebellion of 1798—The
Union—India—The Colonies—Patriotism of the Old Whigs
—Scotland—The British Allies—The policy of Subsidies—
Condition of the European States—War a question of
finance—Posterity was to pay the balance—Pitt's futile
attempt to make peace—British Allies conquered—Mutinies
in Royal Navy—Battle of Camperdown—Napoleon in Egypt
—Nelson and Sidney Smith—Napoleon's *coup d'état*—He
turns on Austria and Russia—British refuse peace—The
Netherlands.

IX. BRITISH FOREIGN POLICY DURING THE NAPOLEONIC
WAR—1800–1807 165

    Napoleon as First Consul—His reforms—His fresh victories—The Armed Neutrality again—Acceptance of some of its principles—Peace of Amiens—Napoleon's acts during the Peace—Prepares to invade England—The "*Detenus*"—Rupture of the Peace—Europe required certain lessons—British preparations for defence—Efficiency of the naval defence—Pitt resumes office—Napoleon's strategy—British resume their old strategy—Napoleon's first plan—Disposition of the British fleets—Nelson's defective blockade of Toulon—Napoleon's second plan—His third plan—His final plan—French and British strategy compared—Villeneuve escapes—Nelson in pursuit—His foresight—Calder's action—Villeneuve loses his chance—Nelson's strategy—Trafalgar—A new era in the war—Motives of Napoleon's policy—Austerlitz and Pitt—British commerce—Mahan's treatment of the subject—Hard but necessary fate of neutrals—Depots for British goods—Growth of British resources—They desire peace—But resolve to fight it out—Struggle was not with French people, but with Napoleon.

X. BRITISH FOREIGN POLICY DURING THE NAPOLEONIC WAR
(*continued*)—1807–1808 198

    System of Subsidies broken up—How to supply its place?—Failure of Pitt's successors—Abolition of the Slave-trade—English responsibilities for slavery—Canning's training under Pitt—His special merit—Napoleon and Spain—The "Spanish ulcer"—Canning's Peninsular policy the outcome of his popular sympathies—Seizure of the Danish fleet—Defence of that act—The state of the Baltic—The "Continental System"—French seizure of Portugal—British "Orders in Council"—Their concentration of trade—Effect of French policy on the Continent—Seizure of Spain—Canning accepts the challenge—His reasons—The secret of his power.

XI. BRITISH FOREIGN POLICY DURING THE NAPOLEONIC
WAR (*continued*)—1808–1814 219

    Sir Arthur Wellesley succeeds Canning as representative of Great Britain, after a period of discontent—Torres Vedras—Revival of European spirit—Gloomy prospects of the French—The resistance of Russia, which suffers under Continental System—Tempted by the war in Spain—Austria and Prussia—Invasion of Russia—Wellington's advance—The Russian strategy—The catastrophe—Rising of Europe

—The War of Liberation—The Truce fatal to Napoleon—
Allies defeated at Dresden—Napoleon defeated at Leipsic—
Rising of the West Germans—Diplomatic difficulties—Allies
press on—Wellington at Vittoria and in France—The Allies
cross the Rhine.

XII. BRITISH FOREIGN POLICY FROM 1814 TO 1827 . . 239

Napoleon's Abdication—The Bourbons—The new Charter
—Talleyrand—The Czar Alexander I.—Dismemberment of
France prevented—Napoleon's escape—Advances to Paris—
His strategy—Disadvantages on both sides—British made
fewest mistakes—Battle of Waterloo—The final Abdication
—St. Helena—Estimate of the two generals—The Congress
of Vienna—Moderation of the Allies—The Kingdom of the
Netherlands—The Treaty of Vienna—Continuity of British
Foreign Policy—Its course inevitable—The American War of
1812—Its causes—Foresight of the American Government
—Results—The "Holy Alliance"—Canning's return to office
—Oppression of Spain, Greece, Italy, and Poland—Reactionary Congresses—Canning deals with Spain and Portugal
—And then with Greece—Congress of Verona—Battle of
Navarino.

XIII. BRITISH FOREIGN POLICY AFTER 1827 . . . 261

The Turks in Europe — Virtual Protectorate of Great
Britain—The "Eastern Question"—Troubles in the Peninsula—Separation of Belgium and Holland—Final services
of Talleyrand — Palmerston pursues Canning's policy —
Question of Intervention — The "Spanish Legion" —
Triumph of Constitutionalism—The Slave-trade abolished
—The state of Italy—Austrian influence—Secret Societies
—Pio Nono and Garibaldi—Victor Emmanuel—Louis Napoleon — Palmerston and Cavour — French intervene —
They annex Savoy and Nice—Garibaldi in Sicily and Naples—
Victor Emmanuel "King of Italy"—Palmerston's policy
truly British—Defence of it—Poland, Switzerland, Portugal
—Egyptian invasion of Turkey—Attitude of French and
British towards Turkey—Crimean War—Beaconsfield and the
"Eastern Question"—Russia and Great Britain in the East
—Pacific rivalry of the Powers in Africa—British Colonies
—The British in Egypt—Conclusion.

INDEX 289

THE HISTORY

OF THE

FOREIGN POLICY OF GREAT BRITAIN.

CHAPTER I.

THE PRINCIPLES OF BRITISH FOREIGN POLICY BEFORE AND DURING THE REIGN OF ELIZABETH.

THE Foreign Policy of Great Britain has no doubt become more plainly visible, less interrupted, more easy to follow, since the Middle Ages, but we are apt to lose sight of the fact that its origin lies in the circumstances of the Norman Conquest. Its gradual development has not been due to the ambition of particular dynasties or sovereigns, the incitement of ministers, the passions of the people, or the growth of colonies, but to the necessities of self-defence. Every part of British Foreign Policy is, indeed, reducible to the one fundamental fact that Great Britain is an island, and, we may add, an island which lies so close to Ireland that it has been proved impossible to consider them as separate countries. *Early foundations.*

Again, an unfortunate delusion prevails that the modern attitude of Great Britain towards other nations is a thing of yesterday. That is the consequence of too narrow a view of English history. The reigns of the four Stuart kings form such a contrast to the reigns which followed that we are apt to forget the policy of their predecessors. It is not till we have learnt to regard the conduct of the Stuarts as exceptional, as a contrast to what went before as well as to what followed after, as a *gran rifiuto*, an apostasy from the English traditions, that we can take in the whole sweep of history. Henry VII., Henry VIII., and Elizabeth, under the new circumstances of their times, fairly represent those traditions, those laws, those unwritten laws from which the Stuarts diverged. But this introductory sketch requires that we should ascend higher still, to the Normans and Plantagenets.

The problem which presented itself as primary and elementary to the conquerors from beyond the sea, and all the more when they began to amalgamate with the already mixed race which they had conquered, was how to prevent any such catastrophe from occurring again. Four invasions of Britain had been successful. The Romans had conquered the original Celtic settlers; the Anglo-Saxons had conquered the Romanised Britons; the Danes the Anglo-Saxons; the Normans the Danes and English. For more than a thousand years the British Isles had been a prey to one invader after another. The dividing sea formed rather an advantage to the attack than to the defence. With a sparse population and often a feeble government, no one could tell where the enemy would make the assault, and the organisation of a navy sufficient for the patrol of the seas was rare indeed. The resistance of the islanders was generally stubborn, and even heroic,

The four invasions.

but in each of the four cases the defenders were overborne.

These conquests had left in the mind of every man, woman, and child in the island an indelible mark; for the misery which had ensued in each case was terrible—terrible not only from individual suffering, but from the changes in laws, language, and land-tenure which accompanied it. Hence, after the Norman Conquest, we see that a common danger to conquerors and conquered alike united them in measures of defence and political order much more quickly than might have been expected; and the main principles of national defence which have been handed down from those times became a fixed policy. They were two in number. A standing naval force must be organised under the Crown; and alliances must be maintained with the neighbouring Continental Powers which were opposed to the enemies of England. The last of these two political doctrines resolved itself for many centuries into the requirement that the coasts extending opposite to the south-eastern shores of England should be, if not in the hands of the English sovereign, at least in the hands of friends.

An indelible mark.

Necessity of a standing navy and Continental alliances.

These are still fundamental principles. The Norman and Plantagenet monarchs represented the last requirement in their own persons. The territories they possessed in the land of the Franks, which was then a congeries of practically independent States, added to their insular possessions, gave them at first a decided superiority over the French kings, but of course forced them into almost incessant hostility with the growing monarchy. Thus the kings of France came to be the hereditary enemies of the

Early kings Continental potentates.

English; and, as they incorporated more and more of their own feudal States, developed in their turn a superiority which at last settled the question. But it was a long process. For three centuries an almost independent Aquitaine and a scarcely less independent Brittany grievously blocked the way of the French monarchs.

The English left the matter to their kings, who were overweighted in the conflict, till parliamentary government brought the people generally to a different view of their obligations. Periods of fluctuation, owing very much to the varying character of the kings on both sides, marked these centuries; but the above principles of defence, though now and then sorely tried, answered their purpose. The expedition of Louis, Prince Royal of France, was rather the effect of a political alliance with an English party than a national invasion; and though in Richard II.'s feeble reign sundry coast towns were burnt, no invasion of England took place either then or ever since. The navy may seem to us to have been insignificant, but it was better than that of other nations. The "Royal Navy of the Cinque Ports" was permanently at the disposal of the Crown; and when need arose it was supplemented by the king's ships. And, further, the intimate English relations with Flanders which had begun before the Conquest, as well as the far less intimate relations with Brittany, supplied the want of direct power which the earlier hold upon Normandy had given. For neither Normandy nor Picardy had sufficiently good ports or length of seaboard to be very dangerous enemies, while the Low Countries were inhabited by races of much the same

English navy best of its time.

nationality as the English, and were closely united by the bonds of trade and commerce. The customers of the English occupied the great Flemish towns, and were generally superior to their feudal lords, who were supported by the French. So the basis of a very useful alliance was always at hand. The French were peculiarly vulnerable on the Flemish frontier, and when Edward III. enforced the ancient right of the English to the Sovereignty of the Seas, his claim was acknowledged as a matter of course by the people of the Low Countries and of Brittany.

The Flemish alliance.

Thus, as the centuries rolled on, whatever alliances were made with the Emperor, with Spain, or with other Continental Powers, were made against France. This was a very simple Foreign Policy. It was dictated by the necessity of keeping England free from invasion, and by the difficulties involved in the retention of the provinces which came to England with the Normans and Plantagenets. By the middle of the fifteenth century these provinces had been torn away from England and united to France. The Plantagenet dynasty was worn out; and it was reserved for a stronger family to formulate the system of Balance of Power, which was to place the protection of England on a more civilised basis.

Rise of Balance of Power.

The new system could not of course be formed until its materials had come into existence. The fifteenth century witnessed the arrival of France, Spain, and Germany at a position of unity analogous to that which England herself attained about this time. The conquest of Wales, the lordship of Ireland, and the diplomatic management of Scotland, due to the sense of the Edwardian failures to

Consolidation of States. conquer that country, gave a certain solidarity to the Island-State. Spain was consolidated by the union of Castile and Aragon, France by the absorption of Gascony, Provence, and Brittany, and Germany by the measures of Maximilian. Each of these States now started on a fresh career, and the Foreign Policy of England came to be summed up in the doctrine that it was her business to balance them one against the other, and so provide for her defence by diplomacy instead of war. For this purpose she must be united at home and strong on the sea. Hence the development of the Royal Navy.

We need not stop here to register the part played by the principle of Balance in the earlier history of the world, the remarkable exemplification of it in the ancient States of Greece, the necessary abeyance of it during the many centuries of the Roman Empire, or the smaller adumbrations of the principle in the Middle Ages by the policy of the Popes, who learnt to look for the safety of the Papal States in balancing their German enemy by the Sicilian Normans, or other Italian States, or France. Nor in mentioning the adoption of the principle by Henry VII. and his son, must we for a moment compare the steady, practical application of it by Elizabeth with the tentative and shifting policy of her father and grandfather. Nevertheless that policy led the way to Elizabeth's successful diplomacy; and we must notice the work of each before we come to the Stuarts, who broke through the Tudor traditions.

The chief difference between her combinations and those of her predecessors is to be found in the changes made by the Continental Reformation, which were only beginning to show themselves towards the end of Henry VIII.'s reign; but the real cause of the system attaining its extraordinary development in Europe is to be found in the advent of the Emperor Charles V. to power. Universal empire could only be warded off by State-combinations. The meaning of the term Balance of Power is really Self-Defence; it is not too much to say that it has been the saving of Europe. When it had done its work the term fell into disrepute. It was open to abuse, and was abused; but it has been succeeded by an international system of much the same sort under a different name, by International Law, by the "Concert of Europe," by arrangements made at Congresses for the smaller by the greater Powers, and to some extent, though still but feebly, by arbitration. *Cause of the adoption of the system of Balance.*

Henry VII.'s experiences before he came to the throne had taught him the necessary statesmanship for the work which lay before him at the very time when the consolidation of States was achieved or being achieved, and was producing its national effects. To his training in exile, to his long residence in France, and to his wise choice of ministers must be attributed his adoption of the policy of Balance which had indeed been initiated by France and Spain. The collapse of Brittany about that time, and the Yorkist hostility of Flanders to Henry as a Lancastrian, had broken up the ancient, well-accustomed barriers of England against France; for by the aid afforded on either side of Calais, the invasion of France by that route had been, and was part of, the political defence of England. Very soon afterwards, however, came the diversion of French *Henry VII. saw his opportunity.*

enterprise (1494) in the direction of Italy, and the struggle in that peninsula between the three consolidated nations, Spain, France, and Germany. Henry VII. seized the opportunity, and definitely commenced the *Balance of Power*, which Elizabeth, surely not unconsciously, as some have said, but deliberately, advanced to the dignity of a system.

A few words on the method of working that system under the Tudors will display the gradually unfolding Foreign Policy of England before the Stuarts departed from it, and by so doing helped to destroy their family. Henry VII.'s Foreign Policy is often described as a mere outcome of his ambition to secure his dynasty by forming the closest possible alliance with Spain, which was the rising Power of the world. No doubt that country was alive from head to foot; the expulsion of the Moors and the discovery of America seemed to point her out as the leader of the nations, and her conquest of South Italy gave her the command of the Mediterranean. This is quite true as far as it goes, but it is much more important to note that Henry regarded that great Power as the best means of making up for the loss which England had sustained by the unification of France. This was the efficient cause of his policy. The ancestral enemy which had expelled the English from their hereditary possessions in Aquitaine, and now exhibited itself as a compact France, was to be kept in check by Spain in the south; and the coasts of the Netherlands, which were now divided between Germany and France, were to be kept secure by balancing these Powers against each other in the north.

The union of Spanish and German interests which came to exist in the Low Countries, through the marriages of Maximilian and his son greatly added to the weight of Spain, and forced France itself, when Charles V.'s imperial position became more and more alarming, to seek her safety in occasional alliances with England. Thus, before religious con- *Henry VIII.* siderations began to exercise influence on inter- *and Eliza-* national politics, the Balance of Power, though *tended it.* definitely formed, but by no means as yet an elaborate system, only required sovereigns of sufficient ability in England and France to substitute its principles for an endless war of revenge and mutual injury between the two countries which bordered the English Channel. These sovereigns were found in the English Henry VII., Henry VIII., and Elizabeth. But the French were not much behind the English; for to them, under the impending weight of Charles V.'s position, the art of Balance became a matter of life and death. Nor was Francis I. afraid to apply the idea in a way which was then thought scandalous, an alliance with the Turks; it had become a necessity. It should also be observed that the system was synchronous with the Renaissance, with scientific diplomacy, and with international law, of which Venice was the first exponent. Thus it took root.

In the Tudor reigns, then, we trace the same outlines of Foreign Policy, the religious question coming forward as a chief ingredient in the last part of Henry VIII.'s reign and the whole of Elizabeth's. We do not of course enter here into the details of Henry VIII.'s fluctuating alliances—first with Spain against France, then with France against the powerful Emperor Charles V. (who had come to hold the greatest empire known since the days of

Charlemagne), and then with the Emperor against France. It is, however, necessary to observe that the balance which he and Wolsey effected gave a time of rest and progress to England which exercised a vast influence on the spread of the Reformation, and made the system acceptable to the English people. The great increase of intercourse between the German and the English reformers, just at the moment when such intercourse was required, is not often noticed as it deserves to be. The translations of, and commentaries on, the Bible made abroad thus found an entrance into English towns and seats of commerce, and paved the way for the anti-Papal movement which accompanied Henry's growing quarrel with Rome over the question of his divorce from Catherine of Aragon.

Passing over the exceptional but happily short reigns of Edward VI. and Mary, during which France recovered all that England had previously gained, we come to the policy of Elizabeth, which exemplified the doctrine on a large scale and in a complete manner. She found herself in an infinitely more dangerous position than that of her father and grandfather. Mary's marriage with Philip II. of Spain, and his succession soon afterwards to his father's enormous empire — still enormous, even though the Empire properly so called had been assigned to his uncle Ferdinand,—had been followed by Mary Stuart's marriage to Francis, who almost immediately afterwards became King of France. Thus both of the great Roman Catholic Powers which Elizabeth had to fear stood at her very doors in a position hostile to her government. Philip having made an offer of his hand to Elizabeth, and been firmly refused, became her enemy for the rest of his life, and turned to Ireland as the best entrance to England. The French king and his beautiful Scoto-French wife actually quartered the arms of England with their own. Elizabeth's policy was then settled for her at once, by necessity; for England was as yet no match for these two Powers united; and the doctrine of Balance, already familiar, came to her rescue. They must be played off against one another; and this she contrived to do by every device in her power, aided by the ablest ministers a Crown ever commanded, for the rest of her life.

A necessary policy for Elizabeth.

A reign of nearly forty-five years by such a consummate sovereign did much more for the Balance of Power than the rudimentary efforts of Henry VII. and Henry VIII., both of whom were constantly baffled by the mistakes of their ministers, and by the astuteness of the Continental sovereigns. Elizabeth's rigid economy and careful administration enabled her to shun the rocks on which they had run, to satisfy her people that she would not tax them more than she could possibly help, and to rise triumphant over every obstacle. The struggling Protestants of Europe wanted a head, and though she took care never to help them except in extremity, they knew well that they could trust her if affairs became desperate. And this new element of the Balance, religion, which weighed but little under her father, now became a leading factor in the necessary combinations. Both in France and Germany the Reforming party rose in arms against their Papist persecutors, and the religious wars which took place in both countries were the salvation of England while it remained in Elizabeth's hands.

Her policy of declining to give any further assistance than was absolutely necessary has been severely attacked by various writers, but it was largely due to the penetration of a highly educated mind, trained in critical times, which taught her the wide difference between the Anglican Reformation, based on the practice of the Primitive Church and the Bible, and the new Protestant departure of Calvin, which broke altogether with antiquity, and recognised the Bible not only as the ultimate reference, but as the sole guide of religion and politics.

Her motives and means of action. Elizabeth knew also the importance of not exasperating the moderate Roman Catholics both in Court and country, who were, as the saying goes, Englishmen first and Papists afterwards. Nor did she forget that, being a woman, she had resources which gave her a peculiar advantage; and by encouraging different suitors at different times, as policy dictated, she accomplished what armies and navies would have failed at that time to do. These were her chief motives and means of action. We are not bound to defend them all alike, but at any rate they were so satisfactory to her people that it was dangerous for any successor to pursue a different course. Englishmen had learnt to feel that they were themselves an integral and necessary part of the Continental system: they were proud of holding the Balance of Europe, and of holding it so cheaply. Their commerce was rapidly growing, and the nations which would have checked it found themselves incapable of hostile action. Prospects of American colonisation were opening out in many directions. The closely guarded New World of Spain was pierced again and again by Hawkins, Drake, and the nautical chivalry of England; the Armada had called forth the whole skill and energy of the seafaring population, and by the end of the reign this imposing Spanish empire, which had sprung up like Jonah's gourd, had shrunk and withered in premature decay.

Henry IV. of France had been saved from destruction by Elizabeth's aid; and though she detested and despised both his apostasy and his debauchery, she had established a lasting political friendship with her diligent pupil. He was still reckoning on her patronage to form his own Balance of Power when she died. Further, the Reformed people of the Low Countries had been saved from Spain, and yet prevented from falling into the hands of France; and thus the safety of the Channel was firmly established. Who could wonder that all this sank deep into the minds of the English people, that they bore with their queen's imperiousness and the occasional narrow escapes of the nation caused by the over-refinements of her statecraft, and that at her death they considered the Foreign Policy of the country to have been fixed for the future beyond recall by the successful Tudor policy of more than a century? It is hardly necessary to point out that this Foreign Policy was guarded and accompanied by the equally definite home policy of keeping the British Isles united, or at least as closely united as circumstances permitted. Whatever else happened, the foreigner was to find it as difficult to gain a footing in Scotland or Ireland as in England itself. The French were driven out of Scotland almost as soon as they landed, and the Spaniards in Ireland received no quarter.

The effect of her Foreign Policy.

Note.—For a more complete estimate of Elizabeth's place in history, see "Commentaries on the History of England."

CHAPTER II.

BRITISH FOREIGN POLICY UNDER THE STUARTS AND CROMWELL.

The Stuarts reverse Elizabeth's policy. THE country had no choice but to place James VI. of Scotland on the throne vacated by Elizabeth. The Foreign Policy of England, which now became "Great Britain," may be summed up as a reversal of that of Elizabeth; and the conviction of the nation to that effect had much to do with bringing on the Great Rebellion and the subsequent Revolution. The Stuart policy was an embodiment of James's favourite motto, "Beati Pacifici," accompanied by a criminal defiance of the British Constitution in the matter of Parliaments, and a leniency towards Romanism which ignored the hostility of the Papacy. It paved the way for the adoption of his system by the Stuart family to the third generation. The best ideas, if applied under circumstances which do not admit of them, become the worst possible. Toleration was excellent in itself; but the removal of those restrictions on the free exercise of Papal power, which had been found necessary in order to preserve the Reformation, was at that time, and for long afterwards, fatal. To assert the power of the Crown was a duty, if the corresponding duty of holding free Parliaments and protecting their privileges had been combined with it. Peace was the greatest blessing to humankind—"peace on earth, goodwill towards men"; but such is human nature, that peace can never be assured except by preparedness for war. If a nation is unwilling to fight for an honourable peace, other nations are sure to combine against it.

It was James's peculiar education and habits of mind which prevented him from perceiving these obvious propositions. Learned and thoughtful, he was pedantic and obstinate to the last degree. He was one of the best talkers in the world, and courtiers knew better than to contradict him; but when it came to action, the motives which swayed him were fear, prejudice, and private affection. Thus he was fooled by Spain throughout the whole of his reign. He never found out that his ministers were bribed till it was too late, and consequently he was made a mere tool or instrument on which that Power could play as it pleased. Never was any foreign minister more completely in command of the English Court and policy than Gondomar. He reported that the English were a nation of shop-keepers, ready to be bought and sold like goods over the counter. So low had the great England of Elizabeth already fallen. *The causes of this reversal.*

And yet this was a period when the Elizabethan policy was most especially needed. Without the patronage which she had granted to the German and French Protestants they were no match for the concentrated energy and power of the Popes, supported by Spain, Austria, and Bavaria. We can best perhaps understand how pressing the need was by studying in Sully's "Memoirs" the position of Henri IV. towards the Balance of Power. Sully *The ideas of Henri IV. and Sully.*

acknowledges that Elizabeth had been the instructress of his master and himself in that policy, and quotes her saying that "nothing could resist the union of France, England, Sweden, and Denmark, when in strict alliance with each other." It is remarkable that she did not mention Holland, which made in her reign its immortal struggle against Philip; but in Sully's list of the two European factions, as he calls them, it appears. On the one side, he says, were ranged the Pope, the Emperor, Spain, Spanish Flanders, parts of Germany and Switzerland, Savoy, and almost all Italy; on the other were France (a Roman Catholic Power), the British Isles, Denmark, Sweden, Venice, the United Provinces (as Holland was then called), and the other parts of Germany and Switzerland. The great Powers of western and northern Europe were to work towards a system which should put an end to this state of things, and form a general Council for the good of all. Each must be powerful enough to be respected by its neighbours, and each intimately concerned with the external policy of every other.

For this purpose each State must be internally strong and well-ordered, or independence would be impossible. Thus each was to have an interest in the prosperity of the rest. Together they were to impose peace and harmony on the smaller States, to impose it by force. The corollary from this proposition was that war must necessarily take place if any one of the greater Powers became too powerful to be bound by the public opinion of the rest, and proceeded to absorb neighbouring States in contempt of the Public Law. War and violence ought never to be resorted to without an absolute necessity. Sully excluded the eastern portion of Europe from consideration. "Poland, Prussia, Livonia, Muscovy, and Transylvania I do not take in."

What James I., in obedience to his misapplied motto, failed to do, what Henri IV. died before he was able to do, and what Sully formulated for posterity, Richelieu effectively did for Europe as it then was. He saved the Protestant princes of Germany, and established France for the first time, and not England, as the acknowledged holder of the Balance. England dropped out of consideration; and the comprehensive Peace of Westphalia in 1648 made no mention of her whatever. That famous treaty did however imply the principle of Balance, and the Peace of Utrecht in 1713 placed the very words in the forefront as part of its preamble. *Balance of Power held by France.*

The absence of England from her proper place as one of the Treaty Powers had a terrible significance. It was within a few months of Charles I.'s execution. No one knew whether the nation which had been the holder of the Balance would ever raise her head again; all respect for her Government had disappeared. She had become the laughing-stock of Europe. James had, under the influence of his own mean spirit and Gondomar's dexterous diplomacy, declined to help, either with men or money, the Elector and Electress Palatine, though their cause was not only that of fainting Protestantism against the crushing powers of the Papacy and its satellite monarchs, but was big with the most pressing danger to Great Britain, her safety, her commerce, and her prosperity. Lectures of advice perpetually read alternately to his children of the

Palatinate and to their destroyers, but followed up in no single instance by action, were the derision of all men. In vain the more gallant gentlemen of England and Scotland rushed abroad, and heroically attempted to stem the tide. What could individuals do? But their labours bore fruit. As soon as James died a Protestant leader appeared in Christian IV. of Denmark, and soon afterwards in Gustavus Adolphus; and the English and Scotch soldiers became in no small degree the leading spirits of the victorious Protestant forces. What sort of respect could these men entertain for the Stuarts, and how could they but join their enemies, or at least stand aside, when the Great Rebellion broke out?

Charles I. adopts his father's mistakes.

But it may perhaps be rejoined that James did go to war at last, just before he died. But on what account? A mere personal affair of Charles and Buckingham, who persuaded the king to take up the quarrel which they had brought on themselves by their absurd conduct in Spain. It was a miserable joke, which came to nothing; and Charles, on his accession, contrived to add a war with France to the existing one with Spain, so that he was at war with the two greatest Powers of Europe at once, without army or navy at his back. What could be worse than his and Buckingham's treatment of Rochelle and the French Huguenots?

We need not enlarge further on the Foreign Policy of Great Britain during the reigns of the first two Stuarts. But how was it that Cromwell did not perceive that the true Balance had changed, that the policy of Richelieu had elevated France far above its old position, and that Spain should rather have been the Power to receive support in

Cromwell supports France instead of Spain.

order to redress the Balance? This has often been asked; nor can it be accounted for on any grounds of reason, but rather from a desire to obtain popularity by attacking the old enemy of Elizabeth's time. But in fact Spain had never recovered from the disastrous war she had waged in those days against England and Holland; Austria instead of Spain had taken the lead in the aggressive movements which precipitated the Thirty Years' War; and France had emerged from that war so triumphantly that the tyrannical grandeur of Louis XIV. was the direct outcome of Richelieu's position. To Cromwell it was of course a temptation to share the spoils of Dunkirk and to appropriate the West Indian possessions of Spain, a convenient but short-sighted policy, laden with future troubles. The Balance of Power was lost; Spain never regained her place; while France became for a century and a half the one great threatening champion of the Papal system of Continental tyranny, and of rivalry with England in colonies and commerce. The old chronic state of almost continuous war between England and France resumed its terrible monotony. One or other of them would have to go down, and Cromwell's memory must bear its full share of the blame. As if to burn the lesson of a true English Foreign Policy more deeply into the English mind, the Restoration only added to the disgraces which the earlier Stuarts had inflicted on the country, and which Cromwell's success against the Dutch had brought out into full relief.

The three Dutch wars in the times of the Commonwealth and of Charles II. form an episode in the history of English Foreign Policy. They could *The Dutch wars an episode.*

hardly have been avoided, or at any rate not the first or second. The Dutch had made rapid strides in nautical power since their revolt from Spain, and their commercial interests had prospered at the expense of Spain and Portugal to such an extent that they would brook no rivalry. The claim of England to the Sovereignty of the Narrow Seas was the occasion of the quarrel which the Dutch themselves sought, with a full determination to fight it out. This ancient claim had sprung from the circumstances of the Norman Conquest, and had been asserted and defended by the Plantagenets and Tudors, while even in the miserable reign of James I., the ships of England, still governed by Elizabethan traditions, fired on the French ambassador's own ship for not saluting the flag. Of course it was not relinquished by Cromwell, and the Dutch knew that the refusal to salute would be made a cause of war.

Behind this, however, were the rivalries in commerce, proceeding to serious issues at Amboyna, and increasingly exhibited in all parts of the world. The Dutch and English were the only two people who could be called nations of seamen; they were also equal in courage and capacity; they had each passed through a desperate war in which they had gained military training and high military ideals. It was clear to both sides that the sooner the struggle was over the better. But the Dutch did not reckon on the extraordinary reserve of strength England possessed in the tried generals and colonels, who turned into admirals of the first capacity almost at a moment's notice. Excellent as the Van Tromps and De Ruyters were, they were overmatched by Blake,

Monk, Montagu, and their comrades, and the English ships were for once the superior war-vessels. This was partly owing to the fleets raised by Charles I.'s ship-money, and partly to the talents of the family of Pett, who were born shipbuilders, and set the fashion for Europe. Later on, the superiority in ships went over to France and Spain.

Never were fiercer battles fought than in those three Dutch wars. In the end the English retained the "honour of the flag," as it was called, the proud emblem of their dearly-bought Sovereignty of the Seas. But the two later wars in Charles II.'s reign were more concerned with the Balance of Power than the first, which was a mere bull-dog fight for superiority, carrying in its train imperial issues. However short-sighted Cromwell's policy, his success in that war, as in every other warlike operation undertaken during his headship of affairs, had, it must never be forgotten, the effect of re-establishing Great Britain and Ireland as one united Power—a Power which was no longer to be trifled with, as it had been for two generations. Now for the first time the Mediterranean Powers were given to understand that Great Britain was resolved to open out her commerce in that sea, and that if they could not suppress the piracy of the Barbary States, there was one country which intended to do so.

"The honour of the flag."

The British and the Barbary pirates.

It requires an effort of imagination to realise the immunity enjoyed in the sixteenth and seventeenth centuries by these barbarians, whose corsairs, during periods of British feebleness, made even the British Channel unsafe for traders. Even in the time of the early Hanoverian monarchy the prolonged peace made it impossible for British officers to obtain any distinction in their profession save by successful battles with these pests of mankind. The lessons taught them by Blake and Narborough were soon forgotten; the profits were enormous, the price of European slaves continuously remunerative. Neither France, Spain, nor Italy could afford the fleets which were necessary to engage the strong fortifications and well-equipped squadrons of Algiers, Tunis, and Tripoli; and the Knights of Malta, once the salvation of Europe, had sunk into imbecility. Thus Great Britain, under the noble leadership of Blake, honourably commenced her career in the Mediterranean, which, under the circumstances of the struggle with Louis XIV., developed into a policy of supremacy in that sea.

The Restored Stuarts pensioned by France.

The Restoration gave the Stuarts back to England, but only to act, like the first two monarchs of that dynasty, as beacons to denote the fatal shoals of politics. Nothing could have been more unfortunate for the generation over which they ruled, however useful to their country in the end, than their enforced education in France. Their banishment from England during the impressionable period of youth had produced much the same effect upon them as it had upon their ancestor, Mary Queen of Scots. They had learned to regard the world from a French point of view, and were prepared to accept Louis XIV. not only as a mighty protector, attracting by the force of personal dignity, despotic power, and a brilliant Court, but as the dispenser of funds available for guilty pleasures or political bribery. Still more had the religious question now come to be the leading factor in affairs; and the bigotry of their mother, like that of the Guise family in the case of Mary, left an impression which no efforts of the English tutors and companions placed around them by Clarendon were able to combat. Charles II. and James II. came back to their country neither English nor Scotch, but French; neither Churchmen nor Presbyterians, but Roman Catholics at heart; and, what neither their father nor grandfather had been, debauchees—of the French type.

Remembering these results of their sojourn in France, our surprise is not so much excited by the entire absence of the principles of Foreign Policy laid down by the Tudors, as by the fact that the restored princes remained so long upon the throne as they did. Instead of any notion of protecting the weaker Protestant States from the growing tyranny of Louis XIV., both princes became his pensioners, and both kept down the freedom and Protestantism of their subjects by all the means in their power. Parliaments became as corrupt as themselves—one even obtained the name of the "Pension Parliament," pensioned like the king by Louis,—and the only wars in which they engaged were instigated by Louis as a means of crippling the only rival he had to fear, the gallant Dutch. These he vainly attempted to conquer by land, and now resolved to conquer, by means of the pensioned English, at sea. Not indeed that the Dutch were unwilling to renew the contest with the English, which was by no means conclusively fought out by Cromwell. In this second furious war, Monk, Montagu, Prince Rupert, and James, the future king, inflicted such losses on the Dutch that Louis XIV., fearing his enemy would cease to exist, and so no longer be able to balance Great Britain and her navy

The French attempts to ruin the Dutch and the British.

if Charles should resist his influence, declared war with England to encourage the Dutch. His officers were however instructed not to interfere with effect; and both the combatants, soon perceiving that the policy of the French was the simple one of letting the sea-rivals destroy one another, patched up a peace.

The third war was waged on much the same grounds. Louis in 1674 directed his pensioned vassal Charles II. to finish off the struggle with his obstinate neighbours, and sent a French fleet to support the British; but he took care to do no more for them than he had previously done for the Dutch; and after more battles the last Peace was made, which again mulcted the Dutch in a large sum, and found them willing to relinquish the dispute as to the flag. These sturdy seamen now lost the great position which they, like the Spaniards previously, had held for nearly a century; and the field was left clear for the rivalry of Great Britain and France by land and sea.

<small>Holland ceases to be a Great Power.</small>

CHAPTER III.

BRITISH FOREIGN POLICY UNDER WILLIAM III.

HAPPILY for the world, the alliance between William of Orange and Mary, James II.'s daughter, commenced a new era of amity between the lately enraged combatants, and led to the united action of the two peoples, British and Dutch, under William III. In other words, the Revolution of 1688 once more opened up the way to the resumption and development of the Tudor Foreign Policy. The British Isles were to be strongly compacted under one Government; France, the disturber of the peace, was to be opposed by alliance with the oppressed States of the Continent; the British Channel to be secured by close union with Holland and the Austrian Netherlands. The fleet was to be increased to an extent which should make it more than a match for the revived, or rather new, navy of France; and England was to be the central figure in the array of the European resistance to Louis XIV. This Foreign Policy was to be sustained by Free Parliaments, from which supplies were to be obtained, and by the alliance of the Royal power with whichever of the two great parties, Whig or Tory, would join heartily with the Crown in the revival of the old policy. *Tudor Balance resumed by William III.*

These parties were sometimes united in that

cause, but much oftener opposed. The Whigs alone, on motives sometimes elevated, sometimes corrupt, threw their weight continuously and consistently into the scale of war, in the reigns of both William and Anne. It was they who had led the van in the deposition of James II.: it was they who determined to run any risks rather than allow him, or his family after him, to endanger the policy which they represented: it was they who, having earned a true and real right to the gratitude of the nation, kept their position for three generations, long after they had ceased to be necessary or even useful; and after breaking up into many feeble and discordant parties, had to give way at last when, under the wholesome influence of the two Pitts in succession, the foundation and subsequent defence of the modern British Empire took place.

<small>The service done by the Whigs.</small>

By the time of the English Revolution in 1688 Louis XIV. had come to the end of the first, the longest, and the only victorious period of his career. The League of Augsburg had just been formed with some trembling hope of at least checking his terrible march to universal empire. Europe had long cowered before him; one man, and only one, seemed capable of leading the Alliance, and he was overmatched. William saw plainly that his only chance of taking up the championship of Europe effectively was to do so as King of England. Nothing is more worthy of study than the processes by which the old Foreign Policy was revived,—the headlong self-destruction of James II., the patient prudence of his nephew, the disappearance of Monmouth as if to make way for William, the incapacity of the Irish Romanists, the fatal errors of the Grand Mon-

<small>The "Deliverer."</small>

arque, who allowed a transient offence taken by James to throw out all his military strategy, and leave the way open for William to effect a bloodless invasion.

Not one word too much has been said in praise of the benefit conferred upon England and the world by the Revolution. From the 5th of November 1688 dates the return of England to her old place,— the place assigned by Burke in the following words: "The Balance of Power has been ever assumed as the known common law of Europe at all times and by all Powers. In all those systems of Balance England was the Power to whose custody it was thought it might be most safely committed."[1] This is indeed a little too sweeping and rhetorical. Our survey of the Foreign Policy of Great Britain in the sixteenth and seventeenth centuries has shown plainly enough that England suffered an eclipse under the government of the four Stuart kings. To retrieve their errors, no matter at what cost of blood and treasure, became an imperative duty. How otherwise could the British Isles have escaped when all their allies were destroyed, or become the slaves of a tyrant, himself the slave of the Pope and the Jesuits? There were, and always have been, vulnerable points enough in the circumference of the British Isles. To turn the long line of coasts into a perpetual encampment, instead of warding off the enemy by sufficient fleets and by assisting Continental allies, was a policy only worthy of a child. The nation had long become aware of the evils of a departure from the principles entwined with its whole earlier history, and exemplified in chief by

England saved by the Revolution.

[1] Third Letter on a Regicide Peace.

the great Elizabeth. It remembered also only too well what it had suffered from the military tyrants of the Commonwealth who had achieved the liberty of the land, but substituted a slavery of their own.

Fine conduct of the English people.

Seldom have the English people presented a finer spectacle than at the Revolution. They would bear, not without frequent and sullen resistance, the wrongs they suffered from the restored Stuarts up to a certain point, but when, added to their ignoble Foreign Policy, and to the open breaches of the Constitution shamefully committed by Charles and James, the people found themselves exposed to an open undoing of the Reformation, they arose, we might say, as one man. But even yet they remembered their history in past times. They were most unwilling to proceed to extremities. If they could shuffle off the incorrigible James, and lodge him with his French relatives, it would be enough. They would brave the danger to which they would be exposed by his league with the enemies of Great Britain. Ashamed of the personal ill-treatment to which he had been exposed by the rough seamen of Faversham, they acknowledged William's treatment of him as befitting the circumstances. It was enough to disarm the royal traitor; they would go no further.

Again, they were quite aware that they must run many risks, suffer many indignities, pay vast sums of money, shed the blood of their best and bravest, in the cause which they deliberately adopted: but this was somewhat in the nature of sacrifice. They must give up something to secure the whole, and it was better to do so before the whole was lost. The Reformation had been founded in blood and martyrdom. Time had healed the wounds it had left. The spread of education and literature, small as it seems to us in these days, had convinced the people that they could not have done better; and the bitter fruits of even a reformed Romanism were only too patent to their eyes and hearts. And so the old Foreign Policy, the old processes of Elizabeth's reign were once more repeated. It seemed natural and glorious. It would be the safest course in the end.

The first thing—by far the most important thing —was to create once more the unity between the two British Isles which James II. had broken up. All the kings of England had perfectly understood that the separation of the two islands must mean the destruction of the larger. The smaller one was so close that it could not be neglected, and it was so small that it could only succeed in obtaining independence by the help of other Powers. Thus it had come to pass that as soon as Henry II. was free to act he settled it upon the political system of the day, under the feudal lordship of his English and Norman subjects. Thus also his Plantagenet successors used such limited forces as were at their disposal to govern the native Irish from the Pale as a centre, the only portion they could call their own. *Unity of the British Isles recovered.* *Ireland.*

During those times the earliest intruders from outside the limits of Ireland were the Bruces from Scotland, and the mischief they caused was a lesson for the generations which followed. The Civil Wars of the fifteenth century were Ireland's opportunity; hence the troubles which the Lancastrians experienced from Ireland while it was the stronghold of the House of York, of which the countenance given to Perkin Warbeck in Henry VII.'s time was the latest fruit. The Tudors, with their keen vision of politics, and their resolution to secure England by ranking her with the Continental Powers, saw that Ireland was their vulnerable side; and under painful experiences of the use which Spain could make of the island as a means of attacking England, subdued the whole of the native tribes, and brought them under the direct government of the Crown. James I. took the further step of providing for the defence and safety of the island by planting colonies from Scotland and England in the northern counties; and Cromwell found himself obliged, when he began to establish order after his ruthless victories, to carry further the same process, known as the "Cromwellian Settlement." Lastly, James II., the Roman Catholic pensioner of France, made no scruple of attempting to establish the French as the military defenders of the island against England. William's victories once more established English supremacy.

This sketch, simple and undeniable as it is, contains the alphabet of English relations with Ireland throughout the five centuries which ended with the Revolution. When at the end of the eighteenth century the French were once more called in by the Irish rebels, the time had plainly come for a more complete incorporation of the two islands than had previously existed. The so-called Grattan's Parliament had now of course to be dissolved, and a single Parliament in the greater island to be the one Parliament of both. Divided counsels had grievously endangered England, and constantly attracted her mortal enemies to Irish shores. It had been so for more than five centuries: it could be so no longer. Self-preservation was the one all-powerful argument, all-powerful over every other consideration of race or sentiment.

Like his predecessors, William had also to establish a practical unity with Scotland before he could deal with Foreign Policy from a secure basis. The personal union of the two crowns under James the Sixth of Scotland and First of England, was the direct consequence of the Tudor policy under which Henry VII.'s daughter Margaret was married to James IV. of Scotland; and that marriage made it more easy than it had previously been to establish during the next century, in a country which refused to be conquered, the necessary diplomatic influence. But a mere personal union, though a great step in advance, was very far short of an incorporate union; and the Great Rebellion, in which the outraged religious passions of the mass of the Scotch people, fostered and led by the soldiers who had been trained in the Swedish service, placed the Scotch on the side of the Parliament. This gave them a position such as they had not held since the battle of Flodden Field. But Cromwell's victory at Dunbar over Leslie in 1653, and Monk's remarkable government which succeeded it, had done much to restore the united action of both countries, and the death of Claverhouse, who represented the Stuart persecutions, removed the only impediment to the peaceful government of these fierce and warlike Presbyterians. William established his position by removing all the obstacles which had been placed in the way of a free exercise of the favourite form of religion; and Anne had no choice, when she formed the Union of 1706-7, but to establish and protect it from future assaults on the part of the English.

Scotland.

William secures the Channel.

Thus William's base was secured on the same principles as those of Elizabeth, but far more firmly than she had found possible. He then collected all the Continental allies who were available, with himself as king of England at their head, and confronted, by land and sea, the Autocrat of Europe. Louis had played into his hands. He had lost his opportunity of attacking William on his passage to England in 1688; and not only so, he was fatally ill-advised in allowing Ireland to be conquered without making effective use of his own fine fleet and finer admiral. When he perceived his error, he was still more mistaken in not leaving the admiral to his own judgment; for it can hardly be disputed that Tourville might have turned the affair of Beachy Head into a decisive victory. Admiral Herbert has been defended by one or two distinguished writers from the previous animadversions of Macaulay and almost all other authors, including Captain Mahan, but it is tolerably clear that Herbert was unequal to the situation in which his courageous exploits and political courage had placed him as William's first available admiral. Admiral Russell, though a no less unsatisfactory representative of the British Navy, did succeed in beating Tourville, who had only half his force, and who fought because Louis had ordered him to do so. Under the circumstances of the Revolution it was at first extremely difficult to find the right men for naval command. The seamen were distinctly with the Revolution, but the higher officers parted most reluctantly with the old *régime*.

However, by the efficient help of the Dutch fleet, William was at least able to keep the Channel clear of the French and transport his troops to Holland. This also was an essential condition of the renewed British Foreign Policy. The security of the Channel along the Dutch and Flemish coast was now provided for by the advantages of William's position; and at the head of the Protestant German principalities, assisted by the Danes, he fought battle after battle for the freedom of an enslaved Europe. Defeat made no difference to a man of William's cool resolution, leading troops like the English and Dutch, who were as obstinate as himself. Thus after the great struggles of Landen and Steinkirk, the victory of Namur convinced the French that the odds against them were too great. The Peace of Ryswick in 1697 marked the resumption of the old doctrine of Balance of Power, so long in abeyance, and of England's old place as its champion and director. *His military Headship of the Allies.*

Perhaps the best index of the revived Foreign Policy of Great Britain is to be found, later on in William's reign, in the Partition Treaties, in their subsequent failure, and in the violent revolutions of English sentiment. The Partition Treaties exhibit the system in its most mature form; but though natural enough to attempt, they represent an overstrained application of a good thing. Louis's position had been assaulted with such difficulty that the prospect of adding Spain to his dominions on the death of the imbecile monarch of that country was intolerable. The Continent was to be cut about and arranged under different sovereigns in order that the catastrophe might be averted. This hazardous policy, contingent upon secret treaties, was of so delicate a nature that we may fairly assume that *The Partition Treaties made for the sake of the Mediterranean policy.*

it would never have been entertained for the mere purpose of Balance. At the bottom of it lay the determination of the British Government not to allow their people or those of other northern nations to be excluded from the Mediterranean. Spain at that time carried Italy; the Levant trade would be ruined, and the maritime influence of other naval Powers would be crippled, perhaps destroyed, by the colonial preponderance which would be acquired by France. The first Partition Treaty was too decidedly against the interests of France to be permanent. She was only to have South Italy and the province of Guipuscoa,—which did indeed give her the means of coercing Spain,—while Spain, the Netherlands, and the Indies were to go to the Electoral Prince of Bavaria, a youth who was supposed to be less dangerous than the great kings; Lombardy was to go to the Archduke Charles. The death of the young Electoral Prince broke up the treaty. The second Partition Treaty gave Spain to the Archduke, who was to give up Lombardy to the Duke of Lorraine.

Spain bequeathed to Philip of France.

Both of these treaties, when discovered by the English people, not only found no favour for their attempt to secure English interests, but were believed to be entirely to the advantage of Holland and Germany. The Spaniards were still more disgusted at the way in which their country had been disposed of by these secret arrangements, and, in spite of the obvious danger of Spain becoming a province of France, the dying king was persuaded to leave his vast empire to Louis's grandson Philip, who was indeed the nearest heir. No scruples stood in the way of Louis. The treaties went for nothing in his mind, and he accepted the bequest at once, thus regaining for his House more than he had lost in the late wars. William's unpopularity in England at the time was such that he had to accept this entire failure of the plans of his whole lifetime, and retired to Holland, apparently to die, a victim to his patriotic schemes and lifelong struggles for the Balance of Power. He had placed Great Britain once more on her true standpoint of Foreign Policy, at the head of the European confederation, as the custodian of the Balance; he had healed the breach between the two great maritime nations of the same blood and temper, so lately furious rivals, and thus provided for the future redress of the Balance; he had set Great Britain and Ireland upon a course of united action; he had started at least the former upon a career of liberty, internal peace, and financial prosperity, and he had latterly recognised a great man, capable of fulfilling the destiny of the British people, in Marlborough, from whom he had been separated by the intrigues of the wife and evil genius of that prince of generals. Such must have been the consolatory retrospect of the hero; and it might have formed some compensation for the otherwise overwhelming sense of failure, even though he must have been well aware that the bitter feeling of the English had some justification in his immoral life, his shameless grants, and his morose attitude towards the islanders, whom it was clear that he only valued from political motives.

Louis XIV. grasps at the Spanish Empire,

But what a marvellous change do we witness in the very next year following upon the French acquisition of Spain for Philip. The death of James in 1701, and the immediate attempt to snatch the

and at the British Empire,

hoped-for prize of the British Isles by the recognition of the youthful Pretender as king, turned the English suddenly round to their old alarm and distress at the aggrandisement of the French, and revived their old sense of gratitude to their Deliverer. The adoption of the cause of James's son by Louis acted as if by magic. Its effect was surely a great compliment to the grand position which William had obtained. His death could not be long delayed; Marlborough's splendid genius was little known, or even suspected; and the influence of the Jacobites in England and Scotland was believed to be far stronger than it really was.

by which he ruined France.

The insatiable ambition of Louis was greatly reinforced by the increasing bigotry of his old age, and the low level of statesmanship at the Court, where servility had long been the passport to power and employment. If he could have used his long experience with any portion of his earlier vigour, he would have seen that his declaration of renewed hostilities could only have the effect of establishing Great Britain in the career upon which she had been set by William, and of destroying the fabric which he had himself so persistently reared on the ruin of his neighbours. He gave way to the temptation, and ruined France. Certainly that great nation has suffered enough from kings and emperors.

Great Britain accepts the challenge.

As Louis knew the value of time, he began at once by driving the Dutch garrisons out of the frontier towns, so that England had no choice. She rushed to war, to the renewal of the war which had already cost her so many millions of money and thousands of men. But she had seldom entered upon a conflict with her people more closely united.

Whigs and Tories, combined under their heroic king, now at last repaid him for all his labours. He hastened to place Marlborough in command of the allied forces in Holland, not only as the one capable man at his disposal, but as the friend of the Princess Anne, to whose one surviving son he had been governor. Thus every circumstance combined to make available the great man who was able to sustain the Balance of Power, and who was also the natural person to place in that position without exciting any reasonable jealousy. Faction was silenced by the acts of the common enemy. The processes of war and the support of war were still familiar and accustomed. Officers, men, and munitions were still at hand, tried and prepared. Again, as the young Duke of Gloucester died just before this time, it must have been no small satisfaction to William that the Succession to the Crown had been established by the Act of Settlement in the line which he had so strongly recommended. Though some of the provisions of the Act were distasteful enough to him, the choice of George as Anne's successor was of itself a decisive step towards securing the persistency of Foreign Policy which we have traced through preceding ages.

The termination of William's reign in March 1702, *Death of William III.* suggests that we should pause for a moment to review the condition of the Continent at the opening of the eighteenth century. We saw how the Elizabethan custodianship of the Balance of European States formed, after a long and checkered struggle of forty-five years, an established system which grew both out of former precedents and out of the immediate dangers which pressed so terribly and so visibly

The state of the Continent at William's death.

upon England that they could be surmounted in no other way. We saw how the Reformation, bringing not peace but a sword, had caused religious questions to assume an importance before unknown in the strife of politics. It was only the imminence of danger at the hands of Louis XIV. which stopped the tendency to make these religious questions the one cause of conflict throughout Europe. They still kept a great and important place, but only amongst other troubles. By degrees the default of England under the Stuart sovereigns convinced the Roman Catholic Powers, such as Austria, that if they were to retain any independence, they must stifle the religious sympathies which the Jesuits had revived, and join the Protestant Powers in the common cause against France. We trace the principle to France herself. France had never shown a scrupulous disposition on this point. Her long-descended "Gallican Liberties" had implanted a certain independence of the Papacy, and even a habit of defiance. In this respect Venice went along with her; and the vast influence of the great Venetian writer, Fra Sarpi, extended those sentiments over a large part of Europe. Francis I. had gone so far as to ally himself even with the Ottoman Turks, as well as with the Protestant Powers of Germany, against Austria; and the Huguenots, forming a great political power within the kingdom itself, seemed, under the leadership of Henri IV., to be about to turn France into a Protestant State.

That, indeed, was found impossible; but Henri IV., though he changed his faith to keep his crown, adopted, as we have seen, a policy of Balance which was to place France as well as England at the head of the Protestant States against Spain, Austria, and the other Papal Powers. His acceptance of the principle that the Balance was not to be exclusively Protestant as against Rome, but that even France, which would not accept a Protestant king, might lead it, was soon afterwards adopted by Richelieu, who placed the Protestant kings of Denmark and Sweden at the head of new combinations along with France, and by their help succeeded in bridling the Roman Catholic Powers of Spain and Austria. Thus it came to pass that France was prepared to mount to the headship of Europe under Louis XIV., who contrived to neutralise both Dutch and English until the Revolution of 1688. By this time, however, Austria also had learned the lesson. Bavaria, which had always kept steadily to the Papal side, had become formidable by erecting herself upon the ruins of the Palatinate, and threatened Austria by her frequent alliances with France. *The Balance loses its dominant religious character.*

None of the German Powers in the neighbourhood of the Rhine had ever been really incorporated with the Empire; the system of Circles was too loose to hold them together; and the division effected by the Reformation exposed them to intrigues from both the Imperialist and the French side. In fact, this system of facing both ways was ancient enough in Germany. It had always been so more or less since the break-up of the Roman Empire. The Rhine might seem to have formed a natural boundary between the Gallo-Franks and the central parts of the German Empire; but, in fact, it promoted the formation of independent States stretching from the North Sea to Italy; and the wars of Europe have to a great extent proceeded from the contentions *The German States near the Rhine.*

to which this circumstance has given rise. We trace it all through the Carlovingian period. Lotharingia or Lorraine was but the shrunken remains of a mighty though ill-compacted State, the *Regnum Medium* which so long haunted the fancy of diplomatists.

Once in later medieval history there seemed a probability of these provinces being moulded into a single middle kingdom between France and Germany under Charles the Bold, who brought Flanders and Burgundy to a threatening headship over the coveted remainder; but with the victories of the Swiss and Lorrainers over their rash invader ended all these projects, leaving the growing strength of France, Austria, and afterwards Prussia, to acquire such of the provinces as each could compass at the end of wars and treaties. The last revival of these ideas associates itself with Revolutionary and Napoleonic France, when, under the name of the "Confederation of the Rhine," was disguised the annexation by France of all the countries which lay between that Power and the great German States. How long it lasted we all know; and we have ourselves witnessed the success of the counter-move of Germany, which by the incorporation of Alsace and a part of Lorraine has settled the question of possession for this century at least. But the idea still survives in the neutrality of Belgium and Holland, Luxemburg and Switzerland.

The Allies of Great Britain.

Thus when William III. died the British allies included Austria, thoroughly alarmed for her existence, along with Holland, Flanders, and the Western German Powers. Russia and Prussia had not yet come on the stage, though they were about to do so. Peter the Great was already preparing to place himself amongst the Great Powers of Europe, and Prussia, bursting the shell of a mere Electorate of Brandenburg, was intent on appearing as a principal in the struggle which was impending. The Poles had hitherto played too great a part in Northern Europe to allow of any rapid expansion of these States; while the yoke of the Tartars had scarcely been as yet thrown off in the south and centre of Eastern Europe. But the Ottoman Empire, though used by Francis I. to form his scheme of Balance in the west, had, owing to the growing strength of Persia, gradually withdrawn from the system, and for a time could only pretend to a sort of balancing position in Eastern Europe, of which far less organised arrangement the Poles, Livonians, Prussians, and Russians formed part. We shall not be able to notice the merits and faults, the use and abuse of the Balance in the west of Europe till we arrive at the Peace of Utrecht. But we may at this break in our history call attention to the fact that the system with which Great Britain was so intimately concerned was no artificial product of a corrupt age, bad in initiation, futile in execution, and fatal in its legacy to subsequent ages, —and this is the way in which it has been described in recent years,—but the result of self-sacrificing and far-seeing public spirit, honourable to those nations and sovereigns who threw themselves into the ranks of its supporters, and in the long run beneficial to all their best interests.

Usefulness of the Balance of Power.

CHAPTER IV.

BRITISH FOREIGN POLICY IN THE EARLIER PART OF THE EIGHTEENTH CENTURY.

Marlborough at the head of the Allies. WE enter upon the more modern portion of our survey with the path made clear before us by the action of William III. In the very year of his death all the threads of his alliances were gathered up in the masterly hands of Marlborough, a Foreign Policy then considered by the nation as entirely its own. It was no longer—at any rate for a time—regarded as that of William and the Dutch, a policy which the English felt they ought to pursue as a duty, but which they feared would produce no immediate advantage to England itself. With a popular queen, "entirely English," they believed that affairs would wear a different aspect; and they were right. The clouds which had hung over Marlborough were soon, under the blaze of his great achievements, dispersed.

We see again the Home Policy, which was the necessary basis of the Foreign Policy, carried to a prosperous issue of a superior kind to that of the Tudor, or the Cromwellian, or the Revolution eras. *Tranquillity of Ireland.* Ireland was tranquil, though under the Penal Laws and the "Protestant Ascendancy,"—a painful system to contemplate, but a system which the recent Civil War between James II., the Pope, and the French on one side, and England on the other, had rendered necessary.

In Scotland William's government had left some rankling sores unhealed, especially his discouragement of the Darien expedition, and his refusal, when it failed, to right the sufferers. The injured sentiment of the Scotch found expression in various ways, and convinced Anne and her ministers that divided and independent national politics could no longer be permitted. The Union of 1706, concluded in 1707, was the result of English pressure put upon Scotland, a severe though pacific pressure, which the Scotch were unable to resist, and yet marked by a spirit of mutual accommodation which made it a model for the Irish Union under George III. It was a great step in the onward course of Great Britain, and required only to be supplemented by the resources of genius at the hands of the elder Pitt. All three portions of the British Isles now contributed to the enterprises undertaken for the whole, and Marlborough felt his rear secured, not only by land but by sea,—for the French made no attempt upon England such as those which failed in the time of William.

Union with Scotland.

Marlborough's allied forces were gathered together in the Netherlands, "the cock-pit of Europe." While he placed his main reliance on the British and Dutch, he commanded, like William, the troops of Hanover, Prussia, Hesse, and Denmark; and the Imperial troops under Prince Eugene of Savoy, as soon as they had secured their frontier on the side of Hungary and Italy, were preparing to operate on the Danube with the allied forces. Marlborough, in spite of the enormous difficulties attending upon the control of the alliance, established his superiority sooner than was expected. The troubles proceeded chiefly from the Dutch, who were no longer fighting under the Stadtholder-King who had formerly led them to battle. Crippled at last by the two tremendous wars for existence which they had waged against Philip II. and Louis XIV., this small but invincible nation had seen the commerce, by which they had been enabled to hold out, absorbed by the English, and not unnaturally declined to be for ever the cat's-paw of other countries. It would be enough for them to protect their own frontiers, and give a reasonable assistance to the allied forces which stood between them and destruction.

The Dutch portion of the Allies.

The dilatory measures and feeble instructions which now hampered the alliance would certainly have broken down the combinations of any one but Marlborough. He had, however, carried his point of making Great Britain a principal in the war, and not a mere auxiliary, as the Tory party desired; and thus, with his Whig friends in the War Offices, he obtained supplies, and triumphed over his enemies at home and abroad. Nothing short of this could have resisted the French, though their best marshals were no longer available, and Louis's great ministers had passed away. It was well that William had laid the foundation of a European resistance to the disturber of the Balance, and that a Marlborough was at hand to raise it to a still higher level under the headship of Great Britain. The capture of Venloo, Ruremonde, and Liége in 1702, of Bonn, Huy, and Limbourg in 1703, convinced Europe that important events were at hand; and happily the

Success of Marlborough's campaigns.

great Captain, who "never lost a battle nor failed to take a fortress," had contrived to shroud in secrecy the concerted movements which in 1704 led to the battle of Blenheim. The result of that splendid victory was to save Germany from the hands of France, of the subsequent victories to drive her out of Flanders. Nothing prevented the conclusion of the war at the gates of Paris but the party strife which prevailed in England, and the errors into which Marlborough was betrayed by the influence of his wife.

The effect of these unrivalled campaigns was to destroy the position which Louis XIV. had attained, to restore the European Balance, and to change the war with France into an external peace, during which the latter country secured her ends by statecraft much more fully than she had done by war. The actual gains of Great Britain derived from the successful campaigns of William III. and Marlborough sink into insignificance when compared with what might seem their legitimate reward; but we have to look further, and must notice the evidence of British Foreign Policy afforded by the War of the Spanish Succession. It is there that we shall find some compensation for diplomatic and political failures.

To forestall invasion, to redress for that purpose the European Balance, and to provide such a superior naval force as might keep the British Channel clear and protect British commerce,—these were the primary objects of the great war. The course of events had led up to a distinct policy of a further kind. Spain had become after the accession of Philip V. all but a province of France; and the Germans had a common interest with the British in

War of the Spanish Succession.

breaking up this union. The commerce of the latter in the Mediterranean had grown during the previous century to a great height in spite of the pirate squadrons of North Africa, to whom British officers, at the head of fleets, and Benbow in a private capacity, had read some impressive lessons. Turkey and Persia had discovered the benefits of the Western trade, and while Spain was independent, her energies, enfeebled by the Elizabethan victories, had been concentrated on the preservation of her American empire. Portugal, indeed, taught by her period of enslavement under Philip II., had formed quite recently a closer commercial union with Great Britain by means of the Methuen Treaty; but the policy of William III.'s Partition Treaties was as urgent as ever, and demanded the measures which were now taken in the Peninsula.

The policy of the Austrian Succession in Spain was at once proclaimed as the pivot round which the English fleets and armies would revolve, supported by such limited forces as Austria could spare to the aid of her Archduke Charles (now to be styled Charles III. of Spain); and advantage was to be taken of the ancient and only half-healed feud between Castile and Aragon to establish the Allies on the Aragonese side of Spain and in the Balearic Isles. The Germans once settled in force upon the land, the sea would be safe for British navies; and between them the French hold on Italy might be paralysed. In short, British Foreign Policy now added the systematic defence of the Mediterranean, for the purpose of promoting British commerce, to the earlier elements of the system.

Systematic defence of the Mediterranean.

This branch of the war ran parallel with the

greater one which Marlborough waged on the Rhine and Danube, and it only wanted a master-hand on the spot to have been equally successful. Lisbon gave a ready entrance into Western Spain, and Barcelona, taken by the fortunate audacity of Lord Peterborough, still more facilitated entrance by the east, since, as the ancient capital of the Catalans, it formed a centre for the old racial rivalry of the two great divisions of Spain. Here the British fleets might be expected to play a part which was denied them in the north, and the Mediterranean might become a British lake. These hopes were destined to disappointment. Perhaps the chief cause of the failure, or rather the want of immediate success in the pursuit of these objects, was the starving of the Spanish War both by Great Britain and Austria under the pressure of the greater campaign. The Catalans had been too completely incorporated by Castile during several generations to lend any important aid; and neither of the two foreign Powers, Britain or Austria, obtained any real popularity. Catalonia rebelled in order to obtain its own laws, or *fueros*, of which the union with Castile had deprived it; but these people had made a good exchange when Spain became a united kingdom; and their sentiment was an anachronism. *General failure of the Allies in Spain.*

The circumstance which rendered the success of France in the Spanish Peninsula of little importance to Britain was the capture of Gibraltar in 1704. It was scarcely noticed amidst the tumultuous rejoicings over the battle of Blenheim, which took place in the same year; but great as the results of that victory were, the capture of the Rock may be considered a more important event, for it turned out to be one *Capture of Gibraltar.*

of the main steps which carried Great Britain to the headship of Europe. As the justice and expediency of its retention were, soon after the Treaty of Utrecht, much disputed, and the policy of it, even in recent times, deliberately attacked, this may be the place for putting that event into its proper place as a part of British Foreign Policy; and we may so far forestall the Peace of Utrecht by which its seizure was ratified.

Importance of Gibraltar. The Rock of Gibraltar, taken, as it was said, almost in a frolic, by Sir George Rooke, and the island of Minorca, with its fine harbour of Port Mahon, occupied by Sir John Leake, were the sole acquisitions made by Great Britain in Europe which appeared to her credit after the enormous efforts she had made to avert " the great danger which threatened the liberties and safety of all Europe from the too close conjunction of the kingdoms of Spain and France." This is the expression used in the Treaty of Utrecht. They appeared to bystanders to be a mere barren and inadequate return for the vast expenditure of men and money which had issued in the victories of Marlborough and Eugene, to say nothing of those of Peterborough, Stanhope, and Galway, which might be supposed to have been neutralised by the successes of Berwick and Vendôme. But Queen Anne and Bolingbroke were not so far wrong as people supposed. At the moment the French and their allies could hardly believe in the good news that, after having been humbled in the dust, they had got off so cheaply; and the French, as principals, were not moved to any great distress at the loss having fallen upon Spain; but as the memory of the conditions on which these places had been conceded and of the British sacrifices which they represented became dim in the eyes of Spanish patriotism, the position of the victors on the impregnable Rock grew to be intolerable; nor, though France put a better face on it, could she digest the painful fact any better than Spain.

With France it was not indeed, as with Spain, a matter of wounded pride, but it was a standing injury to her strategical position; and all the more distressing since one of the few abiding advantages of Louis XIV.'s grand but unfortunate policy had been to establish Toulon as a powerfully fortified naval arsenal. These two British acquisitions, but especially Gibraltar, were thus felt by France, as soon as she began to recover from the war, a most palpable grievance. They were the sure guarantee of an independent British commerce with Italy, Africa, and the Levant, and an efficient means of protecting that commerce against what were then its most terrible enemies, the Algerine and other pirates. Thus they became the regular stations for men-of-war, unwelcome intruders into those inland waters. They were of still greater importance, inasmuch as Gibraltar, with Port Mahon as its support, was in the exact position to cut off, whenever war broke out, all communication by sea between the southern ports of France and her western seaboard. *Seriously felt by France,*

Spain was equally cloven in two. Gibraltar, jutting out into the sea at her southernmost point, barred the way between her eastern and western ports, and stood sentinel over queenly Cadiz, the emporium of all the wealth of Spanish America. *and by Spain.*

D

With such a station for her ships, Great Britain was in a position to suck away the sole remaining nourishment of the old imperial trunk. Spain, however, being already in decay, was willing at times, under the pressure of adverse circumstances, to forget the affront; but her more powerful neighbour, still keenly reckoning on a glorious maritime future, would never allow her to forget it. France was ever standing by, reminding her of the disgrace she had suffered, and offering by secret treaties to support her in her efforts to recover her lost possessions. In vain was Spain forced by Great Britain to confirm the tenure of the obnoxious intruders by repeated treaties. The same causes continued to act; the same fretful disgust betrayed itself over and over again. It must be admitted that the feeling was perfectly natural. Gibraltar was the visible forfeit paid for irreparable errors.

But it is not easy to comprehend at first sight how it was that the British Government could forget or make light of conquests of such vital importance to British commerce and influence; for as a matter of fact, both George I. and his ministers did beyond question commit themselves more than once to a policy of restitution. The excuse for them is that they knew better than any one else the perils which beset the Hanoverian Succession in England, and the delicate relations in which Hanover stood to the nations by which it was surrounded. These were the dangerous and irremediable conditions of the case. During, for instance, the panic of 1715, George I., little understanding at that time what he was doing, went so far as to offer of his own accord to restore Gibraltar. His Prime Minister,

George I. made a mistake on this point;

Lord Stanhope, in 1718, urged it as a means of making an arrangement with Alberoni, the aggressive Prime Minister of Spain. The short war of the latter year, caused by the enterprise of that rash Cardinal, did indeed annul what had passed, and the Quadruple Treaty confirmed the British tenure; yet after all this we find George I. in 1721 actually promising once again to restore it "at the first favourable opportunity, with the consent of my Parliament, upon the footing of an equivalent."

Happily that equivalent was never settled; still less did "my Parliament" ever dream of giving its consent. The people of Britain, whatever their Government might devise for them, had never for a moment lost sight of their true rights and interests. It was the representative of Marlborough's great services. They were clearly right. The Spaniards forgot that it was as a virtual portion of France that they had suffered. The general and violent indignation of the British people, as soon as ever these secret proposals became known, made of course the consent of Parliament impossible. The most insulting language was used by the Queen of Spain, the virtual sovereign of the country. "Either give up Gibraltar," said she, "or relinquish your trade to Spain and the [West] Indies." The British had no idea of giving up either the Rock or the trade. Both rights had been honourably won; both had been secured by repeated treaties; they knew the value of both. The expense of keeping up Gibraltar, reckoned at £50,000 a year, was insignificant. They felt the insult still more when, in 1726, Spain, without any Declaration of War, actually laid siege to the English stronghold. This

The British people never did.

Spanish siege of Gibraltar.

at last put an end to any notion of compromise. The Spanish attack of that day failed, and all subsequent attempts have shared the same fate. Long afterwards, in 1757, the elder Pitt in a moment of depression offered to exchange Gibraltar for Minorca as the price of the Spanish alliance, but happily Spain declined. The idea has never since found any serious expression.

<small>Control of the Mediterranean.</small>
Here, then, we fix a distinct landmark of British Foreign Policy. The Mediterranean was to be kept open not only by such alliances as were possible with the holders of the two peninsulas which jutted out into the midst of it from the Continental base, but by British stations which should guard its fleets at the entrance. It should henceforward be in the power of Great Britain to control the commerce of the inland sea, and to provide for that purpose fleets which might rest upon a secure basis.

<small>Spain and Great Britain in the West Indies.</small>
And this brings us to another great factor in British Foreign Policy which sprang into a new phase of existence during the early part of the eighteenth century, and requires a much more minute notice. Like the growth of control in the Mediterranean, an almost unperceived movement had been going on for some generations in West Indian waters. The progress of English commerce and nautical power in those seas dated in practice from Elizabeth's triumphant struggle with Philip II.; but its foundation was laid in the patronage of the two Cabots, father and son, by Henry VII. and Henry VIII. It extended over many years; for the son, Sebastian Cabot, was the chief adviser in nautical affairs of Edward VI.'s ministers; and their position is of importance in this survey. Under

their auspices the English learnt to consider themselves the arbiters of English interests in North America, just as much as Spain and Portugal considered themselves the controllers of the South. But the central portion, including the Mexican Gulf, lying between North and South America, with the Pacific on one side of it and the West Indian Islands on the other, could not in the nature of things be treated as exclusively Spanish,—not at least after the North American colonies, planted in the seventeenth century, had risen into important and populous communities.

And here we should remember that there was a fundamental difference between the colonies of the two European races. The Spanish—for the Portuguese colonies, which were of the same kind, need not be considered here—were either mining settlements, of the greatest value in that age when the supply of gold and silver was scarce, or else the mere administrative government of enfeebled native States which had been conquered by a Cortes or a Pizarro. There was no thought of emigration on any large scale from the mother country. The administration of these native States might be compared to the old English administration of Gascony, or the modern English government of India. But the English colonies in North America were like the settlements of Greece and Rome in ancient times, like those of the Jutes, Saxons, and Angles in Roman Britain, and like those in Canada, Australia, and South Africa, which we now call "The Greater Britain." They were real emigrations; and in New England they were even migrations of whole bodies of people, men, women, and children, agricultural,

The nature of the British colonies in America.

and for life, perfectly English in their municipal, their commercial, and their religious type. What was still more important, they brought with them all the nautical habits and traditions of the parent race, and they possessed long lines of coast and frequent harbours for their development. They inherited the spirit of Raleigh and his paladins. How could it be expected that they would submit to be excluded from the adjacent waters of the Gulf of Mexico and the West India Islands?

<small>Their relations to the mother country.</small>

Further, their English parents had conferred on them inestimable advantages by governing and keeping order in the different colonies, though not always by the best men,—but where has that not been a cause of complaint?—in protecting the interests of the colonies when they could not yet stand alone, and in sharing with them the ancient English institutions, as well as the political and domestic improvements of the times. We are not accustomed to measure the condition of the American colonies of England before the war which issued in their independence, but we must set ourselves to the task if we are to understand the growth of British Foreign Policy. What we have to do at present is to observe the impossibility of preventing the colonists from taking advantage of the lax relations which had long existed between themselves and the Spanish colonists planted at different ports along the shore of the Mexican Gulf. And though the prevalence of the buccaneers during the Restoration and Revolution periods had *eo nomine* come to an end, the enterprising spirit on which smuggling processes are based could not but survive in all these seas.

Let us, then, trace the circumstances which brought

on the conflict between the two mother countries, Britain and Spain, first while peace was still supposed to exist, and then when the war of 1739 broke out.

The victories of Elizabeth's reign had been forgotten, and the Peace of 1604, made by James I., had allowed Spain to pursue her American policy undisturbed. She on her part took no notice of the growth of the English colonies in America, and seemed to hope that no future Drakes or Hawkinses would ever appear in those vast seas which she called her own. But as a matter of fact, all through the reigns of James I. and Charles I., British and Dutch vessels were in the full career of what the Spaniards called "depredations," and during Cromwell's Spanish war not only was Jamaica captured by the English, but Spanish commerce and the safe carriage of Spanish treasure were grievously interrupted by Blake at Teneriffe, and by others. Not however till 1667 did Spain condescend, even tacitly, to recognise the existence of those who had been so long forcing their way into her strongholds. In the treaties of that year and of 1670 were laid the bases of the subsequent intercourse. It was the reign of Charles II., and the attitude of the two nations had changed since Cromwell's war. The ambitious hostility of Louis XIV., coinciding with the recent evidence of a serious power for mischief in the British American colonies, was drawing Spain into unwonted alliance with Britain. Hence favourable conditions of trade, and especially of West Indian trade, were at last granted by Spain, and expressions used which, whether intentionally or not, were open to more than one construction. It is necessary to examine these treaties.

Attitude of Spain as to British commerce.

Favourable treaties of the seventeenth century. The first treaty (1667) began by referring to the Treaty of Munster in 1648, by which the Dutch—thus long before the British, and no doubt owing to the profound depression of the latter at that time—had been admitted to commercial privileges. These were now extended to the British; but there is nothing whatever here which throws light on any claim to the Right of Search. Indeed it was by no means clear that the privileges of trade conceded to the British, which the Spaniards afterwards held to apply to European ports alone, did not by the very terms of this treaty apply to their colonies. In the second treaty (1670) the restrictions which provided that there should be no mutual trade between the colonies of each Power without special licence, were not far separated from the fifteenth Article, which declares that "liberty of navigation ought in no manner to be disturbed where nothing is committed against the genuine sense and meaning of these Articles." A clause concerning the Right of Search is here for the first time inserted; but it is carefully guarded from abuse, and specifically stated to apply only to a search for arms, ammunition, and soldiers. Even this was, it seems, intended to apply principally to the prohibition of British ships from supplying the States of Barbary with military stores. Yet—and this shows why a close examination of the treaties is necessary—it was the Spanish interpretation of this one article, in the times of which we are now speaking (1720–1739), which formed the *casus belli* in 1739. Spain interpreted it to mean the Right of Search for contraband merchandise in American waters, and there, not only when "close to the ports," but out of sight of land, in the open sea.

This illegal system of search, exercised, not under the supervision of captains or admirals of a superior class of men-of-war, but by a low class of officers in *guardacostas*, was carried out in the most barbarous manner. Year after year merchant ships were taken at sea, laden not with "arms, ammunition, or soldiers," but with the British goods which the Spanish colonists were eager to buy at highly remunerative prices. The captains were often sent to Spain, where they were immured in the proverbially vile prisons of that country, and no doubt often, like Captain Jenkins, mutilated. It is remarkable that this, perhaps the most famous of all mutilations of the human body, has for much more than a century been stigmatised as a "fable." It was called so by Burke, using it as an illustration of his argument for another war, on the idea that though the old war, based on this "fable," was one of "plunder and extreme injustice," the Revolution-War with France was justified on every ground of justice and expediency.

(margin: Right of Search.)
(margin: Jenkins' ear.)

No one thought of disputing that great man's statements, especially when he declared that he had made an accurate study of the subject, and had based his epithets on the "candid confessions of many of the principal actors against Sir Robert Walpole, and of those who principally excited the clamour which brought on the war." He has been followed by every subsequent writer and compiler. And yet the story had not originally been considered a fable, nor indeed till a generation had passed away. However, quite recently, Professor Laughton, turning over some documents in the Record Office, discovered one which proved that the "fable" of Jenkins' ear" was no fable at all, but actual fact.

CHAPTER V.

THE EVENTS WHICH LED TO THE WAR WITH SPAIN IN 1739.

THE special instance of Jenkins and his ear—with his dramatic exhibition of the well-preserved member, wrapped up in cotton, before the House of Commons, and his reply to a question from the House, "I commended my soul to my God, and my cause to my country"—was only one out of a thousand incidents which brought on the famous war of 1739, and settled the Foreign Policy of Great Britain very much as it has remained ever since. It was the secret treaty with France in 1733 which encouraged Spain to make a mock at the remonstrances of the British. *Walpole's peace policy.* To this we must add the error of Walpole's later administration, which had degenerated into a base and un-English system of staving off war by absurd devices, and buying peace at any price. Let us deal first with the encouragement given by France to Spain.

We have noticed the unprovoked attack made on Gibraltar by Spain in 1726 and its failure. Walpole's plan of dealing with it was to treat it as a childish act of spleen, not the least to be considered an act of war, but as requiring that a fine should be *Hosier's blockade of Porto Bello.* levied on the offender. The harbour and fortress of Porto Bello, where the galleons met after having received the annual supply of gold and silver from the miners, was blockaded by a considerable fleet under Admiral Hosier. Not that the orders given to this officer were made known to the people, who were appeased for the moment by the demonstration of force; but there is no doubt that the Admiral had orders not to attack the forts, which however were captured by Vernon in 1739 with only six large ships. This blockade was very disagreeable to Spain, but it was also very costly to Great Britain. It was galling to the Spanish Government to find that its supplies could be stopped, and that it had no fleet ready to prevent the stoppage; but it was also gratifying to feel that this was the worst the supposed mistress of the seas could do, and that it was only a temporary infliction.

But how about the cost and humiliation to those who inflicted the punishment? The sad story has left an indelible mark on English history, and it need not be repeated in detail. Never was such a blunder made by even the most incompetent Government. The fleet of old ships, worn out during a long peace, might have performed their service well enough had they been despatched straight against an enemy. As it was, kept cruising for months off this petty fortress in the deadly Gulf of Mexico, the ships rotted to pieces, and the entire armament dissolved away: twice over were nearly the whole of the crews destroyed by fever—for the ships had been manned afresh at Jamaica; the fine old admiral, as well as his successor, had succumbed; and along with them ten captains, fifty lieutenants, and between 3000 and 4000 inferior officers and seamen. The cost of men and money was equal to that of at least three general

Catastrophe of Hosier's fleet.

actions such as were in those days fought at sea. The catastrophe sank deep into the souls of Englishmen, and was never forgotten. Twelve years later Glover's celebrated ballad of " Hosier's Ghost" sounded the knell of Walpole's administration.

Secret treaty between France and Spain. Walpole found the difficulty of dealing with the so-called Right of Search increase enormously after the secret treaty in 1733 between Spain and France, of which we have spoken. It ran as follows: "Whenever it seems good to both nations alike, the abuses which have crept into commerce, especially through the English, shall be abolished; and if the English make objection, France will ward off its hostility with all its strength by land and sea." This treaty was not known to the world before it was published by Ranke in quite recent times; but its fruits were visible enough in both continents. The very year after it was formed, the tranquillity of Europe was broken by the union of France, Spain, and Sardinia against the Emperor, and that issued in placing the Spanish Charles upon the throne of Naples and Sicily. Great Britain, still entirely in Walpole's hands, looked helplessly on while a friendly Power, the Empire, was overpowered. The House of Bourbon now reigned supreme over the whole west of continental Europe, and the two great peninsulas of Spain and Italy, which commanded the Mediterranean, were mainly in the same hands. The continued tenure of Gibraltar and Minorca wore now, of course, year by year, a still more intolerable aspect in the eyes of these Powers; and the resolute policy of France to use the Spanish alliance for the purpose of pushing forward the colonial empire which she was bent on acquiring, began to show itself in the formation of forts and settlements along the rear of the English colonies in North America, and in fresh enterprises which threatened the British position in India.

The next year, 1735, placed France on a still higher pedestal. With remarkable sagacity the aged Cardinal Fleury, then at the head of affairs in France, contrived to complete by the Treaty of Vienna the crowning achievement of his country's ambition. By securing the reversion of Lorraine and Bar, which soon fell in, France at last rendered herself secure on her eastern frontier. She was now—it might almost be said without a war—at a summit of power which Louis XIV. had beggared the resources of his nation in the vain attempt to reach by means of wars which had lasted, almost without intermission, throughout his prolonged reign. This success had been obtained by the neutralisation of Great Britain and Holland. But Holland had far the best excuse for non-interference: she had been quite exhausted by the gigantic wars in which she had saved Europe, and from which her people have never since recovered. Have they not gained for ever the respect of mankind for their past services in the cause of freedom?

It was this threatening attitude of France, standing behind Spain, which daunted Walpole, to whom the secret treaty seems to have been known, and inspired the timid policy which we are now to trace as regards the West Indies. The diplomatic successes of the Prime Minister had indeed procured the blessing of peace for the moment; but they had laid a sure foundation for an inevitable war. By withdrawing his country from her accustomed place in

France under Cardinal Fleury.

Great Britain withdrawn from Continental affairs.

Continental affairs,—that is, from the place obtained in the Tudor and later Stuart reigns of William and Anne,—and by allowing her to be insulted and betrayed in both hemispheres, he had encouraged a weak nation like Spain, which must have collapsed had she been treated from the first with becoming spirit, to carry insult and defiance still further. In the complicated relations of the trade between the two countries in the West Indies and Spanish America there was a rich abundance of occasions for the display of the bitter hostility which rapidly developed in both nations. Not only was the commerce of the London, Bristol, and other merchants largely engaged in pushing its way to these regions, but also, as we have already said, that of the hardy settlers of the North American coasts, men who earned their bread by the sweat of their brows, or covered the sea with their trading vessels.

High spirit of the British colonists.

It was these men who gave the tone to all the English of the New World, and suffered with rugged impatience the insults and trade restrictions of a people for whom they could entertain but little respect.

Nor should it be forgotten, in tracing the quarrels of the eighteenth century, that even in the West Indies the English had already had to bear their part in connection with the European wars of the previous age. Men like the two Christopher Codringtons, lords of rich sugar islands, and each in succession placed by the British Government as "Governor-General of the Caribbean Seas," had in the reigns of William and Anne led great expeditions against the French, and cultivated with some success a military spirit among the planters; while the undaunted Benbow had taught the enemies of the English that they might easily try the temper of his people too far. We should also remember that the theory of maritime freedom was steadily advancing along with the civilisation of the age; and however the English might resist at home the claims of Grotius for the Dutch in the Narrow Seas, it is not to be supposed that the doctrines of the *Mare Liberum* were unheeded in their application to Spain and the distant American waters, where no claim to exclusive rights had been acknowledged like that which had been conceded to the English as their domestic inheritance for seven centuries.

Add to these considerations that not only the English but the French and Dutch had settled in the seventeenth century on the West Indian Islands and the adjacent coasts. Thus it is quite intelligible that any practical operation resulting from the old Spanish theory that the American coasts and seas extending south and west from the northern shores of the Gulf of Mexico were exclusively their own, must have appeared to the British people and their colonists an absurd, insane, and most injurious anachronism. They had never acknowledged the right of the Pope to give away continents or oceans. The nations of Europe were already mixed up together inextricably within those distant seas; and each of these nations, as yet in the early stages of the colonising process, looked with more than a parental eye on its promising offspring. How could constant smuggling and everlasting disputes fail to arise in such circumstances between Spain and the new-comers? Nothing but the most liberal policy between contiguous colonies, and between the States to which they belonged, could possibly have kept the peace. But the condition of Europe during Walpole's so-called pacific administration was very far from pacific.

<small>Spanish exercise of "Right of Search."</small>

It was with these English colonists, numerous, active, and self-reliant, quite as much as with the English themselves; it was with that English flag,—the honour of which had been carried so high that the claim for an ancient mode of paying it respect in the Narrow Seas had led to sanguinary combats and terrible wars,—that Spain, a Power no longer of first-rate rank, resolved to deal as if she were undisputed mistress of the ocean. What must have been the feelings of the English, both at home and abroad, when they found the Spanish *guardacostas* presuming to exercise the so-called "Right of Search" on the high seas—*i.e.*, out of sight of land—upon British vessels proceeding on their legitimate traffic from one English colony to another? What must they have felt when they were perfectly aware that no such right existed by treaty? What when they found this practice become customary without their own Government interfering to prevent it?

It was even stated over and over again, though perhaps never proved, that the Spanish *guardacostas* had actually sailed into English ports and carried off English merchant vessels under the eyes of English men-of-war. At any rate, the instances of their barbarous treatment of Englishmen caught smuggling were numerous and undoubted. The number of those who died in Spanish prisons, which were worse still on the Spanish "Plantations" than in Spain itself, was frightful. No doubt there were many cases not very different from that of Captain Jenkins;

but in spite of cruelty and losses, the English and their American colonists found the profits too great to be relinquished, and the struggle went on year after year; while Walpole, upon each occasion of complaint, minimised the affront, and provoked fresh insolence by exhibiting a pusillanimous dread of giving offence. People asked if this was the way to secure peace. Did any nation ever yet succeed in retaining its independence by allowing injury and insult to pass unnoticed? By degrees these just and natural sentiments extended to the whole nation, and at last forced Walpole himself to demand redress. There was something to be said for Spain in her attempt to prevent the British from trading with her colonists, but her mode of operation was intolerable. The war which she provoked could hardly be called "a war of plunder and extreme injustice" on the part of the British." *Walpole takes no notice.*

Here then we have before us the grounds of the war which led to such immense issues, and which have been so obscured during the last century and a half. We have discussed the validity of the Spanish claim to the Right of Search in the open sea, and shown that it was not grounded on treaties. We have seen, further, that the system of "smuggling," on which the claim was justified, had itself a considerable amount of moral justification. It may be well to carry this explanation a little further. During the whole reign of Charles II., and even to the close of the seventeenth century, the same spirit which had dictated the unwonted liberality of the Spanish Treaties of 1667 and 1670, derived from the dread of France and the consequent friendly approach towards Britain, brought about an entire relaxation *Systematic smuggling.*

of those treaties, a relaxation which grew into a custom, and of course became associated with the idea of right. "A flourishing although illicit trade was, by the connivance and indulgence of Spain, carried on between the English and Spanish Plantations";[1] nor was it till the accession of Philip of Bourbon to the Spanish throne, as Philip V., in 1700, that any change took place, nor scarcely even then,— for Spain was torn to pieces by the Succession War,— till the Peace of Utrecht in 1713.

Change from quasi-free to restricted trade.

The truth is that a state of things had arisen which could not possibly continue without an explosion. Further, a new system of relations was adopted by Spain and accepted by Great Britain at the Peace of Utrecht, a system of definite and absolute restriction of trade, which, after the lapse of three generations of mutual intercourse, virtually amounting to free trade, was unworkable. Let any one consider what that lapse of time meant, the number of families and communities which had grown rich in this trade, and had handed it down from one generation to another; the money sunk in the trade, the many channels by which the British colonies and the mother country had communicated with one another in this connection. That the absolute restriction of this trade, with the one exception of the Assiento, forming part of the Peace of Utrecht, should have been acceded to by Queen Anne and her Tory ministers is not usually (though it might well be) charged among their faults. They might be excused on the ground of a sanguine hope that the new plan would be suffered to bear as lax an interpretation as the old. The sequel proved them

[1] Coxe's Walpole, i. 558.

EVENTS WHICH LED TO WAR WITH SPAIN. 67

to be entirely in error. Philip V. was not only a hostile Frenchman, but he became a thoroughly hostile Spaniard as well. His sympathies flowed from both sides in the anti-English direction, and it was no wonder. The former friendliness between Spain and Britain had been extinguished in the late war, with its disastrous result to Spain in the capture of Gibraltar and Minorca.

Here was Philip's opportunity. By the Peace of Utrecht the old permission to trade by licence had been annulled. What was the famous Assiento which had taken its place? It was a contract for supplying the Spanish colonies with a certain number of African negroes, a contract made with Spain by the English South Sea Company. To it was attached the privilege of annually sending a single ship of a certain burden, laden with European merchandise, to Spanish America. Was this privilege to be literally interpreted? The Spanish Government would have been wise had they reflected upon the impossibility of undoing the work of their predecessors, and, by a mere edict from the mother country, attempting to force backwards the stream which had so long been running in the direction of freedom and mutual advantage; but under the circumstances it was natural that such reflections should find no place. The effect is described by the excellent historian Coxe in the following words:— *The Assiento.*

"The letter of the American Treaty was now followed, and the spirit by which it was dictated abandoned. Although the English still enjoyed the liberty of putting into Spanish harbours for the purpose of refitting and provisioning, yet they were far from enjoying the same advantages [as before] *Working of the new system.*

of carrying on a friendly and commercial intercourse. They were now watched with a scrupulous jealousy, strictly visited by *guardacostas*, and every efficient means adopted to prevent any commerce with the colonies except what was allowed by the annual ship."[1]

It was not therefore surprising that British merchants and colonists refused to be bound by the letter of the treaty. Considering the trade as already theirs by long prescriptive right, and not a mere matter of indulgence, they adopted, in concert with the Spanish colonists, all sorts of petty methods of evasion. They " continually put into the Spanish harbours, under pretence of refitting and refreshing, and in many places almost publicly disposed of European merchandise in exchange for gold and silver. Other vessels sailing near their ports and harbours were repaired to by smugglers, or sent their long-boats towards the shore and dealt with the natives. The Spaniards declared that the 'Assiento annual ship' was followed by several other vessels which moored at a distance, and, as it disposed of its cargo, continually supplied it with fresh goods; that by these means and by the clandestine trade which the English carried on they almost supplied the colonies; and the Fair of Panama, one of the richest of the world, where the Spaniards were accustomed to exchange gold and silver for European merchandise, had considerably fallen; they monopolised the commerce of America."[2]

It is obvious that as there were two parties to these transactions, the attempt to interfere with what both people were alike resolved to have was

---

[1] Coxe's Walpole, i. 559.   [2] Ibid., i. 560.

as hopeless as to fill the cask of the Danaids. The confusion into which matters fell is well described by Lord Hervey. "The Spaniards had often seized ships which were not smuggling; and many of the Spanish governors connived at the English smugglers for money. Thus merchants were often secure in ports where they ought not to have found any [security], and insecure on the seas."[1] The Spanish-American coast was open for hundreds of miles; there were but few settlements; the hope of profit, the sense of danger, the love of adventure, and the belief that right was substantially on their side, produced of course the effect of stimulating this illicit commerce in exact proportion to the severity of the means adopted for putting it down. It must also be noticed here that there had been more than one short interval, even since the Peace of Utrecht, when Spanish quarrels with France had for a time again produced a relaxation of the restrictions imposed by that Peace, and given rise to a variety of misconstructions of the same nature as those already mentioned.

Hopelessness of improving the system.

Thus failure after failure, especially dating from the year 1727, when the blockade of Porto Bello had exasperated both nations, only made Spain more obstinate, and blinded her to the true nature of the means to which she now resorted. The 'Craftsman' in 1729 by no means exaggerated the English sentiment when it said, "It looks indeed as if all the Powers of Europe, both friends and foes, were confederated against us and resolved to unite their endeavours to deprive us of all our trade at once."[2] As the English placed their own interpre-

Incessant Spanish insults.

[1] Memoirs, ii. 485.   [2] Vol. iv. 196.

tation on past treaties, on the recent numerous and intermittent relaxations, and on their own "customary rights," so also did their opponents on the Treaty-right of Search. It was indeed, as now applied, a pure invention. The able minister, Carteret, Lord Granville, justly remarked that "in all the negotiations which preceded the Convention our ministers never found out that there was no ground or subject for any negotiations; that the Spaniards had not a right to search our ships; and when they attempted to regulate them by treaty, they were regulating a thing which did not exist."[1]

So matters went drifting on. At length it became clear that nothing short of an entire concession of the trade on the part of Spain, or at least an absolute relinquishment of search upon the high seas, could avert war. "The English traders regarded the extension of their business, as hitherto allowed, a possession honestly won, looked upon all interference with it as an unjustifiable act of violence, and claimed the assistance of Government against it."[2] Nor can it be reckoned as any fault on the part of the British that they made no attempt to stop the smuggling which went on upon shore. That was not their business, but the sole concern of the Spaniards—a difficult task indeed, for the line of coast was long, the expense of a proper naval coastguard considerable, the great value of the mutual exchange to both parties suggestive of every sort of collusion. The case, on its technical aspect, could hardly be put better than it was in 1737 by Mr. Benjamin Keene, the British ambassador in

[1] Quoted by Lord Chatham, Parliamentary Debates, 1770.
[2] Ranke's History of England, Oxfd. ed., v. 398.

Spain: "Upon the whole, the state of our dispute seems to be that the commanders of our vessels always think that they are unjustly taken if they are not taken in actual illicit commerce, even though proofs of their having loaded in that manner be found on board of them; and the Spaniards, on the other hand, presume that they have a right of seizing not only the ships that were continually trading in their ports, but likewise of examining and visiting them on the high seas in order to search for proofs of fraud which they have committed; and till a medium be found out between these two notions the Government will always be embarrassed with complaints, and we shall be continuing to negotiate in this country [Spain] for redress without ever being able to obtain it."

In other words, each nation considered itself injured, and neither would stir a finger to remove the cause of complaint. Each adhered to its own notion of its obligations. The British were satisfied with the formal execution of the Treaty of Utrecht; the Spaniards asserted a right to which they had no claim by treaty or otherwise. The bellicose policy of the Spaniards in searching British ships on the high seas, instead of controlling and punishing their own colonists and the British smugglers on or near the shore, must therefore be considered the cause of the war. It was a plain issue, and no room should have been permitted for any confusion of claims. War should have been declared on the first occasion when the capture of a British vessel was made on the high seas and reparation refused.

War becomes necessary.

The state of things produced by these opposite views of the case was aggravated by the action of the Spaniards in a matter which admitted of no doubt. The British had a double right of trade in another part of the West Indies altogether independent of the disputed trade on the Mexican coast. The right to cut logwood in the Bay of Campeachy and to collect salt at the island of Sal Tortuga had been always taken as implied in the various treaties, and rested upon precisely the same ground as that by which the British held the island of Jamaica or any other settlement in those seas. Presuming on impunity, this right was now not only questioned, but the British salt-fleet had been actually attacked by two Spanish ships of the line, and only saved by the courage and conduct of Captain Thomas Durell, commanding the Scarborough of twenty guns, in charge of the convoy. This fine officer gallantly employed his two colossal enemies so long that thirty-two out of thirty-six vessels made their escape; as, after seeing his convoy in safety, he did himself.

The "Patriots" in Parliament take up the subject.

In short, for some time not a year had passed without a series of the most bitter complaints from the British merchants, often, no doubt, exaggerated, but in the main well founded, and emphasised in Parliament by Walpole's opponents, the "Patriots," after the bitterest fashion. This furious spirit by degrees extended itself to the country generally. The feeling that there was something behind the audacious action of Spain became rooted, and the timidity of Walpole was felt to be intolerable. A careful study of the Parliamentary Debates of the years 1737 and 1738 reveals the minister in the un-English attitude of an apologist for the grievous wrongs which he himself admits his country to have sustained, on the avowed ground that it would not be safe to resent these wrongs. And yet such was his command of Parliament—we know only too well how it was maintained—that it took two whole years after he had confessed his disgraceful position to oblige him to recognise, in the only way now left, the outraged dignity of the people of England.

Thus the scene of the last Act shifts to the House of Commons, and it is worth our while to follow it, for we are dealing with the events out of which sprang the modern British Empire. Not that the complaints against the Spaniards had been hitherto unheard in Parliament, for a continuous dropping fire had been long levelled at Walpole. They culminated in 1737 under the form of a Petition of West India Merchants to the House of Commons. This famous document insisted that "for years past their ships have not only been frequently stopped and searched, but also forcibly and arbitrarily seized upon the high seas by Spanish ships fitted out to cruise under the plausible pretence of guarding their own coasts; that the commanders thereof, with their crews, have been inhumanly treated, and their ships carried into some of the Spanish ports and there condemned with their cargoes, in manifest violation of the treaties subsisting between the two Crowns; that the remonstrances of his Majesty's ministers receive no attention at Madrid, and that insults and plunder must soon destroy their trade." It concluded by demanding full satisfaction, and insisted that no British vessel should be detained in the future, nor seized upon the high seas by any nation on any pretext whatever. *Petitions to Parliament.*

Next year (1738) still stronger petitions formed

the basis of the debates in Parliament. The principal one took an historical survey of the subject, reminding the House of its own futile proceedings, since it had frequently acknowledged the justice of the British complaints; and it "addressed the Crown" for satisfaction. It contained the following remarkable passage: "The Spaniards have paid so little regard to his Majesty's most gracious endeavours that they have continued their depredations almost ever since the Treaty of Seville (1727), and more particularly last year have carried them to a greater height than ever, they having arbitrarily seized several ships with their effects belonging to his Majesty's subjects on the high seas in the destined course of their voyages to and from the British colonies, amounting to a very considerable value; and that the captains or masters of some of the said ships were, according to the last advices of the petitioners, and are (as the petitioners believe) at this time, confined by the Spaniards in the West Indies, and the crews are now in slavery in Old Spain, where they are most inhumanly treated."

In spite of his well-drilled majority, it was impossible for Walpole to prevent the House from coming, under the influence of Barnard, Wyndham, and Pulteney, to Resolutions which endorsed the petitions. In this memorable debate the Prime Minister was forced to admit: "That our merchants have fully proved their losses, and that the depredations which have been committed are contrary to the law of nations, contrary to the treaties subsisting between the two Crowns,—in short, that they are everything bad and without the least pretence or colour of justice."

Walpole begins to give way.

The Resolution which he proposed and carried ran as follows: "That the freedom of navigation and commerce which the subjects of Great Britain have an undoubted right to by the law of nations, and which is not in the least restrained by virtue of any of the treaties subsisting between the Crowns of Great Britain and Spain, had been greatly interrupted by the Spaniards by pretences altogether groundless and unjust. But before and since the execution of the Treaty of Seville and the declaration made by the Crown of Spain pursuant thereunto for the satisfaction and security of the commerce of Great Britain, many unjust seizures and captures have been made and great depredations committed by the Spaniards, which have been attended with many instances of unheard-of cruelty and barbarity. That the frequent applications to the Court of Spain for procuring justice and satisfaction to his Majesty's injured subjects, for bringing offenders to condign punishment, and for preventing like abuses for the future, have proved vain and ineffectual, and the several orders or *cedulas* granted by the King of Spain for restitution and reparation of great losses sustained by the unlawful and unwarrantable seizures and captures made by the Spaniards have been disobeyed by the Spanish governors or totally evaded and eluded. And that these violences and depredations have been carried on to the great loss and damage of the subjects of Great Britain trading to America, and in direct violation of the treaties subsisting between the two Crowns."

It has been necessary to wade through this long but weighty Resolution in order to make the British case clear beyond dispute. That it is necessary may be gathered from the difficulty which foreign authors have found in admitting the justice of the war which was by this time inevitable. Not that it is surprising to find the unpatriotic verdict of our own historians accepted abroad; but it is high time that the policy which issued in the formation of the modern British Empire should be vindicated by reference to the original documents and Parliamentary Debates of the time. This must be the apology for dwelling at such length on the particular series of events which determined the Foreign Policy of Great Britain.

Walpole's disgraceful conduct

Perhaps in the whole range of British history there will not be found an instance of the representative of the Government lowering the dignity of the nation to a more disgraceful level than Walpole with his servile majority did on this occasion. It seems incredible that the mover of such a Resolution should recommend a continuance of the timid forbearance which had been hitherto displayed. It was no longer a question of fact. The House had examined the witnesses of the petitioners, and reported that they had proved their case. Yet Walpole still harped on the same string. He was still bent on "obtaining satisfaction and full reparation by peaceable means," and declared that " we ought not to involve the nation in a war from the event of which we had a great deal to fear." " Some branches of our Spanish and Mediterranean trade might, if the war should be of any duration, be irrecoverably lost,"—a doctrine he had still more unblushingly expressed in a former speech, when he told the House that " it may sometimes be for the interest of a nation to pocket an affront," and when he shadowed forth the dangers which a war with Spain would bring on from other potentates of Europe, "since if the Spaniards had not private encouragement from Powers more considerable than themselves, they would never have ventured on these insults and injuries which have been proved at your bar."

Sir William Wyndham had no difficulty in deducing a different moral from the Prime Minister's "long account of the late treaties between Spain and us, whence it appeared that we had been for above twenty years not only negotiating but concluding treaties in vain, and without the least effect," and he scornfully denounced the system of "fitting out formidable squadrons without proper instructions for enabling them to follow words with blows." Sir John Barnard refuted the argument that a nation could rely on her former achievements if at the same time she declined to enforce respect. Pulteney, with all the thunder of his eloquence, insisted "that the time for reparation had long passed away," and that "the suffering our American trade to be ruined was not the way to protect our Spanish, Italian, and Turkish merchants"; which argument Mr. Plumer followed up by insisting that "the more our trade decays the less will be our power to assist ourselves, and the less ready will our neighbours be to assist us; and that every British subject ought to choose to live upon bread and onions rather than see the House of Bourbon give law to Europe; for an open and declared war was better than a cruel and contemptuous peace." Wyndham had previously laid down the only safe law for an independent nation in these words: "When the insult or attack appears from the very nature of it to have been

Attacked on all sides.

committed by public authority, satisfaction ought to be sued for by ambassadors: it ought to be immediately taken by fleets and armies, properly instructed for that purpose." Equally significant passages might be quoted from the Debates in the House of Lords.

A "gracious answer" from the Crown was an echo of the Addresses from both Houses of Parliament. It will however be scarcely believed by those who have not read the Debates that even in May of this year (1738), when the subject came once more before Parliament, Walpole announced his intention to oppose any Bill "which may tend to plunge this nation into a ruinous and perhaps doubtful war," and frankly propounded it as his opinion that "we were not a match for the Spaniards and French too." To which Pulteney replied that he hoped that the time had not arrived when it might be said: "Your seamen are to be enslaved, your merchants plundered, and your trade ruined, because if you take one step to prevent it France would interpose." "We have already been insulted by our enemies; we shall soon be despised by our allies; we shall be considered as a nation without rights, or what is the same, without power to assert them." The people of Great Britain did not believe that they were unable to confront united France and Spain; and they turned out to be right.

<small>Address to the Crown.</small> Again the House "addressed the Crown" in becoming terms, and the words used on the occasion by the famous Speaker Onslow are worth noting. "To encourage the Spaniards," said this truly representative Whig statesman, "to rummage our ships is to give them a right to the Sovereignty of the Seas,

as it was always deemed by Great Britain; and it was never allowed by any of your Majesty's predecessors." Again a "gracious answer"—in precisely the same terms as the Address—issued from the Crown, and again one of those expedients on which the minister seemed to live from year to year, a compromise with Spain called (from the king's palace) the Convention of Pardo. In this document the honour of Great Britain is disgracefully sacrificed to suit Spain; the word "satisfaction" for the wrongs done is studiously omitted, the payment which had been previously agreed upon by way of compensation for Spanish depredations is juggled away, and the vital question of the "Right of Search" wholly evaded. Spain, as was observed in the House, instead of giving reparation, had succeeded in obtaining a general release.

This final blunder settled the fate of the ministry and their policy. Convicted out of his own mouth, the whole country turned against Walpole. It was no personal question, no division of Whig and Tory. Nor is there much solid ground for attributing, as Burke has attributed, the universal sentiment of the nation to the literary skill of certain writers of prose and poetry. They expressed what was already a deep and wide-felt national grievance; the people were thankful for any spokesman. They welcomed the prose of Bolingbroke and the verses of Pope and Thomson, Johnson and Glover, just as they did the oratory of Pulteney, Carteret, Wyndham, and Barnard, and even the rough seamanlike harangues of Vernon, as the language of Englishmen. It was Walpole's obvious duty to retire, but he failed to perceive it. On the contrary, he took the fatal

Walpole's final blunder.

The statesmen and poets who aroused the country.

course of attempting to put in practice the policy forced on him by his opponents.

The best proof that Burke was wrong in attributing so large a share in producing war to the poets of the day is to be found in the fact that the only men who really made their mark, Pope and Dr. Johnson, did not publish till 1738, the year after the whole country had been aroused by the West Indian Petition and the debates in Parliament. Glover's "Hosier's Ghost" did not of course appear till after Porto Bello was taken. The passages from Pope and Johnson are here transcribed. The other minor poets are Glover in his "Leonidas," not a very likely poem to arouse enthusiasm; Nugent in his "Odes to Mankind and to Lord Pulteney"; Thomson in his "Britannia," his "Liberty," and his tragedy of "Agamemnon"; Mallet in his "Mustapha"; and Brooke in his "Gustavus Vasa."

Pope's lines occur in his "Satires and Epilogue":—

> "And own the Spaniards did a waggish thing
> Who cropt our ears and sent them to the king."

Again:—

> "Nay, hints 'tis by suggestion of the Court
> That Spain robs on, and Dunkirk's still a port."

Johnson's lines occur in his "London":—

> "Struck with the seat that gave Eliza birth,
> We kneel and kiss the consecrated earth,
> In pleasing dreams the blissful age renew,
> And call Britannia's glories back to view,
> Behold her cross triumphant on the main,
> The guard of commerce and the dread of Spain,
> Ere masquerades debauched, excise opprest,
> Or English honour grew a standing jest."

Again :—

"Here let those reign whom pensions can incite
To vote a patriot black, a courtier white,
Explain their country's dear-bought rights away,
And plead for pirates in the face of day."

Again :—

"But lost in thoughtless ease and empty show,
Behold the warrior dwindled to a beau,
Sense, freedom, piety refined away,
Of France the mimic and of Spain the prey."

Again :—

"Has Heaven reserved, in pity to the poor,
No pathless waste or undiscovered shore,
No secret island in the boundless main,
No peaceful deserts yet unclaimed by Spain?"

But none of these found so much favour with the vulgar as the famous line, ascribed to Atterbury, and at this time reproduced :—

"The cur-dog of Britain and spaniel of Spain."

Walpole's fate still pursued him. Even when he had made up his mind to lower himself so far as to become the mere agent of the Opposition, he showed to the last his entire misapprehension of the true state of affairs. The Spanish Government having most unwillingly signed the Convention, proved at once that it had no intention of keeping it; but no Declaration of War came from England. An order for reprisals was thought sufficient. This, however, was soon seen to be a wholly untenable position; and at last the momentous document, so long delayed, went forth to the world. That Declaration of War, issued by Walpole on October 15, 1738, *Walpole declares war.*

F

contains the best commentary on his own repeated defence of the policy of peace. It pronounced that the treaties had been "habitually violated"; the claim of Spain to the Right of Search is stated to be "unwarrantable, groundless, dangerous, and destructive to England and her colonies." British subjects had been treated with great cruelty and barbarity; exorbitant duties and impositions had been laid on trade; ancient and established privileges had been broken; and the late convention manifestly violated. War was declared to "vindicate our undoubted rights, and secure to our loving subjects the privileges of navigation and commerce to which they are justly entitled."

After such an exhibition of the absence of self-respect, it was impossible that the country could for any length of time confide the conduct of the war to its long-accustomed chief. The painful process by which Walpole was at last hurled from power need not detain us. We are only concerned with the defence of the British people from the charge made by Burke that the war which had such immense issues was a war of "plunder and extreme injustice." We have seen that there were at least two sides of the question. His error seems to be due to his having fixed his attention on one cause only of the quarrel between Spain and Great Britain, the struggle for the West Indian trade; whereas we have seen that the issues, as Walpole only too well understood, proceeded as much, or more, from the side of France, Gibraltar, and the Mediterranean. The best excuse that the great minister ever ventured to make for himself was that his policy was the best under the circumstances.

Walpole forced to resign.

At any rate it turned out most disastrously. His country had bought peace for a short time at the cost of a future struggle for existence. France and Spain resumed the position from which they had been hurled in the great wars of William III. and Marlborough, and the work had to be done over again.

We must not leave this subject without fairly facing Burke's statement that he had conversed with many of the principal actors against Walpole, and with those who principally excited that clamour, and "found that none of them, no, not one, did in the least defend the measure [of declaring war] or attempt to justify their conduct." This seems to be too specific a statement to be set down as mere rhetoric; but it must not be taken for more than it is worth. Nor can we suppose it possible that Chatham could have been counted as one of the "many principal actors"; for his glorious career opened with the debate on the Convention of Pardo, and he was from beginning to end identified with the principle of supporting British independence against France and Spain. No doubt some of the "principal actors" were originally governed by party spirit in the first instance, and not having a clear conscience in the matter, forgot in later times how much ground they really had for their action.

Burke's statements accounted for.

We must also remember the period of gloom and depression which fell upon the nation soon after the war commenced, and which scarcely lifted till Pitt threw over the scene the illumination of his glory. This period synchronised with the most impressionable part of Burke's life, a period when Englishmen

looked about regretfully for such a leader as even
Walpole, with all his faults, had been, and were
slow to understand that they had the greatest
statesman of his century rising to power in their
very midst. The "ringing of bells" for joy at the
war was soon, as Walpole predicted, succeeded by
"wringing of hands." The ecstatic burst of national
delight at Vernon's success was the one short-lived
moment of exultation, to be succeeded by many a
bitter disappointment. The very next year after
the war commenced saw France abetting Spain.
Three years later Prussia ranged herself on the
same side. In 1744 the mask was dropped, and
open war commenced with the enemy whom Walpole, unlike an Englishman, had dreaded.

Gloom of the succeeding period. What a dreary history is that of the succeeding Administrations. What a state of naval anarchy did Mathew's action off Toulon reveal. What millions appeared to be wasted on the Continent. How disgracefully was England governed when the Rebellion of 1745 broke out. What a humiliating treaty was that of Aix-la-Chapelle. What a painful period of half-peace, half-war, succeeded that so-called Peace. And how hard it was to convince the nation that nothing could possibly restrain their enemies from attempting to recover the position they had attained in the previous century but a desperate and determined struggle for supremacy. It was twenty years before victory decisively declared itself on the British side. This was not much, perhaps, for the founding of an empire; but during the extreme tension of the process, how many statesmen must have shared the misgivings of the people, and brooded with sad reflections over what might easily have come to be reckoned the madness of those who had provoked the conflict.

If, then, we may fairly acquit the nation of embarking on the war with Spain after the fashion of pirates, out of a hope of plunder, and fully aware of its "extreme injustice," let us ask ourselves what must have been its sentiment when France—first covertly and then openly—appeared on the scene. With that country the British had had no quarrel since the Peace of Utrecht. In order to keep on good terms with it, their Government had thrown overboard nearly all its ancient traditions, and borne with a strange equanimity insults from Spain which at any other period would have produced instant war. France had no common ground in the complaints made by the Spaniards in the West Indies, whether just or not. From the British point of view, it ought rather to have sided with them. And yet it must be admitted that the French policy was grounded on something deeper than appeared on the surface, and that it was not unnatural under the circumstances. It was none the less galling to the men whose memory of the times of William and Anne had not even yet been obliterated. *Provocation on the part of France.*

Nor did it mitigate their resentment to find, as the true nature of the war developed itself, that the cause of the Pretender had once more, under the influence of his special friend Cardinal Tencin, the Prime Minister of France, become the leading factor in French counsels. The old intolerable pretension to force a Popish sovereign on their country, so far from being abandoned, was now to be enforced by the bayonets of the chief general in Europe, Marshal Saxe. If any doubt had remained as to the necessity of war with Spain, the conduct of her far more dangerous ally strengthened the national conviction from day to day. In short, if we observe the whole course of the proceedings of the two Powers, banded as they were together by a secret treaty, we shall find it not only impossible to admit that the war was one of plunder and injustice on the part of Great Britain, but, on the contrary, we shall be constrained to declare it a war of self-defence, a just and necessary war, just both morally and politically, a war only too long delayed, a war which carried in its train the history of the world.

<small>War just and necessary.</small>

CHAPTER VI.

BRITISH FOREIGN POLICY DURING THE WARS WHICH FOUNDED THE EMPIRE—1739-1763.

WE are now, then, face to face with an enlarged "Foreign Policy of Great Britain" which we must both connect with and differentiate from the policy of preceding times. In order that we may see our way more clearly, let us recapitulate. We have traced the origin and fundamental principles of this policy in the dread of invasion by foreign Powers, which, during the early times of English history, had been attended with success on no less than four different occasions. That dread had become an integral part of the English inheritance. We have watched the development of these principles under the prolonged rivalry of the growing House of France with the Norman and Plantagenet kings of England. We observed the great change in the relation of States to one another which took place at the opening of what we rightly call "Modern History"; and saw that the system of Balance as understood by England and France, under the leadership of the Tudors, grew naturally and beneficially out of that change. We saw how in Elizabeth's hands it became the salvation of her country, and how the Stuart sovereigns deliberately apostatised from it. We watched its resumption under Wil- *Recapitulation of the history of British Foreign Policy.*

liam III. and Anne, and traced the fresh departure which it took in their wars; for to their time belongs the additional policy of guarding the Mediterranean in defence of the expanding relations with the Levant which grew out of the successful struggle with Louis XIV.

We have now arrived at a still further step in the progress of this Foreign Policy. The somewhat minute detail into which our survey of the Walpolian era has necessarily run will not have been thrown away if we have been thus enabled to measure what a momentous change was produced by the contest with united France and Spain, and to observe that the *laissez-faire* policy of the British peaceminister, at first so wise a leader, and then so ignobly foolish, brought it on. Nothing can be more plain than that a decided line of conduct on Walpole's part, conceived in the spirit of earlier and later statesmen, would have induced both France and Spain to pursue a different policy. It is, indeed, quite true that if the country had not been awakened out of its sleep by repeated insults and grievous losses, it would have borne with more impatience the taxes necessary for war. And it cannot be doubted that the struggle which was heralded by such gloomy presages, and which more than once produced a national feeling akin to despair, was, in fact, the process by which the modern British Empire was founded. But those considerations are, as we say, after date. Placing ourselves in that generation, we are called upon to measure the agony, the suspense, the loss effected by the conduct of a corrupt Government; and the course of our inquiry has demanded that we should not shrink from the exposure.

We may then sum up the enlarged British Foreign Policy now before us, engraved by this struggle in every British heart, in the famous words—"ships, colonies, and commerce,"—a policy new and yet old. We have seen how far it was old. It was new, inasmuch as the country fondly took for granted, after it had leaped to liberty at the Revolution and had under the new *régime* brought the despot of Europe to his knees, that its course as a naval, a colonial, and a commercial Power would be progressive and unchecked. Great Britain had not put forth these things as its aims, for the wars had been defensive; it was a mere accident that they had brought prosperity in their train. It was now seen that everything was to begin again; and it was also gradually borne in upon the national mind that there was an alarming European conspiracy formed in order to deprive the envied Mistress of the Seas of the ships, colonies, and commerce which she had prematurely supposed were beyond the reach of attack. Year after year unfolded more and more the serious nature of the attempt; nor, though the struggle was intermittent for short periods, was it relinquished till Nelson won the battle of Trafalgar in 1805.

<small>Ships, colonies, and commerce.</small>

During the century which had elapsed before the war of 1739 the American colonies of England had been—one might say, silently—growing up into vigorous manhood, and for the latter part of that time had been as much concerned with the Spanish quarrel as the British themselves; they were now threatened with extinction or conquest by the combined efforts of France and Spain. The East India Company also, having by this time established its rights and privileges in the three Presidencies of

<small>Dangers besetting Great Britain and its dependencies.</small>

India, found itself in the greatest danger from the French. The masterly way in which these insidious movements had been made, almost unknown, and unopposed by the British Government, is the most remarkable part of the situation. It was hard to make ordinary observers believe the actual facts of the case. But it had now become impossible to deny that the war was a struggle for national existence, a war for ships, colonies, and commerce as the outworks of the defence of the realm. There were not wanting those who still sighed for isolation, still wondered why Great Britain could not keep to herself without meddling with foreign affairs, why, in short, they could not roll back the stream of time. It took many years to convince the nation as a whole that the obligations into which it had entered, and the interests bound up with its daily life, demanded sacrifice. But the stern teaching of failure and disappointment gradually forced its way, and the frequent glimpses of victory led at last to a glorious consummation. As at the time of the Revolution, it now again became an axiomatic part of Foreign Policy to treat the combinations of European States as an essential factor in the safety of the British Isles, the British colonies, and the British commerce.

Deplorable state of the Royal Navy. Perhaps the most convincing proof that the fundamental conditions of such a European policy were inextricably mixed up with all the other necessary conditions of British safety, lies in the miserable effects of the weak and degraded condition of the Royal Navy when the war at last began. An officer of merit in his day, Sir Charles Wager, too easily giving way to the prevailing temper, had allowed the naval service to fall into the state which the readers of "Anson's Voyage" will remember from the account of its disasters. The type of ships remained as it had been in previous generations. When the contest for the command of the Mediterranean began in earnest, it was found that not only the French but the Spaniards had possessed themselves of a superior type to that of the British; and it was only by servilely copying those which had been captured that the unequalled crews of the latter found themselves fairly matched with their enemies. The errors made in the choice of such officers as Mathews and Lestock to command the fleets on which depended the safety of the country, were an additional proof, if any were required—and these did not stand alone—that the feeble Government of that period had lost sight of the ancient landmarks just at the very time when the Bourbon Powers were mustering their forces on all sides, and closing round their former conqueror.

Under the great officers whom the course of the war gradually drew to light, and whom the king and the people forced to the headship of the Royal Navy —Anson, Hawke, Warren, Pocock, Saunders, and their pupils Howe and Keppel—the service raised its head again, and gave the elder Pitt the material he required for founding the modern British Empire in the Seven Years' War (1756–1763). In other words, the recovery of an imperial position by the British people was marked by the welding together of the old and the new elements of Foreign Policy. The latter could not exist in safety without the former, and the key of the whole was to be found in the efficiency of the sea-forces. The security of the country from invasion was to be guarded as of old by sea-supremacy; the coasts of the Low Countries

Reform of the navy the keystone of the national success.

must be in friendly hands; the colonies must be saved from absorption by the French and Spaniards, who had been for so long a time laying their hostile plans; India must be kept free for the development of British trade and government; the Mediterranean must be retained at any cost by a sufficient fleet and by the help of its fortified depots at Gibraltar and Minorca. For the latter of these Malta, later on, became the substitute.

So it remains.

As the colonies increased in number, and the wars of the century strengthened the British position, this policy became so natural that its necessity was never seriously disputed. It has only been obligatory on British statesmen to review the situation from time to time, and adapt the dimensions of the Navy to the changing armaments of other nations, so that it might at least be a match, as of old, for any other two combined. This, we see then, is not in any sense a discovery of to-day. It may have been too much put out of sight under the influences of a long peace, and Captain Mahan's "Sea Power" has no doubt been useful in reviving a wholesome public opinion on the subject; but the most elementary knowledge of English history is sufficient to establish a perfect familiarity with the principles involved. At the same time, however, it must be remembered that the remarkable book above mentioned has had and will have a general effect on the other nations of the European world, and in that way a reflex effect upon Great Britain by no means altogether to its advantage. When the plain and irrefutable doctrine of "Sea Power" becomes common property, Great Britain will not be left alone to translate it into action, but will assuredly find herself under the same necessity of a constant increase of sea-armaments as the Continental nations already experience with respect to their land-forces. However deplorable, there is no escape; for to the former lines of Foreign Policy already detailed there has been added during the last half-century the necessity of providing for the sustenance of an immense population which depends on food supplies imported from foreign countries. *[Additional question of food-supply.]*

Let us then resume our illustrations of the change, or rather growth, of British Foreign Policy ushered in by the war of 1739. We have in this chapter to trace it as it developed itself in the capable hands of the elder Pitt, and under the great chiefs whose noble succession culminated at the end of the century in Lord Nelson.

It will be observed that in describing the processes of growing public opinion in connection with our subject, we have said nothing about the army, and very little about the policy concerned with the coasts of the Low Countries. As to the former, we may remark that the long peace which succeeded Marlborough's campaigns interfered with the training of military, even more than of naval, officers, and that the renewal of war exhibited the poverty of the country in that respect to a still greater extent. Such generals as Lord Stair and the Duke of Cumberland on the Continent, and Braddock in America, were much of a piece with the unsatisfactory, or at best commonplace, admirals who were alone available for command at sea. It was not till the war itself had formed and brought to light a Wolfe and an Amherst, a Clive and a Coote, that any confidence could be placed in the men who were to command *[The army could not keep step with the navy.]*

the excellent material which the nation has always produced at demand. But what could any of them have effected had not Anson, Hawke, and Boscawen stopped the French reinforcements on their way to America, and shattered the fleets which were about to invade England, or if Warren in the West, and Pocock in the East, had not secured that freedom from interference by sea which gave the talents of the generals a fair field?

It is worth remarking that each of the earliest battles, one on each element, which displayed the want of generals and admirals, brought to light at the same time the man who was to exercise surpassing influence on the coming struggles. We cannot, of course, compare the influence of George II. with that of Chatham; but it is not too much to say that the great minister could have done nothing without the king, who, having proved himself a hero at Dettingen, used the whole power of the Crown in support of the one man whom he found fit to take the helm. It was George II. who, arriving on the spot in time to remedy the errors of his general, led in person the magnificent charge which turned a defeat into a glorious victory—though he had to retreat from a want of supplies, which was not his fault. Again, it was Captain Hawke in the Berwick, who shone out so far above every other actor in Mathews' miserable battle off Toulon, that his rise to the headship of the navy commenced from that day. There was plenty for him to do.

George II. and Lord Hawke.

But we may still further say about the army and its influence upon Foreign Policy that, with the exception of the fine officers brought to the front in the Seven Years' War, it made no advance like the navy in the supply of first-rate talent. The war with the American colonies was waged by generals inferior to George Washington, and the only Englishman who might have matched him, Lord Cornwallis, was so ill-supported by his colleagues that his surrender at Yorktown, which practically closed the war, ought scarcely to be regarded as his fault. When the great Revolution-War with France demanded that all disposable talent should be employed in order to deal with the military enthusiasm of the Revolution, the old Teutonic practice of the German Courts prevailed; and the king, so much to be commended in most respects, prevailed on even Mr. Pitt for a time to give the command of the British forces on the Continent to the Duke of York. But that serious error had at least the effect of showing the colonel of one of his regiments what ought not to be done; and he never forgot the lesson. This was the future Duke of Wellington.

As to the coast of the Low Countries, it is enough to say that the principle of alliance and amity between Great Britain on the one side, and the Dutch and Flemings on the other, which had been retained through so many centuries, and which, when temporarily broken by the Dutch wars, was so fully renewed by William III., remained not only unimpaired but strengthened after the Peace of Utrecht. For the purposes of Marlborough's "Grand Alliance," indeed, the Dutch, as we have seen, were far less serviceable than they had been under their own Stadtholder; but that was chiefly because their strength had been exhausted during the consuming conflict which they had sustained against the two successive tyrants of Europe. Their fortunes might *Alliance with the Low Countries.*

have been repaired if the British had not pushed them out of the position which they had fondly hoped would have been their own, the dominion of the sea and the leadership of the colonial world. But their short-lived ascendancy had been acquired during the collapse of Britain under the Stuarts, and, as it happened, the Dukes of Brunswick brought with them to England that Hanoverian influence over the Dutch which had already stood them in good stead, and used it with the greatest skill and energy.

<small>Hanover in relation to Holland.</small> This influence was, as we now perceive—though the fact has scarcely found its way into our English histories—far more than a set-off against the Continental "entanglements" which the possession of Hanover brought with it. It was in the character of the great leader of outraged Europe, during the anomalous condition of the Empire, that Great Britain had won and extended her position under Marlborough; and Hanover, as we shall see, was to form in a sense a fulcrum for the support of the lever by which Chatham moved the world. The change of the allegiance of the Netherlands from Spain to Austria helped to knit the bonds between the inhabitants of the opposite coasts, and the best possible proof of their political connection was afforded when the French Revolution broke out. It was the union between the militant Republicans of France and the democratic portion of the people of the Low Countries which brought home to the British the danger to which they were exposed; and France declared war in consequence of the younger Pitt's remonstrances. That also we shall examine more in detail. Since the Peace of Vienna the bonds have been still more closely interwoven; and to safeguard

the independent position of both Holland and Belgium is one of the obligations which bind Great Britain to place herself as the active auxiliary, when required, of any particular State or States on the Continent.

We may take as the text of the Foreign Policy of Great Britain, at the time when the war broke out in 1739, a well-known passage from Ranke's luminous "History of England" (v. 405): "The fall of Walpole was not the fall of an ordinary minister, but the fall of the political system based on the first union of the House of Hanover [under George I.] with the Regent of France. It was a return to the policy which had at that time been abandoned—the policy of war against France and the Bourbon interest of Europe; and that at a time when these had the upper hand both by land and sea." We have seen that on almost every side the interests of Great Britain were endangered, and that Walpole had not been deprived of power a day too soon. We have noted the almost despair of the people at finding their navy reduced to such a state that no dependence could be placed upon it, and the general sense of fury at discovering that the Bourbon family were acting on a steady principle of co-operation and aggression, while there seemed to be no one at the head of affairs to cope with them.

Gloomy prospects for Great Britain.

France was now protected on her eastern frontier by Lorraine, and the Mediterranean seemed about to realise the condition, dear to the French through so many centuries, of becoming a French lake. The last days of the country which, as Burke says, William III. had taught to regard herself as "the arbitress of Europe, the tutelary angel of the human

G

race," seemed to be drawing near. What was to prevent the commerce, by means of which the people of Great Britain had been nursed into prosperity, from being swept off the face of the sea? The foundations of the British Empire were thus laid during the influence of a general sense of alarm and insecurity, and the Continental Powers soon found out that when this feeling was once predominant the character of the people broke out much in the same way as of old.

The Rebellion of 1745 was of great service to England. The British were not themselves aware how much benefit they had derived from what seemed so disastrous at the moment, the Rebellion of 1745. The Union of England, Scotland, and Ireland has been for many centuries, and always must be, the first and most essential condition of success in entering upon a European war. The Union with Scotland under Queen Anne had been a noble beginning; but the practical independence of the Highlands had survived that operation, and was not extinguished till the battle of Culloden. Now at last, over mountain and plain alike, the law reigned supreme, and the power of the feudal chiefs was abolished. Now at last these gallant savages were disarmed. From this time forth they fairly set out with characteristic energy upon that race of education and civilisation in which their Lowland brethren had had the start of them, and in which the Scotch as a people have outstripped all competitors. They were soon to find themselves amongst the foremost ranks of the British forces when the genius of the elder Pitt called forth their warlike spirit into a legitimate channel by enlisting them as Highland regiments with a Highland costume under Highland officers.

And Ireland, which has so often in history been a dead weight upon British enterprise, was at this same period in a happier condition than usual through the splendid administration of Lord Chesterfield. At this critical moment another obstacle to national progress was thus, at least partially, removed by his means. Nor did the effects of his admirable measures, which kept Ireland so tranquil during the Rebellion of 1745 that troops quartered there were spared for the English emergency, pass away with his period of office. We cannot but connect with it the subsequent rapid increase in the value of Irish land, and the eagerness with which tenants now sought to obtain leases at largely increased rates. Thus agriculture began to supply in some degree the void which English jealousy of the trade and commerce of the sister island had created; and when, after some years, this immediate source of prosperity received a check, a compensation was found in the general reclamation of bog and waste lands, and in a course of general improvement to which the troubles of the latter part of the century, consequent on the Revolt of the American colonies, alone brought a cruel and too-prolonged suspension.

Ireland under Lord Chesterfield.

If we may pause for a moment to explain how this exceptional state of Ireland was brought about by Chesterfield's brief administration in 1745, we must remember that he was "the first Lord-Lieutenant, since the subjugation of the island by William III., to introduce order and economy into Irish finance, to encourage Irish science, and to seek out and employ merit without reference to private or political interest." Ireland, it was publicly said, enjoyed a serenity unknown to the greater part of Europe.

And this success was purchased, not by the depression of the Protestants, whose associations for the defence of the island received Chesterfield's earnest encouragement, still less by the neglect of efficient preparation for soldierly defence if the wave of Jacobitism should break upon its shores. This mixture of firmness and conciliation in the hands of an enlightened statesman accounts for the phenomenon.[1]

<small>Militia organised at last.</small> Add to the practical union of the three countries which made straight the road to empire, the effect of the Scottish Rebellion, in putting an end to the repugnance of the English to establish the national militia, and we cease to wonder at the enormous contrast presented by the country, when Pitt took the helm, to its condition under Walpole and his immediate successors. The memory of the Cromwellian tyranny and of the attempts both of James II. and William III. to establish a standing army had hitherto been too strong to allow the nation to tolerate even the old militia. The people hated and were ashamed of the foreign troops brought over from time to time on an emergency, but were quite aware that some disciplined force was required on such occasions; and the Rebellion of 1745 brought the need home in an unmistakable way. Such an exhibition of national panic as that of "Black Friday" at the appearance of the insignificant force led by the Pretender, and such a revelation of jobbing and corruption as that which prevailed in the highest quarters concerning the forces raised to deal with the invasion, were felt

---

[1] See in the 'Edinburgh Review' for October 1886, an Article entitled "A Century of Irish Government," by the author of this book.

to be a disgrace beyond bearing. But the prejudice did not yield to one assault, nor was the remedy found till Pitt was strong enough to take the matter in hand.[1] He could now work on a secure base.

When Pitt, after having at last surmounted every wave of opposition, was forced to the headship of affairs in 1756, he had no longer to trouble himself about the unification of the kingdom or its home-defences, and saw before him a task which exactly suited his statesmanlike genius. He had, indeed, to throw to the winds his former opinions with regard to Hanover; for he perceived that instead of being hampered with a barren responsibility for an outlying Continental State, that State, under the circumstances of Frederick the Great's war with the rest of the Powers, might be, as it turned out to be, of inestimable value to his own country in the struggle which had been forced upon her. It is difficult to say in which respect the soldierly old George II. was most useful at this crisis—whether as Frederick's uncle taking a leading part in the combinations of Northern Germany against France, or as the keen observer of military and naval conduct at home, encouraging the brave and getting rid of the incompetent. Nor was it a small thing that the shocking feud in the Royal Family should have been extinguished just at this time by the death of Frederick Prince of Wales. It had served one good end, at least, in forming a rallying-point for the opposition

<small>Pitt and George II. at the crisis.</small>

---

[1] The "Establishment of a National Militia" (Hallam's Const. Hist., iii. 262) took place after much debate in 1757. Ever since the Great Rebellion—a period of about a century—the ancient Militia had practically been in abeyance. This was owing to the struggle for its command which had taken place at that time, and which both King and Parliament dreaded to renew.

to Walpole and his feeble successors. The king and Pitt were now left free to take up a Foreign Policy which they had no choice but to pursue, and which, as we have said, was fairly represented by the phrase, "*Ships, Colonies, and Commerce.*"

The words, and the thoughts suggested by the words, are inextricably combined. "Ships" connotes both royal and commercial ships; "Colonies" connotes the ships which are to protect them and the ships which are to convey troops, Government supplies, and commercial cargoes; "Commerce" connotes the exchange of commodities which ships alone can convey. So that, as in the very beginning of national life, the country clearly understood that the Royal Navy must be maintained in a state of efficiency suitable to the times. Each year which had elapsed since the war of 1739 broke out had been teaching its lessons, and Pitt found to his hand the justly celebrated Lord Anson as the organiser of the navy, and Sir Edward Hawke, who had lost no time in justifying the splendid promise he had given, in command of the Channel fleet. Thus a head and a right arm were available for the naval service which were exactly suited to its needs. Not that the great minister was capable of using the matchless British war-weapon without more experience than he had yet acquired. His treatment of the affair of Admiral Byng was unsatisfactory, and his failure at Rochefort in 1757 was much more his own fault than that of any one else.[1] But he made no more mistakes. Selecting, from the junior ranks of generals, Wolfe and Amherst, keeping Hawke at the

Lord Anson and Hawke.

Pitt fails at first.

[1] See the Life of Admiral Lord Hawke, chap. vii., 2nd edition, 1896 (W. H. Allen).

head of the Channel Fleet, employing Boscawen at the head of the Mediterranean Fleet, and Pocock at the head of that in the Indian Ocean, he placed Howe, Rodney, and Keppel in command of the squadrons employed in making diversions upon the coast of France. At the same time he protected the flank of Frederick's Prussian forces by British and Hanoverian troops, judiciously placed under Prince Ferdinand of Brunswick. Further, the king and the united people of the United Kingdom were at his back, and they let him know it; while Parliament made no difficulty as to the expense of his armaments, or the subsidies paid over to the indomitable Frederick. Great Britain and Prussia rose together with a bound. The spectacle of Frederick's extraordinary victories, turning defeats into triumphs over and over again, had a great effect upon the British; and there is no doubt that the vigour and thoroughness of such a statesman as Pitt had a distinct effect upon the commanders whom he employed. *His plans.* *Prussia and Frederick the Great.*

The method by which these high qualities took effect has, however, been often, perhaps generally, misrepresented. Pitt figures in history as a sort of slave-driver, flourishing his whip over men who would otherwise have behaved no better than their predecessors. The true reading of his administration is that he chose the men who had already shown courage and genius, gave them the needful material for success, and threw aside the useless instruments of former times, so that the fine officers in command felt that their services would be appreciated, however far they might depart from the usual fruitless system of routine which had hung like a leaden *Pitt's relation to the officers in command.*

weight upon the services. Hawke, who had discarded traditional rules even in 1747, required no spur to do the same thing at Quiberon (1759), when he broke up the fleet and army which were about to invade the British shores, under circumstances unparalleled in the history of the world. Boscawen, though he failed to keep the French ships within the harbour of Toulon, did not scruple to run them ashore and capture them on the neutral territory of Portugal, being quite aware that the invasion of Britain was to be stopped at any cost. Wolfe was allowed to follow his own plans; nor did he require any spur or slave-whip. And the same may be said of the rest. The judicial murder of Admiral Byng has been made too much of. It found a witty exponent in Voltaire, whose mocking phrase—"*pour encourager les autres*"—has been taken as gospel truth ever since.

There is truth in the phrase, no doubt. The treatment of this sad affair elevated the standard of naval capacity, and acted as a warning to future possible Byngs; but the error of employing so incompetent an officer, who owed his rise to interest, was never sufficiently brought home to those who deserved blame; nor did the evil effect of such partiality prevent the perpetration of the same fault to an almost incredible extent in the later history of the Royal Navy. On the other hand, the great officers of the Seven Years' War were worthy founders of the Empire, *sans peur et sans reproche*. They only required to be left free, and to know that their acts would be favourably interpreted if they gave a good account of the enemy. It may here be remarked that, with scarcely an exception, it was possible for Pitt to find his agents in men of social standing and family position. The Empire was founded by an aristocracy, which was perhaps then, with all its faults, at its best. *The Empire founded by the aristocracy.*

The first part of the programme of Foreign Policy was thus completed. The Royal Navy had swept all others off the sea, and attained to the brilliant position from which it never afterwards receded. Under its wing commerce had flourished. During the earlier and less fortunate war (1739–1748) merchants had indeed suffered very serious losses, but the enemy had suffered more, so that the balance of prizes was estimated to be in favour of Great Britain by two millions sterling. During the uneasy peace which intervened (1748–1756) between that war and the next, British commerce made great strides, and in the Seven Years' War it rose to such a pitch that it enabled the country to stand up against its reverses during the revolt of the colonies, assisted as they were by France, Spain, and Holland. To provide for the security of that commerce had been the main object of the war of 1739, and it had become the leading factor, or almost the leading factor, in Foreign Politics. Throughout the century the development of manufactures by means of canals, new coal-mines, and progressive inventions of machinery, gradually made Great Britain the "workshop of the world"; and thus the place of commerce was more and more firmly fixed as the centre of Foreign Policy round which everything else was to revolve. The people became a "nation of shopkeepers," building up their trade, as the Jews did their walls, with the sword in one hand and the trowel in the other. *A "nation of shopkeepers."*

Perhaps this is most observable in the treaties of

Witness the treaties.
the century, and not least in the great Treaty of Paris, which concluded the Seven Years' War in 1763. In all of them alike the victories of Great Britain were most inadequately recognised. Statesmen and diplomatists contented themselves with securing the entrance of the Mediterranean by Gibraltar and Minorca, so that their ships might pass freely and the Levant trade be uninterrupted; with establishing the exclusive possession of North America and India, which had been won by arms; and with strengthening the West Indian position, though not excluding other nations, so as to prevent a repetition of the state of things out of which the war of 1739 had arisen. The commercial classes were satisfied, and they now represented the public sentiment more than at any previous time in English history.

And it is well to remind ourselves of this fact, for we are very likely to forget it in the literary warfare which waged around these various treaties, and in the political partisanship which coloured the public notices of the times—a partisanship which has, somewhat discreditably to our modern teaching, coloured them ever since. It is also left too much out of sight that in her contests with France and Spain, Great Britain was fighting not only for the primary object of keeping intruders off her own shores, but for the maintenance of the Protestant interest in Europe, and for the freedom of the weaker States (of which Hanover was one) from the domination of the more powerful. She was, in short, the visible champion of International Law, and thus found her duties to her own subjects correspond with her duties to her neighbours. The doctrine of the

Britain the champion of International Law.

Balance of Power was, in her hands, only another phrase for those elementary duties. Her mixed Continental and Colonial position, and her headship of the Reform Communions, developed on her part a persistent hostility to tyrants, which also provided for her own defence. Her support of the weak made her strong. With the internal concerns of other States she had never interfered except when and so far as those concerns affected her own rights, her own safety, her own existence as a nation.

But while we cannot help observing that successes in war were invariably followed by a retreat from the strong but invidious position which the British might have been justified in assuming, it is far from necessary to attribute, with complacent optimism, this fact to the deliberate forethought and judgment either of the Government or people. It is rather the compensation, the self-acting balance, not obvious perhaps at first sight, provided by a free Constitution, the roots of which penetrate to the very structure and composition of the nation. Self-government involves an ultimate appeal to the nation. However ardently a people rush into war, and however just the cause, they soon grow weary of it when the needful sacrifices are brought home to them. That weariness, even though they have achieved success, leads them to accept and approve of terms which are often below the position attained by means of the war. The members of the Government which has carried on the war are generally the last to see this change of opinion or to recognise its justice; but they have to give way, and when they have done so, the popular voice which has forced their hand not seldom turns against them. Yet, in spite of the complaints which naturally fill the air, the right course has, on the whole, been pursued.

<small>British colonies in America the main object of attack.</small>
The affairs of the American colonies occupied by far the largest space in the Foreign Policy of Great Britain during the period treated in this chapter. We have seen that the colonists had a large share in bringing about the war of 1739. They and the British merchants were in full sympathy in their determination to retain their trade with the Spanish settlements; and it was one of the main objects of France, by means of the secret treaty of 1733, to make use of the Spanish footing in North America in order to support its grand scheme of attack upon the British colonies. The three Bourbon thrones of France, Spain, and the two Sicilies, had not been acquired for a mere show of grandeur, or even for the purpose of dominating the Mediterranean. The prospects of a French America and a French India had, under Louis XV., succeeded to the European ambitions of Louis XIV. The English had indeed preceded them in both directions; the Dutch had preceded the English and the Portuguese the Dutch —at least in the Indian Ocean. It was very natural that the French should ask, Why should not France have her turn? And in truth the French and British were now so intermixed in the neighbourhood of the St. Lawrence that their petty jealousies and differences could no more be composed without hostilities than the West Indian quarrels between Spain and Great Britain in 1739.

<small>Attack on them during the peace after 1748;</small>
Thus, whatever might be the unpractical dreams of the British Government when it made the Peace of Aix-la-Chapelle in 1748, the French never stopped for a moment in their career. All they wanted at

that critical time was a free passage for their ships and soldiers between France and her western colonies, undisturbed by the ubiquitous navy of their ancient rival. Their chief attention was bestowed on this main part of their policy. In India Dupleix was encouraged and assisted to follow up the advantages already gained over the British. In the West Indies and on the African coast all neutral territory was claimed for France by the simple process of setting up posts and proclamations, and in some cases by actual occupation. In North America no pains were spared to strengthen the fortifications of the island of Cape Breton, and especially of its capital, Louisbourg; to form extensive alliances with the savage Indian tribes at the back of the British settlements, who were now armed, and to some extent disciplined, for the conflict which would soon begin: and above all, to establish a chain of forts which should connect their prosperous Canadian colony with the Mississippi, and so with Louisiana, and with the forces of their allies, the Spaniards. They were also bent on obtaining water-access to Canada by lake and river to the south of the St. Lawrence, which is ice-closed in winter. *also on India, Africa, and West Indies.*

This was an extremely clever scheme. If the sturdy British colonists who had already given so much trouble, and who were very much more numerous than those of France and Spain, could only be hemmed in by a military cordon in their rear, and checked by great naval and military stations in front, there would be some real prospect of a French America. Jonquière and Galissonière were, as agents for the aggrandisement of their country, only second to Dupleix and Lally in India; *A French America.*

but they have dropped out of general history. It did not much trouble the national conscience that some of these aggressive forts were built within territories which the British had long considered their own. Why should these people be the only colonists to extend and encroach upon their neighbours? The French Indians were not indeed of much service except to cut off a few straggling settlers, and to use the scalping-knife with a scandalous freedom; but considerable bodies of disciplined French soldiers had been stealthily introduced into the new forts. The colonists could make no united, and therefore no effective, resistance; and Great Britain was not at all likely to begin over again an expensive war for such a trifle.

The British Government did, however, in 1749, take one step which showed they were not unaware of the future danger—the foundation of the military colony of Halifax, a thoroughly statesmanlike measure, but it only led to further French aggression.

The French in Nova Scotia. Though the limits of Nova Scotia (or Acadie) had been carefully recognised by the Treaty of Utrecht, the French colonial governor made no scruple of pursuing the same policy as had been decided upon in the case of the older colonists. He seized upon the adjacent unoccupied territory, built forts along the rear of the Acadian colony, cut off their fur-trade, and encouraged rebellion amongst the old French settlers, who, having accepted loyally the terms of the Treaty of Utrecht, had hitherto lived in quiet subordination to the British Government. The Jesuit missionaries were particularly concerned in the spreading of sedition. Thus a petty border warfare had commenced between the colonists of the two nations, in which the British could not but suffer most. The feebleness of the Home Government precluded redress of grievances, and the peculiarly unsatisfactory representation of Great Britain at the Court of France by Lord Albemarle made things worse.

So far had the Pelham administration been from comprehending the full danger of the situation that in 1750 there had been a large reduction of the navy, to which Anson reluctantly gave way, and against which Pitt, from the side of the Opposition, protested in vain. Even the Spaniards renewed their old methods of harassing British trade in the West Indies, and ill-treating British merchants in Spain. In India the genius of Clive had begun to shine through the cloud of gloom which had fallen over the prospects of the British; but no one could possibly foresee what would be the end of the struggle upon the great Colonial question into which the country was being forced. Resolutely, but yet sadly, did the nation enter upon it, for the people trusted Newcastle's Government still less than they had trusted that of Walpole; and the half-measures which were at first adopted were as unsuccessful as such half-measures always are. The French outwitted the British during the Peace on every point. They passed over to North America by ones and twos, so secretly that their number was not even guessed at, a fleet of twenty-five line-of-battle ships, and on board these ships troops of soldiers. Still further, from their vantage-ground at Toulon they sent out a fleet and regiments of soldiers to lay siege to Port Mahon, which was almost taken before the Government received any information. The unfor-

British outwitted by the French.

tunate selection of Byng to command the relieving force, and his distressing failure, filled the measure of the national wrath and forced Pitt to the helm.

<small>Attempt to close the Mediterranean.</small>

This renewed attempt of France and Spain to close the Mediterranean to British commerce was a part of the general attack now organised upon Great Britain, but only a subordinate part. It grew out of the efforts of the British to support the Balance of Power on the Continent, which had seriously exercised their diplomacy and their arms for many years; but the imbecility of the Walpole, Pelham, and Newcastle Governments had stood in the way of any general success. The cause of the Pragmatic Sanction and Maria Theresa had indeed been honourably supported, and British superiority in the Mediterranean had been on the whole retained.

The defence of their colonies in America formed the chief ground of the Seven Years' War, as far as the British were concerned. The invasion of England was soon to exhibit itself as a portion of the enemy's general attack, and thus every branch of its Foreign Policy was brought to the test. This is what makes the Seven Years' War so important a feature in history—important enough on the Continent, but much more so to Great Britain. All that had been hitherto cherished as vital to the well-being and even existence of the nation was in extreme danger, and its triumphant emergence from a sea of troubles, as the war went on, fixed the circle of its future policy. It will be observed that the idea of leaving the colonies to their fate can scarcely be said to have ever entered the British mind. The American colonists had grown up like children,—somewhat troublesome children, round their parents, but they were an integral part of the British nation, with institutions in nearly all respects similar to those of the mother country.

Nor did they regard the mother country in any different light. The idea of separation had never been entertained for a moment. It had been generally felt to be invaluable that there should be a common link between the Colonies and the Crown, that fixed boundaries between themselves should be formed and preserved, and that order should be maintained during the growing period of society, the more so that they had no unity and little mutual intercourse, being kept apart by intense jealousies, arising out of their different origins and constitutions. But now they felt further that, with French and Spaniards closing round them, it was absolutely necessary for them to have the protection of Great Britain; and all the more when their local expeditions against their enemies failed, as they generally did. Without army or navy, and separated by great distances, how could it be otherwise? It is remarkable that some writers should have blamed the mother country for not allowing them to run alone as soon as they were fairly settled. That comes from not understanding the age, or perhaps from transferring the ideas of a small party of modern political economists, now almost extinct, to the society which existed in the middle of the last century. On the contrary, to be left alone was the one thing that neither party wished nor would have tolerated. Their interests were identical, and the loyalty of the colonists to Great Britain—up to the time when events led to separation—was quite as great as could be expected.

British government of its American Colonies.

Mutual interests.

The above sketch will have made plain the out-

The Seven Years' War, 1756–1763, and its effects. lines of the Foreign Policy established by the Seven Years' War, the same indeed which we have been tracing throughout the history of England. It seemed to be fixed for all time by the ascendancy of the Royal Navy, the low condition to which the French and Spanish navies had been reduced, the firm alliance of the Powers which held the Dutch and Flemish coasts in a league with Prussia and Hanover, the constant growth of British commerce, the command of the Mediterranean, and above all, as it appeared at the time, by the unity of the American colonies—now increased by Wolfe's splendid conquest of French Canada—with the mother country. The Empire was founded; but as we do not profess to describe the war here, it is enough for our present purpose to remark that Great Britain had lavished her resources on the protection of her American colonies from the French and Spaniards, and opened up to them a boundless development. We must now glance at the causes of the overclouding of this fair prospect.

CHAPTER VII.

BRITISH FOREIGN POLICY FROM THE CLOSE OF THE SEVEN YEARS' WAR TO THE OPENING OF THE FRENCH-REVOLUTION WAR—1763–1793.

THE reign of George III., which commenced with, or rather by a very little preceded, the Peace of Paris in 1763, brought with it, though insensibly, a great change in the scheme of Foreign Policy traced in the last chapter. The thunders of war had ceased, and Pitt had retired. That it was time he should retire, and so make way for peace, may be called perhaps the sober judgment of history; but there were many, who were unable to take a larger view of the subject, who saw in the Peace only the personal influence of a Court favourite, Lord Bute, over a young and inexperienced king, and who considered the country to have been stopped disastrously in a career of grandeur which would have raised her to a summit of power from which her enemies would never have been able to depose her. We shall not here dwell upon this question. Enough that large majorities in Parliament supported the peace party, and that the great man who might perhaps have composed the differences with the colonies had been reduced to impotence. When he again took office in 1766 his health had given way, and being only a nominal official, the rupture with the colonies which

_{The Peace of Paris, 1763.}

George Grenville had set on foot was carried farther by Charles Townshend, one of the colleagues of Pitt, by that time Earl of Chatham.

Changed relations with American colonists.

Instead, then, of pursuing a Foreign Policy, one leading element of which was to protect and develop the American colonies, the young king and his incompetent ministers found themselves faced by an alienated colonial population. The ideas of the colonists had undergone a great change, partly owing to the fact that there was no longer any hostile pressure upon them from France and Spain, and partly because they had taken offence at the neglect and blunders of the Home Government. These were the underlying elements of discontent, the one discreditable in the abstract to the colonists, but incidental to human nature, the other equally discreditable to the mother country, but incidental to the low political standard of government, which was due to the long and unbalanced tenure of office by the Whig Revolution-families. If any one could have foreseen that a war for independence would arise out of these elements of ill-will, which interpenetrated one another, a very slight attention to the wishes of the colonists would probably have prevented, or at least deferred, the disruption; but the neglect on the part of the British, so far as it did not proceed from mere carelessness, must be considered as the outcome of the insular feeling that enough had been done in the late war for their children of the New World. It was thought that the time had arrived when they might fairly be called upon to pay some of the interest of the National Debt, some portion of the immense expenses which had been incurred in their behalf.

It is difficult, when more than a century has passed away, to place ourselves in the situation. The right to deal with the colonies as if they were a part of the national territory had not yet been practically disputed. Even the seditious "Junius" maintained the right to tax, while Burke declined to deny it, and declared "the constitutional superiority of Great Britain to be as necessary for America as for ourselves, and consistent with all the liberties a sober and spirited American ought to desire." So difficult was it to impress the mother country with the notion that there was a real danger ahead, that even the kindly young king and his easy-going minister, Lord North, when nearly all the obnoxious taxes had been repealed, thought there could be no harm in helping the East India Company by imposing a slight tax on its imported tea. Then came, not without warning, the unappeasable resistance, the burst of pent-up, furious passion on both sides, the blunders and confusion, the horrors of Civil War, and the failure of Great Britain, assailed on all sides. Then was tested the strength of the newly-founded Empire. France and Spain fondly believed that the moment of their revenge had come. Even Holland remembered that she was once the sea-rival of England. No longer was the mistress of the seas to dominate the world. The victories and gains of three generations were to be obliterated. When North America and the West Indies were once reclaimed by the aid of the revolted British colonists, Great Britain should be again confined to the Narrow Seas, and India would surely be recovered under some new Dupleix.

These keen politicians were right enough as to the

European allies of the colonists.

immediate prospect. The assistance of the European enemies of Great Britain did indeed enable the previously overmatched colonists to hold their own; and the power of the British Government was almost paralysed by the sustained opposition of great British statesmen who did not scruple to take advantage, in Parliament and out of it, of the crisis at which their country had arrived. But these politicians had not calculated upon the tenacity of the hold which the history of the past had infused into the very nature of the British people, and above all, upon the king who was their representative, not only by office, but in spirit and sentiment. This tenacity was by no means chiefly founded on animosity to the revolted colonists, but rather upon the fear of the revolt spreading to other portions of the Empire, and especially to Ireland, and upon the disgust occasioned by the unprovoked aggression of the European Powers which had not so long before made peace after a tremendous struggle, a Peace in which the conqueror had granted far easier terms than the circumstances required. Was the whole fabric of empire, built up during the ages with such vast expenditure of industry, money, and human life, to collapse like a child's castle of cards?

Views of George III.

The king, who felt his responsibility profoundly on this point, had been by no means, as often represented, one of those most bent upon harsh measures. That assertion is false. He would gladly have repealed the Stamp Act rather than enforce it with the sword. But colonial independence presented itself as something which it was a solemn duty to prevent at all costs. No inherent right was ever claimed for it; all policy seemed to be against it.

"A small State," wrote the king to Lord North, "may certainly subsist, but a great one, mouldering, cannot get into an inferior situation, but must be annihilated. By perseverance we may bring things to a peace; by giving up the game we are destroying ourselves to prevent our being destroyed." Again, "The country has a right to have the struggle continued till convinced it is in vain." With all classes the war had been popular on these grounds, though prolonged failure had its effect at last. Lord Chatham, who had so vehemently opposed taxation, had often said as much against Independence as any one; and died, as we may say, in the act of beseeching his countrymen never to give way to the demand. Nor did the idea find favour with the colonists till the progress of the war had so embittered the strife that all previous feelings were overwhelmed in the flood of hostility.

The patriotic sentiment that his European enemies must be humbled before any general peace was made, was more keenly operative in fixing the resolution of the king to stand out than anything else, substantially supported as he was on that point by his people, though not by his ministers, who quailed before the combination of foreign foes. The surrender of Cornwallis, scarcely through his own fault, and the failures by sea on the American coasts, had indeed convinced the king that the United States, led by Washington, one of the few great men of all time, had conquered their Independence. It had become plain that the separation of the two countries by the Atlantic Ocean was in those days really the leading feature of the situation. Terms must be made sooner or later. But however that might be, there was to be no cessation of hostilities with the hereditary enemies of Great Britain until their interference had been punished and their pretensions reduced. "We are contending for our whole consequence," wrote the king to North, "whether we are to rank among the Great Powers of Europe, or to be reduced to one of the least considerable. He that is not stimulated by this consideration does not deserve to be a member of this community. We have it not at this hour in our power to make peace; it is by steadiness and by exertions that we are to get into a position to effect it; and with the assistance of Divine Providence I am confident we shall find our enemies forced to look for that blessing."

This letter was written in June 1781 to encourage the fainting heart of the Prime Minister. Only a few months afterwards, the gallant Rodney had conquered the chief fleet of the French, and, not long after that, the Spaniards had shattered themselves to pieces against the Rock of Gibraltar. The Dutch had already been taught to bewail their miscalculations. Hawke and Wolfe had found worthy successors in Rodney and Elliot. The confederated hosts had once more collapsed as in the days of Chatham, and as they were to do again under Chatham's son. The time had come when the war might be concluded with honour. It was concluded in 1783. Never ought the words of George III. to be forgotten: "I was the last to consent to the separation; I will be the first to meet the friendship of the United States as an independent Power."

Peace of Versailles, 1783.

We can now place ourselves where Englishmen stood a hundred years ago, and give the revolted colonists their due meed of praise. They acted as Englishmen might be expected to act. They had carried with them the old English spirit, the old English education in freedom; they rose against what they thought to be tyranny; they learnt with marvellous rapidity the elementary arts of war from the troops sent to reduce them; they established a well-balanced republic—a model for others, and a realisation of their own political needs. Both parties learnt, in the very act of separation, to respect one another. The United States have expanded to an extent which no one could have even imagined in dreams, and spread British institutions over no small portion of the world's surface. As for Great Britain, it has been truly said that she "arose from the war stronger and greater than ever." She exchanged a barren sovereignty for an immense commerce with the new States; and as separation must have come sooner or later, it is possible that its postponement might have brought less satisfactory results. Nor could the renewed struggle with France and Spain have been long delayed. That also was well over when it was; for it was thus that Great Britain secured ten years of rapid recovery and amazing growth under the younger Pitt, and gained an enormous and unprecedented development before the still greater trial of the French-Revolution wars still more terribly taxed her resources. *Effects of the war.*

Thus it will be seen that there is another and a truer view of the Great Revolt than is usually presented in popular books. After the war the British people could say—with more political truth than General Scott's "Wayward sisters, go in peace,"—"Manly children, take your inheritance *Upon Great Britain.*

and prosper." As for the British Empire, which had been founded, as we have seen, in self-defence, it turned out to be all the more firmly planted by the assault of the first great storm which had broken upon it. The British oak, if we may use the simile, struck its roots the deeper for the loss of branches, which by their too great weight had exposed it to danger. It was still young and vigorous enough to put forth fresh branches in their place, and the healthy verdure of the newer shoots soon filled up the void, and concealed the ravages of the hurricane.

<small>Upon the Mediterranean, Canada, and India.</small> For a time, indeed, these newer shoots were few. The loss of Minorca was of small consequence to British commerce, since the Rock of Gibraltar had been proved impregnable, but it had been deeply felt. It was the only drawback to the general satisfaction at the Peace of Versailles in 1783. Twenty years were to elapse before the safe possession of Malta could supply that influence in Italy and Sicily which was required to keep up British supremacy in the Mediterranean. The delay only the more rigorously determined the course of British policy when the nations once more clashed together in mortal conflict. Canada, which, after Wolfe's victory, had been wisely provided with a liberal constitution, had not only remained vehemently loyal during the struggle, but had become the refuge and home of the Loyalists of the United States. It thus presented itself as in some sense a set-off against the loss of those States, as well as a channel for commerce which promised to widen every year; and India, which had been, like the old American colonies, too much overlooked by British states-

men, became, as soon as the Peace of Versailles was made, the concern of rival ministers and rival Governments. Fox's India Bill failed to command national assent; and Pitt's Bill, which he carried as soon as he became Prime Minister, settled, under the great administration of Lord Cornwallis, that magnificent possession almost in the form and system which obtained down to our own day.

With trade opening out in all these directions, the change which had been effected by the loss of the United States was rather a change in name than in reality. The necessity of defending those States from European aggression had indeed passed away, but the protection of the East and West Indies and of Canada remained as much a part of British policy as ever, and took a larger development as more and more capital was sunk in those possessions.

But before taking a survey of the Foreign Policy of the younger Pitt, we must notice a very important ingredient in the war which we have briefly noticed in connection with the American colonies and with Lord Chatham. The so-called "Armed Neutrality" had been sprung upon Great Britain just at the moment when she was reeling in the struggle with the revolted States, and was weighted with France, Spain, and Holland on her back. The Empress Catherine headed the attack on British maritime supremacy, and before long was joined by Prussia—which had not forgotten that the Peace of Paris had been made without her complicity,—by Holland, Denmark, Sweden, Portugal, Naples, and the Empire. France and Spain did not join the league, but gladly accepted its principles. Under

The Armed Neutrality.

the circumstances the stoppage of the British Right of Search was tantamount to the destruction of the means by which she had hitherto grown great. It may be well to place this matter in its true light.

The Right of Search exercised in war by Great Britain, contrary to the falsely assumed right of Spain exercised in peace in the West Indian seas, "had generally been acknowledged as the law of nations," and she was under solemn engagements with other Powers, under which they had "altered the primitive law by mutual stipulations."[1] That "free ships should make free goods" had been allowed under certain special treaties for mutual benefit; but this provision was accompanied by the rule that "enemy ships should make enemy goods." The last was not a rule necessarily connected with the first, but supremely important in its operation, for it formed an effective security against the collusion which must otherwise take place. But what now occurred? By the Armed Neutrality the latter rule was simply abolished, while the former was peremptorily authorised as of universal application; and thus the Right of Search could only be exercised with extreme difficulty. If Great Britain had consented, she would in fact have relinquished the power of preventing supplies of every kind from being poured into France, Spain, and the colonies with which she was in deadly conflict. The universal law was to be broken at a moment when its continuance, however unpleasing to other nations, could alone enable her to bring the war to an end. She defied the Confederacy, and her naval victories

[1] British Declaration, Annual Register, xxiii. 349.

secured her position. With the Peace of Versailles, the Armed Neutrality dissolved;—to reappear when storms once more broke upon the British maritime supremacy. The attempt, however, had the effect of bringing Russia to the front as a great Baltic Power with which British Foreign Policy had to reckon; and this advance of Russia, itself largely due to Chatham's neglect, taxed to the utmost as he had been with the French struggle, formed one of his son's chief difficulties when he accepted the office of Prime Minister at the close of 1783.

The rise of Russia had been steadily progressing since Peter the Great had established her as one of the Great Powers of Europe at the beginning of the century. She had indeed failed in crushing Prussia, though the Empire and France had joined in the attempt; and Frederick had made his country a great independent Power. In 1772 the fatal Partition of Poland took place; and then, when the Empress Catherine found herself firmly placed on the throne, she used her great talents and unscrupulous diplomacy for the purpose of crushing Sweden in the north and Turkey in the south. In spite of her enormous extent, Russia was determined to have further room to expand both in the Baltic and the Mediterranean. Both of the threatened States were, however, unfortunately for Russia, the allies of Great Britain, and the younger Pitt found himself obliged to prevent the success of Russia in both directions, not only for the sake of the British allies, but for the sake of British commerce, which had greatly increased in both seas. The Porte had been in close alliance with the English ever since the reign of Queen Elizabeth. No small share of

The rise of Russia.

Relations between Great Britain and Turkey.

the Asiatic traffic which, as its route through Europe changed from age to age, had left so many marks on the fortunes of the West, had now fallen into English hands. For some generations the "Turkey Merchants" had been the typical representatives of English commercial wealth, and had scarcely yet been eclipsed by the rising fortunes amassed in the East and West Indies.

The alliance of the Porte with France was indeed older than that with England; for a diversion from the side of Turkey had often been a part of French policy in their wars with Austria: and the elder Pitt, as we have said, had, during the mortal struggle of the Seven Years' War, always favoured Russia as against France. Even Fox, in 1783, was deaf to the proposal of France that she and Great Britain should combine to check the aggressions of Russia upon Turkey, and upon what remained of Poland. The alliance of Great Britain and Turkey had, in fact, been hitherto only a commercial connection, but it was felt that the possession of India made it a very important alliance to the former of the two countries, and that circumstances might arise which would call for a more strictly political alliance.

It was this old and valued ally which now lay crushed beneath the heel of the Muscovite. The recent Treaty of Kainardji (1774) had detached the Tartars from the Turks, planted Russia on the shores of the Euxine, and established a Russian Protectorate of the Christian vassal States of the Porte. The Turkish fleet had been destroyed. The Empress had quite recently carried her conquests still farther. The capture of Oczakoff distinctly announced the coming partition of the Ottoman Empire. It was about to follow the fate of the still undigested Poland and Finland.

Still more pressing were affairs in the Baltic, for they were nearer home; and Russia had led, as we have seen, nearly all the nations of the Continent in the cause of the Armed Neutrality. The hostility of Russia endangered the safety of the British Channel; and long before the French Revolution ruled the situation in Europe, she and Austria, under Catherine and Joseph, were sapping away the Dutch barrier which was so important to Europe. As early as 1781 Joseph had begun to work out his wild scheme of giving to the Elector of Bavaria the Austrian Netherlands, while he was to take Bavaria in exchange; and he had gone so far as to dismantle the Barrier Towns, which had cost such vast expenditure in blood and money under Queen Anne. This affected Holland, inasmuch as the French, already in a republican ferment caught from America, and prepared by Voltaire and Rousseau, were overrunning the Netherlands and settling themselves amongst the Dutch. A republican party, as opposed to that of the Stadtholder, had always existed there, and now, reinforced by the French, was about to imperil the protection which England had always considered of vital importance to the safety of the Channel. This insane plan of Joseph's was indeed peremptorily stopped by Frederick the Great. It was his last political act before his death in 1786 removed the one great obstacle to a European revolution; but Pitt had to meet the now imminent danger by again forming the old alliance between Great Britain, Prussia, Sweden, and the Dutch Government, and

Plots of the Empress Catherine and the Emperor Joseph II.

Frederick the Great interposes.

thus he once more checked the designs of France. For the moment the Baltic and the Channel were safeguarded; but the French Revolution occurred almost immediately afterwards, and the republican enthusiasts would brook no denial. That Pitt's measures had even a temporary success was due to the fact that he represented the complete readiness of his people to go to war on the subject, and that is, after all, the only real strength of diplomacy.

Pitt's Foreign Policy up to this point had been remarkably successful. Austria and Denmark had been detached from their alliance with Russia—a great result. But the British people were not prepared to support him and the king in their further measures for the protection of Turkey. It was too far off. If they had been properly supported, the Empress would have found herself confronted by British fleets, and by Polish and German armies subsidised by British gold. The opportunity was lost, and the Crimean War was required, two generations later, to save the East Mediterranean from becoming Russian. But something had been done. The further partition of Turkey was warded off by the dread of British interference; but the suzerainty of the Porte was never efficiently asserted till 1856, when the special protectorate of Russia over the Christian provinces was abolished.

Turkey saved by Pitt.

It was then at last that the collective guarantee of the European Powers was established as the substitute for the Russian protectorate, which had been only another name for gradual absorption. The true principles of International Law were then at last laid down by the consent of all the Great Powers. The

"Concert of Europe" was to regulate its affairs, an idea which had been before the European mind for some centuries. Each, as Sully had said, and which we once more repeat, must be powerful enough to be respected by its neighbours, and each intimately concerned with the external policy of every other; each should be internally strong and well-ordered, or independence would be impossible. Each was to have an interest in the prosperity of the rest. The struggles of the French-Revolution period, which we have here forestalled, only exposed too clearly the need of these principles.

We are now in a position to sum up Pitt's Foreign Policy in comprehensive terms, or rather to remind ourselves of it,—for we have already emphasised it as the necessary policy of the British Empire then and now. It was to combine the principle of the defence and preservation of the united British Isles, of her colonies, and of her now world-wide commerce, with the old-established principles of International Law and Balance of Power. Such European concert as was possible had been skilfully obtained. The aggressions of three States of the first class, France, Russia, and Austria, had been checked without war. The security of the smaller States, which in previous European settlements had been constituted the barriers and "buffers" between their more powerful neighbours,—a security which has often proved itself invaluable,—had been restored as far as was still possible, or at least preserved from threatened injury. In the earlier years of George III. those who were responsible for European concert in maintaining public rights had not perceived, or had neglected their duty. In the nine years of Pitt's

General view of Pitt's Foreign Policy.

brilliant peace administration, the wholesome action of international principles had been once more triumphantly established.

<small>Portugal.</small> One such minor State has not yet been noticed. Portugal may be grouped with the States of the Mediterranean, amongst which it had been the policy of Great Britain to constitute herself an independent, if not supreme, Power. It had long been reckoned as a natural ally. Not only was its chronic hostility to Spain as marked as the chronic hostility of Holland to both Spain and France, and its interests so far exactly coincident with the interests of England on both sides of the Atlantic, but its seaboard was most conveniently situated for mutual commerce, and Lisbon was almost an unequalled port. Perhaps there was no stronger bond of union between any two States of Europe. From the time when English crusaders helped the Portuguese to expel the Moors this friendship had been almost uninterrupted. Though wanting in the characteristics of blood, faith, and social intimacy which had signalised the relations between the English and Dutch, the alliance had not suffered as those had from serious hostilities. The treaties with Portugal which were made by the Long Parliament, by Cromwell, and by Charles II. on his marriage with Catherine of Braganza, were little less advantageous to both countries than Queen Anne's Methuen Treaty, which was strictly an offensive and defensive compact.

By that treaty also the Portuguese wines, imported in exchange for English wool, became the substitute for the wines of France; and so remarkably were public and private interests interwoven in those days, that even Hallam found it necessary to remark that the desire to taste French wines once more had no small influence in carrying the Peace of Utrecht. The generous assistance sent from England on occasion of the great earthquake at Lisbon had kept alive the sense of obligation, and this, a little later, when Spain was employed in one of her frequent attempts to subjugate her smaller neighbour, was still further strengthened by the aid of British troops. No one understood the value of the alliance better than the Marquis de Pombal, the one great minister Portugal has produced; and it was no slight title to British confidence that under his auspices Portugal was the first country to expel the Jesuits (1759).

These amicable relations were too firmly established to be shaken by the momentary adhesion of Portugal to the Armed Neutrality, or by the abandonment of the commercial part of the Methuen Treaty, which Pitt, in his pursuit of commercial equality with France and other nations, found to be necessary. The value of friendly relations with Portugal was soon to be tested.

Thus when the tremendous war with Revolutionary, and then with Napoleonic, France broke out, in spite of all Pitt's efforts, his country had no new tactics to adopt. Her position was understood at home and abroad. She had merely strengthened and adapted to circumstances what experience had dictated. Great Britain had advanced far beyond her neighbours in the development of all the resources necessary for interposition, if that should be needed. She could afford to wait, as she did wait, till every expedient had been tried before she plunged into the gigantic conflict which was not only to settle the question of her independence, but to decide her future existence as an empire.

Strong position of Great Britain before the great war.
This patience was no doubt misinterpreted as tameness, and as the weak repudiation of a glorious past; but calm observers, if any such were left after the French Revolution began, might have remembered that the spirited methods by which the British Empire had been secured of old had not been abandoned. Besides the great colonial war which we have noticed, Great Britain had on two occasions, one quite recent, announced to the world that there was a point beyond which she would not be forced even where the *casus belli* seemed small and unimportant. In the affair of the Falkland Islands in 1770, her instant armament and categorical remonstrance forced Spain to withdraw from her insulting position; and in the affair of Nootka Sound in 1790, almost exactly similar, Pitt followed the old path with precisely the same result. In both cases alike it was an attempt on the part of Spain to find out how far she could go in the way of intimidation. She was manifestly wrong. War, indeed, on such questions might seem absurd, yet the same unhesitating spirit was shown in the prompt exaction of reparation. A firm diplomacy and instant preparations for war secured the neutrality of France and brought the offender to reason.

That governed the war policy.
We are now about to deal with the development of British Foreign Policy at the period of the war of the French Revolution—the unwelcome war which broke in so rudely upon the breathless haste and rush of the British people in their forward progress. It is in reality more easy to describe than in the

foregoing periods; for, as we have said, the outlines of the policy remained precisely as they have just been formulated,—only applied to a new series of facts. From 1793 to 1815 there was but one object before the eyes of king or ministers, parliament or people, and this was to restrain the aggressive action of France, first in her political frenzy, and then in her military ambition. This object was to be attained in concert with the other States of Europe, and yet the problem was to be solved of so co-operating as to prevent any of them from seizing that overwhelming supremacy which could not be permitted in the case of France.

In other words, it fell once more to the lot of Great Britain to be summoned, unwillingly summoned, to the front for the purpose of administering the International Law of Europe. The call was explicit; but it none the less affected the vital interests of Great Britain herself. It was not only that the vast majority of the people felt a genuine disgust at the principles which issued in the horrors of the French Revolution, and a profound sympathy for the oppressed nations which fell under the French yoke; they were convinced that in fighting for others the British were also fighting for themselves. This conviction nerved every arm and inspired every sacrifice. The movement never really lost its first impulse. It was not quixotic; it was never selfish in any but the best and most honourable sense. It was the dictate of judgment as well as feeling, of common-sense as well as philanthropy. Its motives were, in short, mixed, and ought not to have been otherwise.

It is not so very long since it was taken as a

An explicit call to resume the old position in Europe.

Attacks on this policy. matter of course that the policy pursued by Great Britain in the Revolution war was disgraceful and ruinous, that the ambition of Pitt was the real cause of it, that the aspirations of France for liberty justified not only her domestic but her foreign policy, and that the vast National Debt which the war bequeathed to Great Britain was the just punishment for her interference. This was surely the language of party-spirit, of peace-at-any-price, of a mock liberality, shaping a theory for the past in accordance with the views of subsequent popular writers, and totally opposed to the sentiments which had animated the British nation during the mighty struggle. Those views of the past, we may safely say, no longer predominate.

We may attribute the change partly to the inevitable influence of reaction, and the improved habits of examining contemporary literature; but also not a little to particular books, in the front rank of which *Reform Bill politics coloured history.* we may place Lord Stanhope's "Life of Pitt." In the period of the Reform Bill—" sixty years since "—when victory was achieved over the obstructive Tory influences of the previous half-century, history professed to have gone shares with the victors, and the arrows of the 'Edinburgh Review,' multiplied and sharpened in a thousand quarters, found their way to the very heart of the public in England, in the United States, the Colonies, and the Continent. The dreadful past was supposed to be the deplorable result of an unnatural union between an imbecile king and a proud, imperious minister. Though Fox himself found out when too late that he had been deceived, his older opinions, which had become so notorious during the greater part of his career, were once more brought to the front. Even the old Whig admiration of Napoleon had a revival, and found a vivid expression, wholly inconsistent with the ultra-liberalism which formed the rest of the historical programme. He and Fox were martyrs who had been shamefully persecuted by inferior men incapable of understanding their greatness; but the numerous memoirs which have seen the light in recent years have not confirmed that view. In England, at any rate, it is very generally repudiated; but it is none the less necessary to refer to its existence.

CHAPTER VIII.

BRITISH FOREIGN POLICY DURING THE FRENCH-REVOLUTION WAR—1793–1800.

Pitt's views as to the French Revolution. WE begin the Foreign Policy of Great Britain during the greatest of all its wars with a brief statement of Pitt's position at its opening. Only ignorance or party-spirit could fail to note that he was almost the last person in the kingdom to admit that the course taken by France called for war; and that there was everything in the world to dispose him to peace. For more than three years—1789–1793—he guided the country through the extreme excitement produced by the dreadful scenes passing in France. At every pause of the terrible drama his voice was to be heard loudly proclaiming non-interference. He positively refused to join the Allied Powers at Pilnitz. He was obviously and avowedly forced into war at last by the nation, and had no choice.

The ideas which ruled that almost invincible repugnance were open to all the world. As a statesman, he regarded France in the light of a counterpoise to Russia, which was taking advantage of the paralysis of Western Europe to complete the absorption of Poland. He had persuaded himself that the Revolution was only a temporary unsettlement, called for by the financial and social diseases of France, and that she would soon return again to her place in the European Balance, from which she could not be spared. The British nation, led by Burke, interpreted the course of events with more sagacity, and failed to find any element in French society strong enough to arrest its headlong career. The Revolution was already infecting the neighbouring States, and the British Isles more than all others. From the point of view of British prosperity there was every excuse for Pitt's inclination to shut his eyes to the true state of things. To have attained such wonderful success in the development of his country's resources, and now to see the whole object of his life torn away from him by war, was a prospect the horror of which can only be measured by those who have made a study of the work he performed during the first period of his administration.

But the time came when he found that he would have had to relinquish every shred of the political inheritance which had been intrusted to him, every particle of the Foreign Policy he had himself proclaimed to the world, had he shut his eyes to what the French proceeded to do without the slightest consideration for British interests, and yet fully aware of the importance attached to their acts. To put it shortly—they overran the Netherlands, declared the neutrality of the Scheldt, and prepared to invade Holland. On the remonstrance of the British minister they declared war. Pitt had now no alternative. The shores of the Low Countries had always, as we have seen, been recognised as a vital part of the English defence, for their ports dominated the Channel. The action of Great Britain was to be viewed not only from the side of the general considerations of Inter-

War forced by the French.

national Law and national obligation, but from the side of strategy and self-defence.

<small>Pitt had to accept the issue.</small> Pitt had indeed, as a separate proposal, and in the presence of the dangerous advance of Russia, paid some attention to overtures for the French annexation of the Austrian Netherlands. It was one of his few mistakes, and could not have been put into practice; but to allow the virtual occupation of the whole of the Low Countries by a State which, whether professedly hostile or not, would then hold the southern and eastern coasts of the British Channel, the Bay of Biscay, and the Gulf of Lyons, was nothing more nor less than to place a rope round the British neck, and to hand the end of it over to those who were only too ready to do the rest. It was to give up a thousand years of history, to wipe out from past records the thousands of lives, the millions of money, and the innumerable obligations incurred in building up the Empire. It was to open up a frightful future of war, with every disadvantage of place and time, with diminished resources, and a sense of paying a tremendous penalty for the indulgence of a momentary infatuation. Better to take the dreadful plunge at once into the old state of war, subsidies, and alliances, with all its unknown future of debt, distress, and sedition, than attempt to assume the attitude of affected insular indifference, false to every tie of honour and policy, and laden with the heavy certainty of future retribution.

Happily for the world these views commended themselves even to the pacific Pitt. The plunge was taken. The war which had been declared by France on February 8, 1793, broke out; and it is not too much to say that the modern world, as we now find it, was the result of the British Foreign Policy, of which the defence of the Channel shore had always been, speaking generally, a fundamental part. As that policy further developed, Napoleon himself confessed that it was the British, with their naval power, their foreign subsidies, and finally with their operations in the Peninsula, who interposed between him and the triumphs on which he had with good reason taught Europe to reckon. There is every reason for insisting on the cogency of the grounds for war as they presented themselves to British statesmen.

Of course we may well, at this distance of time, indulge the wish that it had been possible to let the French people work out their own Revolution; but we should deceive ourselves if we compared the wise non-interference of modern times in the internal affairs of States with the circumstances of the great French Revolution. It was different in kind from anything which has ever been seen before or since. There was no pretence of leaving other nations alone. Distinctions of race and history disappeared in the proclamation of the brotherhood of man. The republican propaganda openly professed to inculcate its principles wherever its emissaries could penetrate. Every one knows its famous "Declaration to the Nations." This it was which gradually, and almost insensibly, carried away all the defences of peace one after the other, however steadfastly men like Pitt clung to them. Even in 1792 he looked forward to "fifteen years of peace." But how could society hold together if no barrier was to be raised against the influx of paid propagandists, and the flood

Reasons why war could not be evaded.

of sedition which came pouring in from France? Burke was indeed raising the barrier by his extraordinary skill and energy. How could Pitt but give his aid? In short, neutrality was impossible, both on social and political grounds; and this is now very generally understood.

The old Foreign Policy reappears.

Again, then, the principles which had governed the Foreign Policy of Great Britain for so many generations appeared in active operation at the commencement of the new war. Again they were represented by the phrase "ships, colonies, and commerce," under the conditions, which were only gradually realised, of a united people in both islands, of the continued protection of the British Channel, and of the conservation of the European Balance of Power. The Royal Navy was organised on the principle of being a match for all the other navies of Europe under whatever combination; and it protected the colonies which were still left after the American Revolt, as well as India. While naval supremacy brought about the absorption of the maritime possessions of other countries, it also protected in every sea the commerce which multiplied its activities as the ocean became more and more the exclusive property of its mistress. The recurring military expeditions to Holland which characterised the first years of the war, pursued indeed the same melancholy course as in former times; but they at least exemplified the doctrine of Channel-protection, and gradually taught the country that, however marked its loyalty to the Crown, it was no longer safe to put its trust in the inexperienced princes of the blood then available. The descents upon France were in accordance with precedent, but were only

Naval supremacy.

Descents on France.

useful as far as they kept at home French troops which would otherwise have been employed beyond the frontier. It must be admitted that they were even more deficient in local success than those of the elder Pitt; for the loyalist French *emigrés*, who were at first reckoned as an accession of strength, proved to be useless.

Gathered round and bearing up all other considerations with a daily increase of cogency was the undying instinct that, over and above the insular aspects of Foreign Policy, the true and permanent safeguard of British interests was to be found, as of old, in uniting the insulted and endangered nations of Europe against the offender. The new-born Republic, which was breaking through its own limits on every side, and ostentatiously taking the place occupied by Spain in the sixteenth, and by monarchical France itself in the seventeenth century, was destroying the Balance and trampling it to pieces. At any risk the old safeguard must be renewed for the sake of one and all. France was to be attacked on every side,—in the Mediterranean, on its western coasts, on its northern and eastern frontier; and, as the one nation which, by the help of its navy, was able to retain its ships, colonies, and commerce, Great Britain was to find payment for the armies of Europe. If the population were unable to bear any further taxation, posterity must be called upon to bear its share. *Foreign alliances and subsidies.*

And here came in the singular advantage enjoyed by Great Britain in its fund of credit. No other nation possessed anything to be compared with it. A far-seeing sagacity enabled British rulers to perceive that at such a crisis the risk of raising immense loans must be run. The best thing to say about it *British credit.*

is that the risk has been run with success, and that their foresight has been justified. This is not to say that sufficient efforts have been made to keep the National Debt within safe bounds. France and the United States have each in turn read a much later lesson to Great Britain, which ought to be taken to heart; but a good deal has been done to reduce the British debt, and the way to do more has been opened up in recent times. It was emphatically credit,—the British power of raising loans on the public security to almost any extent and without paying exorbitant interest, which saved Europe.

What was the secret of this wonderful credit? It was the product of many things peculiar to England. To name only a few of them, it resulted from steady persistence in the financial system established in the reign of William III.; from the growth of trade, manufactures, commerce; from the multiplication of markets for British produce—and this during war as well as peace; from the security afforded by a ubiquitous Royal Navy; from the social order which, under the peaceable succession to the Crown and the decay of Jacobitism, had made great progress; and in this connection, from what we may call the hardening of the Constitution in proportion as its three divisions,—King, Lords, and Commons,—each in its own place, developed and improved its relations with its co-ordinates and the people. In fact, the Law was King, and went hand in hand with Credit.

The Law was King.

Perhaps if we were to inquire how it was that such a source of power was available at this particular juncture to an extent which eclipsed all previous wealth of resource known to history, we must assign the first place to the fact that Great Britain had not to begin afresh with her Royal Navy, as she had in 1739 after a long period of peace and neglect. A strong link of fine officers connected that sad awakening of the country, and its consequent uprising, with the crisis of the French Revolution. We have seen how the great Lord Hawke, who was so much concerned with founding the Empire, formed a school of which Lord Rodney and Lord Howe, his pupils, were the noble representatives. The elevated standard set by Hawke was never lowered. The whole naval service was impregnated with his spirit, and successive governments proceeded on his maxims. Nelson was a post-captain when Hawke died, and represented on a still grander scale his public spirit and magnanimity. Hood, Jervis, Bridport, Duncan, and Collingwood were only the leaders of a great body of brave and capable men such as the country never had before, and will be very fortunate if it ever sees again. *The Royal Navy at the height of efficiency.*

But it must be admitted that this navy had a special advantage unknown in former wars. The aristocratic French navy of the eighteenth century was peculiarly obnoxious to the Republicans, and was soon deprived of many of its best officers. In the army this would have been of rather less consequence, but the sea is a stern mistress, and exacts an apprenticeship of many years. For the formation of a fighting navy simple instruction and theoretical tuition, however superior they may be, are inadequate: training at the hands of skilled experts versed in the traditions of the service, and the lessons learnt by opportunities of putting theory into instant practice, are absolutely essential in *French Navy demoralised.*

addition. Experienced soldiers may indeed, like Blake, Monk, and others at the time of the English Civil War, be converted into good seamen if they possess the necessary gifts; but mere republican enthusiasm turned out, as might have been expected, to be no education at all, and in some respects was worse than none.

It was no doubt owing to the sense of security inspired by a navy which was, from its own excellence and the deficiencies of its enemy, triumphant on almost every occasion, that the credit of Great Britain stood the immense pressure which was laid upon it. In vain the Armed Neutrality again raised its head. The spectacle of the British nation occupying the seas of the world so as to prevent all others from sharing in a commerce which they alone had a navy to support, and forbidding them by a rigid exaction of the Right of Search from making profit by trading with France, was more than human nature could stand; but till the war was over, and for many a long year afterwards, Great Britain refused to relinquish her advantage. Such a surrender was indeed impossible till quite a recent date. It remains to be seen how future naval wars can be carried to a conclusion under the change which has in later times been effected.

The Armed Neutrality again.

It was in consequence of this sense of security, engendered by naval predominance and financial soundness, that the military failures in Holland were felt so slightly that they had no important effect upon the credit of Great Britain with capitalists. The failure was a distress at the time, but its true significance was much better appraised than it has been in later generations. It was plain enough to

Failures in Holland.

intelligent persons that British generals and armies could not possibly in those days be a match for Continental generals and armies till they had acquired an amount of experience in war under approved masters which an insular State, with a very small standing army, could not afford. But, on the other hand, the French Revolution produced almost at once a nation of soldiers, of whom the very best came to the surface. Distinguished courage and conduct in the field raised the private to the rank of an officer, even of a general or marshal, as a matter of course; and every soldier knew it. Even these, however, failed, as might be expected, just at first; but necessity, the necessity of dealing with an enemy at every point of the frontier, was the stern teacher which elevated the French, almost at a bound, to the first rank of military nations. Their enemies soon found this out, with an astonishment which is pathetic, and at a cost which was terrible. The British suffered far less than any other opponent, and considering the mistakes they made, far less than they deserved. They had at least their ships to fall back upon.

Military eminence of France.

The fact is, that both army and generals had to be absolutely created afresh, to learn in small sections, to learn slowly. They were hampered by a multitude of traditional impediments, by antiquated usages of Frederick the Great's time, by what soldiers call "pipe-clay" and civilians "red-tape"; above all, by the prevailing custom already mentioned of employing members of the Royal Family in the field before they had been trained to their duty, and had proved that they were masters of their art, under exactly the same apprenticeship as other officers.

K

Gradual improvement of the British army.

The standard being thus lowered, it was all the more creditable to Sir Ralph Abercromby, Sir John Moore, and Sir Arthur Wellesley that they—for it was chiefly their work, assisted at the Horse Guards, when no longer on foreign service, by the Duke of York—gradually succeeded in raising it to a higher level. Then at last, after years of failure, they produced a school of officers who proved themselves in the end the worthy rivals of their brethren at sea, and not inferior to the French marshals, as well as a body of troops who "could go anywhere and do anything." Then also, towering above them all, came to the front the man who had been the chief agent in the process, and who, alone in Europe, could be matched with the great Napoleon.

Unfair treatment of Pitt's war measures.

These considerations may be thought too obvious, but they are needed in order to dispose of the attacks which Macaulay and others have made on the memory of Pitt with regard to his so-called failure to wield with effect the forces at his disposal. He did the utmost which his circumstances permitted, and it is as absurd to condemn him for not using the army which he had not got, as to deny him the credit which he deserves for the success of the weapon which he had to his hand, the Royal Navy. The error arises from the refusal to balance against one another the two things which ought to be balanced. In the War of the Revolution, as distinguished from that with Napoleon, each contending side was armed with one superior and one inferior weapon; the true objects of comparison being the soldiers of France and the sailors of Britain. In the latter war the sailors had little to do, for their enemies were soon annihilated; while the armies had come to be fairly on a level as regards efficiency; or rather the demoralisation of the French and the improvement of the British in the Peninsula gradually gave the superiority in both weapons to the latter. This position, in conjunction with the uprising of the Continental nations, meant victory. Pitt had passed away; his successors were feeble; but nothing could now impede the onward march.

So much for the weapons at Pitt's command for the defence of the British Isles, especially of the Channel and of the countries bordering the Channel, for the protection of commerce, and for the support of the credit which could alone enable his country to hold out against the French propaganda. It is remarkable that he should have achieved such a measure of success at a time when his basis of operations, or at least the Irish part of it, was by no means in the condition which was required in order that he might use those weapons with their full power. Unlike his father when he founded the empire, he was hampered and crippled by the rebellious condition of the sister-island. We have seen that the island was in a comparatively healthy state under the elder Pitt,—at least it was in a course of gradual and wholesome improvement, and gave no trouble. But Ireland was not left in peace to pursue a course of self-improvement. Not long before the younger Pitt came into power the principles of republicanism made their way from America, and bore fruit much as they had in France; for in each case there was a soil well prepared to receive them. *Condition of Ireland.*

The Penal Laws against Papists had been a necessary consequence of aggressive and most dangerous

Jacobitism; nor could they be repealed, though in practice they were greatly mitigated. The Protestant Parliament became, however, after the American War, a centre of disaffection; and when France, Spain, and Holland joined the colonists with a view to recovering their losses in the American War, this Parliament, with the help of the Irish volunteers, who had been raised for the defence of the united Empire, practically separated the British from the Irish Government. The two Acts which bound the two Legislatures to one another were repealed under Irish pressure at the moment when Britain was at its most critical condition. This was suicidal on the part of the British Government, but the knife was at its throat, and nothing else could be done. Nor was it possible to retrace the step when peace returned.

Pitt found it necessary to wait till a Union of the two islands could be effected, and in the meantime to check by such means as were still in his power the further development of the Irish aspirations for independence. The Union came about in a way which could hardly have been expected. Pitt's numerous reforms served only to exasperate the Irish. Every year showed that something else was necessary, and the need of corporate union became more and more apparent. Then came the French Revolution, which turned the idea of practical separation into the form of distinct rebellion. Revolutionary societies spread like wildfire over the island, and in 1795 the organisation was practically complete, though the actual rebellion did not break out till 1798. The Irish Protestants, formed into "Orange Lodges," kept it at bay; but the direct interference of the French, and the open adhesion

Ireland torn by factions.

of the rebels to France, brought matters to a point. Was Ireland to be French or English? That was the plain issue. The Jacobin Clubs at Dublin and Belfast ordered regiments of "National Guards"— so called after the French—to be levied, with French uniforms and passwords. The battle was no longer to be fought on the Continent or at sea, but on the shore of Ireland, within a few miles of the English coast.

Then at last, just before it was too late, the British Government, acting on timely information, seized the chosen leader of the Rebellion, Lord Edward Fitzgerald, and without much difficulty put down the armed forces which had risen in Wexford. Lord Cornwallis, whom we have heard of in the American War, and who had spent nine years in India establishing on a secure footing the new order of things brought about by Pitt's India Bill, was now given *carte blanche*, or nearly so, to set the troubled affairs of Ireland to rights on the footing of corporate union. As then established the Union has remained; and from that day the internal difficulties which had so seriously interfered with the Foreign Policy of Great Britain passed away. The "United Kingdom of Great Britain and Ireland" could now act from a secure base, the troops were no longer interned in Ireland as if in an enemy's country, and no small part of their success abroad was due to the presence of brave Irishmen in the ranks of the army. The Rebellion of 1798. The Union.

The organisation of India cannot be reckoned in any strict sense as part of the base from which Pitt's Foreign Policy was developed. But he reaped indirectly the fruit of the treatment of that vast country which he had embodied in the famous Bill carried India.

at the commencement of his ministry. Interpreted and admirably worked as it was by Cornwallis, the designs of the enemy were frustrated just in time. The absence of wise organisation on the part of the British would have given the French a fair chance of proceeding once more with the plans which they had been obliged to relinquish in the reign of George II. And so the waves of hostile aggression rolled off from India as from an immovable rock. So also with the colonies which still remained faithful. They had received suitable constitutions, and clung the more closely to the mother country the more fiercely she was attacked. Her successes were theirs, and her men-of-war formed the ever-shifting and yet constant link between the scattered portions of the Empire. These were days when "Imperial Federation" had not been heard of, but the foundation was laid by the settlement of officers of both services upon colonial lands, granted at the Peace by way of pension—the sensible form in which Government strengthened its hold upon the daughter States.

<small>The Colonies.</small>

It is unnecessary to do more than allude in this place to the enormous assistance which Pitt received in his arduous task from the collapse of his great rival Fox, and the junction of the Moderate, or "Old Whigs," with himself, under the guidance of Burke and the Duke of Portland. Never did the old Revolution-families more nobly prove their right to be consulted on the destinies of their country. The services they had performed at the Revolution had been worn out of memory by the errors of the factions into which they had been split up, They were now reinstated. The influence of Pitt and the teaching of Burke, coinciding with the conviction that the

<small>Patriotism of the old Whigs.</small>

battle for life or death had commenced for their country, separated them from Fox and his friends by a cleavage which could not be filled up. Patriotism took the place of party, and their old leader was left with an insignificant following both in Parliament and the country. Scotland had forgotten its ancient feud, and Ireland, though the weak place of the nation, could be left till the proper time had arrived to deal with its new disturbances. It was this settled Government, this unanimity of Parliament, this harmony of King, Lords, and Commons, which enabled Pitt to grasp the full power of the State, and exhibit his country in its old position before the astonished world. *Scotland and Ireland.*

We must now follow in a little more detail Pitt's use of his weapons of war, of his partly united base, and of the national credit. His plan might indeed be briefly described as war with France and alliance with all her enemies, save and except so far as the Armed Neutrality for a brief period suspended it. In 1793, Pitt having, as we have seen, been absolutely deprived of all choice by the conduct of France in the Low Countries, and her Declaration of War with Great Britain, formed his alliances rapidly with Russia, Sardinia, Spain, Naples, Prussia, Austria, Portugal, Tuscany, and several of the Princes of the German States; not one of which, such was the general financial weakness of Europe at this time, could do anything considerable in war without subsidies from the island-kingdom. The spectacle of such a system of general subsidising is one of the most remarkable afforded in the history of the world; but it had already been witnessed on a smaller scale in the Seven Years' War, and had *Pitt's allies.*

now come to be reckoned as a matter of course. It has indeed been treated—such is the force of habit—in much the same way by modern historians; but it will take a place of its own in the future history of this great upheaval of the western nations.

Discussion of the policy of subsidies.

The only justification for such an anomalous proceeding, open to abuse, and often abused, was the absolute necessity of the case. For it is plain that nothing can exercise so wholesome a check upon the belligerency of a nation as the ever-present fact that it has to pay out of its own resources for war. Nothing can be more demoralising than a system of spending the money of other people yet unborn. What is patent enough in private life is equally true of States.

Looking back on the past, it might indeed be argued that even if the Continental States had not been subsidised by the British, even supposing that the French had in consequence overrun them at the commencement of the war, they would have sooner rallied under the flag of a desperate patriotism and forestalled the days of the "Storm of Nations" in 1813. The weakness of this line of argument consists in the application of modern ideas to the times which now lie far behind us, so much further than the mere lapse of years would suggest. The upheaval has passed away, and the whole face of Europe has been changed by the effects of the French Revolution. But at that time Continental society was still monarchical and feudal. Its frame was fast wearing out, and very much required the influx of the new ideas which made their way from America, and then from France; and yet if those ideas had come down upon the nations like a flood, without preparation, without even such preparation as France had received, who can say what might have been the consequences?

Theories are not of much use, especially as to the past; but a review of actual facts teaches us practical lessons. There was no popular resisting power on the Continent to balance the mad enthusiasm of French revolutionary armies, no popular representation, no exhibition therefore of the popular will, no power of raising taxes to the extent required for a sudden war of an internecine kind. Of all the Continental sovereigns, not one inspired enthusiastic devotion or unlimited confidence; the Powers were divided by old grudges and new jealousies; each feared that the other would accept the French bribes to betray its rivals. Concert without a solid base would have been hopeless. That base was the British Treasury, and Napoleon fell before the indomitable perseverance of his triumphant enemy, the British taxpayer.

The National Assemblies of Germany had become the merest forms. "Nowhere," says Heeren, Professor of History at Göttingen, writing in 1833, "had they been modelled into a true national representation. But the idea of it not only lived in theory disseminated and fostered by the first writers of the day, but was seen to be permanently realised in a neighbouring happy island-state. It could not therefore pass away from practical politics, and was necessarily, during the storms of the following period, the Polar Star which was for ever kept in view in all the aberrations of the times." These words of a very competent observer are such as a writer belonging to the British Isles might have hesitated to use; but they describe the truth. The minds which

Condition of European States.

revolted from the extremes both of despotism and democracy fondly turned towards the British Constitution. But such ideas could not operate effectively at such a moment. A generation must pass away. Dire experience was to teach its terrible lessons. The "first writers of the day" could do little till those lessons were learnt by both rulers and ruled. The resistance must come, if it came at all, from the great feudal societies, just as they were; and nobly they did their duty in standing firm, after many vacillations, to the cause of independence and European concert. But they were unprovided with the necessary funds to meet such an emergency.

A question of finance. Hence the question resolved itself into one of money. The objects of the Continental States threatened by France were identical with those of Great Britain, and the latter alone could pour in the supplies. She must perforce interpose if Europe were not again to be handed over to a frightful tyranny.

But was Great Britain called upon to prevent this frightful tyranny? We have seen that it was at *Responsibilities of Great Britain.* least in accordance with all her previous Foreign Policy and with all the European traditions of Balance that she should do so. There was as yet no system of a standing European Council. And we have also seen that the fulfilment of this international duty had been always found to correspond with a policy of safety to Great Britain herself, and the support of her commercial prosperity. Safety to herself, because France, aggrandised by the conquest of surrounding States, would be a danger of tenfold magnitude compared with France struggling for her own frontiers against a host of enemies sustained by British subsidies. Just as in the struggle of the days of Louis XIV., France did in fact never find herself at leisure to bring her full power to bear upon England. As Wellington wrote to his trembling Government during the Peninsular War, "You may complain of the expenses of war, but if you decline it you will have to meet the invader on your own shores." That was the fundamental conviction. Ever since 1066 it had been so. The Norman invasion was to be the last, and so it has been—has been as yet. With the security of British shores went hand in hand commercial prosperity.

On Pitt has been thrown the responsibility for this stupendous resolution—to make British posterity pay for the salvation of Europe and the safety of the British Empire; but it cannot be too often repeated that he was only the minister and representative of the king, the parliament, and the nation. Never was a policy more deliberately accepted, ratified, and pursued by a people. But it is only fair to Pitt, on whom so much odium has fallen from many quarters, to observe that though forced into war, he was never tired of making attempts to procure peace. It is indeed a question whether the dignity of the nation was sufficiently consulted in these efforts. The first occasion was in 1795, not long after the commencement of the war; but it was perfectly useless, for the French were intoxicated with their surprising successes, and naturally declined to pay attention to such a proposal at such a time. In 1796 the French appeared to have a little more desire to consider the question, but they had no idea of relinquishing what they fondly regarded as the first-fruits of their harvest, the possession of the Low Countries, and, as we have seen,

Posterity to pay.

Pitt's futile efforts to make peace.

Pitt understood too well what the safety and interest of Great Britain required, and what the traditions of her Foreign Policy all through the centuries had laid down.

Nor would he, had he wished, have been able to carry the nation with him in accepting such terms. Burke had once more alarmed the country by his "Thoughts on a Regicide Peace," and public opinion was almost entirely with him. Still more sternly than before he dwelt on the inherently aggressive nature of the French Republic; but he was now able to adduce as evidence the career it had run since the Revolution, its difference in kind from anything yet experienced, not only in its warlike energy but in its social principles; to show that these principles were subversive of all government, all religion, all society; that no country could rest with safety at peace with such a neighbour, so close at hand, and imbued with such a spirit of propagandism; that its doctrines, thus passionately forced by a novel species of missionaries upon all the world, were of the grossest kind; and that Great Britain would suffer far more by a peace which might commend itself as a specious advantage than even by the most disastrous war. These sentiments were more suited to influence the great body of thoughtful people than the political question concerning the Netherlands; but the Government no doubt felt its responsibility for the safety of the Channel and the coasts to be of the first importance, and relegated sentiment to the second place. Sentiment, however, when largely shared by a people, must have its due weight, and no Government can afford to ignore it.

Once more, in 1797, though Napoleon Bonaparte was already flaming in the van of the Revolutionary hosts, Pitt, influenced on these occasions by his friend Wilberforce, whose tender heart fitted him for a philanthropist in the first place, and a statesman only in the second, again attempted to make peace. He was staggered by the default of Prussia, the old ally of the British in the formation of their Empire, but now tottering under feeble government, and severely pressed by the French. Professing to be satisfied with compensation from the Ecclesiastical States, she made a secret compact with France in 1796, by which she gave up the left bank of the Rhine, the bone of contention between Gallo-Frank and Teuton for so many centuries. And it seemed to many a hopeless task to defend the Low Countries, though invaluable to England, without allies; for Austria, pressed beyond bearing, had herself given up their defence; and Spain, which though of no weight as a military Power, had ships and sailors of which France would well understand the use, even this Spain, which had had experience enough of French ambition, had gone over to the ever-growing Republic which struck terror in all directions.

Conquest of British allies.

Worse than all, the one strong arm of Great Britain had in this year suffered for some months a paralysis, which made the most sanguine fear that some grave disaster to the country would happen at the most critical moment of the island history. The Mutinies of Spithead and of the Nore were indeed the most dangerous events that had befallen the nation for centuries. It is said that at one of the crises of this terrible time occurred the only sleep-

The Mutinies in the Royal Navy.

less night of the great minister, whose feeble frame could never have held out to middle life, as it did, if he had not possessed the precious gift of night-rest, even during the most trying events of that momentous period. The grand coalition of European States, not yet four years old, was already half-ruined, and the navies of Spain and Holland were in the hands of France.

The fortitude of British statesmen would have been superhuman could they have witnessed under such circumstances, without dismay, the crumbling away of the Royal Navy. The crisis was, however, met with courage and promptitude, and the mutiny turned out to have been a blessing in disguise. Nothing short of it could have removed the abuses under which that popular service had laboured for years, and when it was over nothing could exceed the vigour and patriotism of the very men who had been concerned in it. With their old furious energy they rushed upon the Dutch fleet at Camperdown, and very few of their victories were more complete. The battle of Cape St. Vincent in February 1797 might indeed have been considered a set-off against the depressing position of affairs which had led to the proposals for peace in this year, for it broke up the plan of uniting the Spanish with the Dutch and French navies in a descent upon England; and it had the still further merit of bringing to the front Nelson, who was about to become the hero of heroes in the history of naval affairs; but its fame had grown dim under the storm of the Mutinies. Napoleon was conquering half the world, and the millions spent in subsidies seemed to have been absolutely thrown away. Thus the international

Battle of Camperdown.

aspect of affairs receded into the distance, and once more an attempt was made to drop out of the European struggle, even at the expense of relinquishing nearly all the colonial conquests which had been made. Why should not Great Britain be allowed to pursue her commercial instincts, and gather up the fruits of her immense sacrifices?

It is not of much use to speculate as to what might have been the result of a Peace in 1797. If the French could have remembered the ancient maxim that "half is better than the whole," they would certainly have left off in their career of conquest at a much better point for the extension of their empire and of their political principles than they secured at the Treaty of Vienna. But no Peace could have lasted under such humiliations as Austria, Prussia, Spain, Italy, and the Low Countries had been forced to undergo. Great Britain would never have given up the struggle for the Mediterranean; Napoleon would never have rested till he had acquired the command of it, and with it the road to Egypt and India. At any rate, the British proposals were scarcely noticed by the triumphant French. The battle of Camperdown announced at once the repentance of the mutineers, and the destruction of the French hopes of a descent upon England with the help of the excellent Dutch seamen.

This failure turned the eyes of the brilliant young conqueror towards the alternative of ruining the only country which he really feared, by blocking her way to India through the roads of Egypt and Turkey, and by setting up at Constantinople an enormous French empire, which might, by the help of a French

The meaning of Napoleon's descent on Egypt.

organisation of the great Mahratta princes, gradually tear away India from the British. That this was the far-reaching plan which dazzled himself and the French Government is even more evident now than it was at the time. All strategic considerations were lost in the blaze and glamour of anticipated success; and certainly if any one could have accomplished the gigantic enterprise it was Napoleon; nor was the Government of the Directory, which was already powerless in his hands, at all unwilling to let him dash himself to pieces on any rock that he might choose to run upon. He made short work of the Directors when he returned from Egypt.

All eyes were now fixed on this new direction of French energy. It was a much less expensive and dangerous process for Great Britain than the former efforts made by her enemy against the coasts of the three kingdoms; for the French had no command of the sea, and with Nelson on the spot were not likely to have a reasonably sound basis of operations. To India the Government turned with confidence; for Cornwallis, having laid the foundations of good order firm and strong, had already curbed the power of Tippoo Sultan, and Lord Mornington was well capable of dealing with the difficulties which Napoleon might raise up by alliance with that treacherous prince.

The real danger arose from the possible success of Napoleon in his designs upon Constantinople; but if not won by a *coup de main*, there was not much chance of succeeding in that quarter. Happily two naval officers, exactly fitted for the work which fell to them, were on the spot, and the rash enterprise fell dead. Nelson's entire destruction of

<small>Nelson and Sidney Smith.</small>

the French fleet at Aboukir, and Sidney Smith's defence of Acre, gave the deathblow to the expedition, which once more illustrated the obvious truth that success can never be achieved in a country which can only be reached by sea, so long as the sea is in command of its enemies. To Napoleon himself the absolute failure of his ill-starred enterprise proved that his theories of reaching Great Britain through the overthrow of her Turkish, Egyptian, and Indian power were mere dreams, and set him once more upon the old, practical, and direct methods of action.

These, however, could only succeed if the reins of power were in his own hands. It was easier to execute a *coup d'état* upon the Government of his own country than on that of the Turks. His countrymen had become used to such things; they forgave him his failure in Egypt, which indeed they proclaimed to be a glorious triumph; for they rightly understood that they had before them the most capable man who had appeared for centuries. They were as ready to put everything into his hands as he was to accept the task. He would at least restore order, and organise the forces set free by the Revolution. His own designs were larger still, and they were soon developed. When he had reorganised France in all the multitudinous details of her civil, military, religious, and social life, he felt that the time would speedily arrive when he might bribe or threaten Europe into a combination against the one disturbing Power which still dared to be independent. *Napoleon's coup d'état.*

But first he must chastise the Continental nations which had presumed to take advantage of his *He turns on Austria and Russia.*

absence in the East. These were Austria in the first place, and Russia in the second. Both in Italy and Switzerland these two Powers had turned the scale against the French, whose conquests had not yet been consolidated; and also in Bavaria, which had often before been more French than German, and which had, up to the time of this last reaction, been reckoned by the French as tolerably safe. Though Napoleon only returned from Egypt on October 9, 1799, he contrived to be recognised as supreme ruler, under the name of First Consul, on December 15 of that year, and ten days later offered peace to Great Britain. This was a transparent artifice to gain time, and Napoleon confessed as much at a later date. Having gained a position from which he could move the world, he would put off the chastisement of his chief enemy for a year or two. But the British Government declined the offer. Perhaps it might not have been so peremptorily declined had ministers foreseen his victory at Marengo and that of Moreau at Hohenlinden. The brilliant general had not yet given proof of his capacity for bringing order out of the French chaos. The weakness of the German Powers was not even yet understood. The desertion of the common cause by Russia was wholly unexpected, for the new Czar Paul had not as yet appeared to be more than eccentric. On the other hand, the Mediterranean had been regained by the battle of the Nile, and the capture of Malta by the British fleets was imminent. Ought the offer of peace to have been accepted?

Some, judging by after events, have thought so. But the British instinct was probably correct. No secure peace could have been obtained. A disarmament and reduction of taxation would certainly have followed a peace, however hollow it might be, and the great general having reconquered his neighbours, all alike despairing and unassisted by British gold, would no doubt have suddenly taken his enemy across the Channel at a serious disadvantage. The same miserable ending as characterised the rupture of the Peace of Amiens would surely have come when the British were far less able to deal with an invasion than they were in 1803, and that before the Union with Ireland had been sufficiently advanced to remove the dangers which had weighed upon the strategy and resources of Pitt during the Revolution-War.

With the accession of Napoleon to supreme power, —for such was his Consulate,—and with the rejection of his specious offers of peace, we may close our survey of the Foreign Policy of Great Britain in the eighteenth century, for we have arrived at the very last week of it. It is remarkable that Napoleon's instalment in power at the head of the French Empire should have been almost exactly coincident with the opening of a fresh age—an age which, in many ways, bears his mark from beginning to end. The age opens, and the centuries which we have specially considered end, with the most tremendous assault of all made by Napoleon upon the British Empire; and we trace, exactly as in the very first stage of our inquiry, the same principles lying at the bottom of the British Foreign Policy,—the determination to be supreme at sea, and the equally fixed resolution to keep what hold was yet possible on the coasts of the Channel. It is true that shortly afterwards, at the Peace of Amiens, the second point was neglected under the stress of the pressure caused by the war, but only for a brief moment. That Peace could be nothing but a truce. It lasted only fourteen months, and then came the final struggle. When the Emperor of the West had been humbled to the dust the old policy was renewed, and the Low Countries became, as they had almost always been, an outwork of the British fortress, guarded, when the rearrangement of European States took place at the Treaty of Vienna, by precautions adopted for their integrity only second to the position secured for Great Britain herself.

The Low Countries.

CHAPTER IX.

BRITISH FOREIGN POLICY DURING THE NAPOLEONIC WAR—1800–1807.

WE have traced the outlines of British Foreign Policy through the centuries preceding the nineteenth, and have observed a remarkable continuity through all changes of dynasties, in spite of the rise of new Continental States and the growth of new habits of political thought. It will not then surprise us to find that in the nineteenth century also this Foreign Policy remains almost exactly the same from first to last. In the following chapters we have to trace it as it was exhibited throughout the period of intense pressure caused by the Napoleonic wars, including the uneasy truce of the Peace of Amiens, to mark its resemblance to the past at the Treaty of Vienna, and to observe the fidelity of British ministers to the old model during the subsequent years.

We have now to deal with Napoleon, though he has only just commenced his wonderful career at the head of all the forces of France, and observe how it was that he succeeded in using his grand position so as immediately to obliterate the failure of his Oriental expedition. The nations of Europe might well take warning that such a genius for war and peace had never yet appeared on the stage of

Napoleon as First Consul.

the world. Even his victories scarcely excite so much astonishment as his almost instantaneous re-organisation of France. Into this we need not here enter, save so far as to say that it made the French a more formidable Power than they had been even under the early revolutionary impulse. Despairing of efficient government under any of the systems which had so rapidly succeeded one another, the French people were easily persuaded that republican ideas could be preserved and extended under the shadow of a monarchy, and that at any rate internal order would flourish under the same strong and able hand which was capable of placing France at the head of the nations. These ideas took such firm root that they survived even the barefaced assumption of all imperial attributes by the man of their choice, and the change of daughter-republics into satellite kingdoms under the government of his brothers and friends. They survived the removal of nearly all the national landmarks, tottering as they already were under the stress of the Revolution.

His reforms. Much may indeed be said in favour of the legal and social reforms effected by Napoleon. Most of them have been permanent, and all bear the marks of extraordinary power and knowledge. His reform, so called, of the Church, conduced equally to the unity and force of his power. Crushing every opposing force, pope, bishops, and clergy, he destroyed the old Gallican Church, and substituted for it an Imperial Church, which could not but become, as it did, Ultramontane to a degree scarcely known elsewhere. A mere Deist himself, he resolved to be the absolute master of unresisting ecclesiastics, and he gained his end. In short, Europe found itself confronted by such an organisation as had never been seen before, and the sense of the danger which was impending weighed heavily on all.

Between Napoleon's accession to supreme power as First Consul and the Peace of Amiens, he contrived, in the very midst of his civil reforms, to win back from Austria and Russia much more than the gains which he had made before his Eastern expedition, and which they had recovered in his absence. The battle of Marengo soon surpassed the triumphs of Lodi and Arcola, and that of Hohenlinden won by Moreau brought about the Treaty of Lunéville, by which France again advanced to the Rhine, and again ruled the "Cisalpine Republic" in Italy. Britain also pursued her accustomed course, balancing—we might almost say checkmating—the European influence attending these successes by securing the Mediterranean and the Baltic with her fleets. The remains of the French army in Egypt were conquered by Abercromby at Alexandria in 1801, thus putting an end to the dreams of French empire in the East; and Malta surrendered to the British fleet—a pregnant fact for the future. In the Baltic the Czar Paul, who had succeeded Catherine in 1796, though his troops had been beaten by the French, was cajoled by Napoleon; and already offended by the British seizure of Malta (where he was Grand-Master of the Knights) from the French, reconstituted the Armed Neutrality. In this policy he was joined by the other Baltic States—Denmark, Sweden, and Prussia.

His fresh victories.

The "Armed Neutrality again.

The attempt to cripple in this manner the force of Great Britain on the element which formed her strength was dealt with promptly at Copenhagen by Nelson, now at the height of his glory, but serving nominally under Sir Hyde Parker, a cautious admiral of the old school. It was one of his greatest achievements; for the Danes were not only, like the Dutch, fine seamen of the same stock as the English, but their fleet was supported by very powerful batteries, lining an intricate channel of the most dangerous character to sailing ships. Nelson's captains and crews were, however, by this time invincible, and the gallant Danes were glad to receive terms which enabled the fleet to proceed on its way to the Russian coast of the Baltic. No further action was required; for the insane Paul was murdered, and Alexander, his son and successor, immediately renewed the British alliance. It is worth remarking that the two finest battle odes in the English language belong to this period. With accidental impartiality Campbell sang the French victory of Hohenlinden on the land, and the English victory of Copenhagen on the sea.

Battle of Copenhagen.

The revival of the Armed Neutrality was useful to Europe and to Great Britain itself in the end; for it taught the latter that though her pretensions were sanctioned by general usage and quite justifiable, the exercise of such powers by one State against all others, she being alone in a position to command the necessary force, was so invidious that some concession had become necessary. The principle that blockades of ports by proclamation were invalid unless there were sufficient ships to enforce them, was now laid down as a canon of International Law. This was rather an apparent than a real loss to Great Britain; and when Napoleon in his turn pro-

Some principles of the Armed Neutrality accepted.

claimed blockades of whole coasts without any naval force whatever to support the proclamation, his action was not only vain and contrary to the new arrangements, but was deemed by all the world ridiculous.[1]

The French successes being thus balanced by those of the British, and both countries being weary of the war and its immense taxation, matters were ripe for the Peace of Amiens. It was felt that it could only be a truce, but that was better than war. Nothing, however, could be much less like a real Peace; for subjects of serious discord presented themselves almost every week while it lasted. It did indeed go on for fourteen months, and it is surprising that it lasted so long. Its terms are characteristic of the policy which we have been tracing. Of the conquests made by British fleets, all were given up

Peace of Amiens, 1802.

---

[1] "On the 17th of June 1801 was signed at St. Petersburg a Convention between Russia and Great Britain, settling the points that had been in dispute. The question of Malta was tacitly dropped. As regards neutral claims, Russia conceded that the neutral flag should not cover enemy's goods, and that colonial produce could not by a neutral be carried from the colony to the mother country of a nation at war. Great Britain, on the other hand, conceded the right of neutrals to carry on the coasting trade of a belligerent, and that naval stores should not be classed as contraband of war. As regarded searching merchant vessels under convoy of a ship of war, Russia yielding the principle, Great Britain accepted methods which would make the process less offensive. Sweden and Denmark followed the lead of Russia, though the Baltic States renewed among themselves the [old] engagements—that the neutral flag should cover enemy's property on board, and that the convoy of a ship of war should exempt merchant vessels from search. These principles were, in point of fact, modifications sought to be introduced into International Law, and not prescriptive rights, as commonly implied by French historians (Thiers, H. Martin, and Lanfrey). For this reason both the United States and the Baltic Powers, while favouring the new rule, were little disposed to attempt by arms to compel the surrender by Great Britain of a claim sanctioned by long custom."—Abstracted from Mahan's "Sea-Power," ii. 57, 58.

except Ceylon, which was necessary to the rulers of India, and Trinidad in the West Indies, which protected the southern access to the British possessions and the trade with South America. Even Malta, the key of the Mediterranean, was to be restored to the Knights from whom the French had taken it; but on the condition that it was to be under the protection of some third Power not named. France on her part relinquished Rome and Naples. This Peace had the sanction of Pitt; but he had himself resigned office some time previously on the question of Roman Catholic Emancipation.

Napoleon's acts during the Peace. The joy of the British at the cessation of the war led the upper classes to disregard all risks in order to gratify the intense passion for foreign travel which had for centuries been characteristic of the aristocracy. Not that any one could be fairly supposed to guess that if the war broke out again Napoleon would detain every English man and woman within his dominions, a proceeding worthy of an Oriental despot. That was only the final act of aggression. We may sum up the previous provocation given by Napoleon in a few words. The British tried to shut their eyes to it, so thankful were they for a little rest; but they soon found that every part of their traditional Foreign Policy was not only threatened, but attacked, while the hostile measures of their arch-enemy were contemptuously displayed without concealment. On the pretext that the refusal of the British to evacuate Malta was an act of hostility and breach of faith, though the stipulated conditions had not been complied with, Napoleon adopted the plan of territorial seizure during peace pursued by Louis XIV. after the Peace of Nimeguen. He took possession of Switzerland, Elba, and other territories, compelled Spain to give up to France Louisiana and the Floridas, sent a threatening expedition to the West Indies, and finally published the report of his agent, Sebastiani, on the condition of Turkey and the Levant,—a distinct indication of the contemplated seizure of Egypt and the Ionian Islands.

Great Britain was also threatened still nearer home. Vast armaments were preparing in the ports of France and the Low Countries; and Napoleon's emissaries were pouring into Ireland, of which Emmett's rebellion in 1803 was the result. When, to crown all, Lord Whitworth, the British ambassador, was repeatedly and openly insulted, the general indignation could no longer be restrained. Perhaps it is enough to remark on this point, that even Macaulay, the fervent admirer of Fox's opposition to the earlier war, admits that "the restless ambition and insolence" of Napoleon were "insupportable," and that a war for the "dignity, the independence, the very existence of our nation was at hand." And thus sorrowfully, almost despairingly, Great Britain prepared once more for war. We can see at this distance of time that there was no real ground for the feeling of despair, and it soon passed away when the issue was again joined. The revenues of the country, swelled by her ever-growing commerce, by the discovery of coal, and by the demand for her manufactures, were equal to those of all the rest of Europe combined. If her debt was also larger than that of all the rest together, it was nothing new. There was no difficulty about credit; and the existence of the Empire was keenly felt to be the concern of future generations as well as of the present.

He prepares to invade England.

Napoleon and the "Detenus."

The reluctance to enter once more upon the war was largely connected with the retirement of Pitt, and with the national perception of the incapacity of Addington for such measures as the times required. Pitt did not find it possible to keep on amicable terms with, and would not take service under him. The eyes of the nation turned to Canning, as the future representative of Burke and Pitt, but he was still young and comparatively untried. Whatever was wanting to inspire the British people with enthusiasm and resolution was, however, given by Napoleon's act above mentioned, the detention in France of some ten thousand British subjects who had taken advantage of the peace to visit France, and his determined refusal to liberate them. Such a course was unheard of; his pretext was ridiculous, and the interference of the act with the domestic life of the whole country brought it home to the people. Never was a greater mistake made by any ruler of men. The nation sprang to arms, and swore to continue the struggle to the bitter end, cost what it might. When once a nation's domestic life is outraged, questions of politics disappear, and, like a bear robbed of her whelps, the most pacific become dangerous. In no better way could Napoleon have enlisted every sentiment of patriotism in support of sacrifices which made themselves increasingly felt as the British lost their money in useless subsidies, and their allies one after another by conquest. Great Britain stood at last isolated,—stood at bay, desperate but proudly erect, while all the rest of Europe grovelled at the feet of the mighty conqueror.

Rupture of the Peace, 1803.

Public opinion, both in Great Britain and abroad, has at last given its verdict on the character and conduct of Napoleon. We are, however, now in danger of forgetting how, in the midst of methods adopted to obtain his ends, in which he offended against every canon of right and justice, he was yet the necessary scourge of Europe; in other words, how much such a scourge was required. Such a scourge was once the barbarous Attila, innocent of modern culture. The corrupt society of the effete Roman world had to be replaced by a fresher and more capable stock, and he led the way. So also the modern world, which had grown up into the place of the old, required in its turn to be penetrated by the idea of liberty, though disguised under the ill-fitting garb of Napoleonism. The foundations of Constitutionalism were laid in suffering and sacrifice. The light of patriotism was elicited from the clash of arms and the severe lessons of adversity. *Europe required a lesson.*

The process was certainly terrible. Great Britain was indeed saved from the actual presence of the conqueror and his irresistible hosts, but none the less was she called upon to face difficulties which seemed to all but the most gallant spirits insuperable, and to suffer losses which appeared irreparable. It was not till the death of Pitt that the country realised to the full the stress of the struggle on which Napoleon had forced it to enter once more, but for the moment the enthusiasm of courage and patriotism surmounted all considerations for the future. The old king was a tower of strength, and though Pitt was content to drill his Cinque Port Volunteers at Walmer, he was felt to be a power in reserve. The whole country resounded with the voice of the drill-sergeant; no divisions of politics or race broke the union of hearts. Feudal times *British defence on shore.*

appeared to have come round again; King, Lords, and Commons prepared for the field of battle; the hunting-men of every county formed and led a cavalry which at least knew how to ride, and the gentry took their place at the head of the local militia and volunteers. Who shall say what the result would have been, even if a considerable portion of the "army of England" had succeeded in securing a landing?

Efficiency of the naval defence. This was, however, virtually impossible. In spite of untimely economies, the Royal Navy was in undisputed command of the Channel, and Nelson was at its head. Whether superintending the defences of the Channel or watching the French fleet in Toulon, all eyes were fixed on the man who had come to represent the ancestral sea-power of England in a personal sense never known before even in the days of Drake, or Blake, or Hawke, or Rodney, or Howe. It was the culmination of all the ages in which the Foreign Policy of Great Britain had been developed and extended upon the basis of the sovereignty of the seas. The labour and the expense of the process had been enormous, but not a farthing of it had been wasted. At the moment of trial it stood the shock, and the storm rolled off to other latitudes.

Pitt resumes office. The imminence of danger forced Pitt to the front once more. It was a remarkable coincidence that he resumed office on the very day (May 18, 1804) when Napoleon assumed the title of Emperor. Not that he had been a mere spectator at any time. That was impossible. While at Walmer Castle, before the Peace of Amiens, he and Nelson, who commanded in the Downs, held frequent converse on the best methods of meeting the combinations which Napoleon was forming for the destruction of the one enemy he had to fear. The recess of the room in which they met is still shown. The two minds most capable at that moment of the insight and penetration which the times required, here perhaps struck out the large ideas which bore fruit when Nelson's day of trial came. At any rate, it was these combinations which, from the moment of the rupture of the Peace in 1803, filled every mind with anxious thoughts, till the battle of Trafalgar broke down the whole hostile fabric just as a spider's web is torn through by a whirlwind.

The general plan of Napoleon was the same which the French had for centuries entertained. It was to decoy away the fleets of Britain by feints of attack upon different parts of her dominions, and to take advantage of their absence to invade the island with an army, under cover of an overpowering naval force. Never yet had such plans been under the control of a consummate genius for war, unfettered by any authority. If success had been possible under the then conditions of sails and wooden ships, it would at this time have been achieved. What may happen in the future under the conditions of steam, iron ships, and torpedoes, who can say? *Napoleon's strategy.*

Until quite lately the combinations of the last few months before the end came at Trafalgar have engrossed the attention of historians. The recent works of Captain Mahan have enlarged the picture. He has laid under contribution the French and English documents of the time, and by their aid has presented to us the shifting phases of Napoleon's mighty plan, as it experienced the changes of events which necessitated its revision, or at least were thought to do so. We may well insert a brief summary of these events, since they illustrate the Foreign Policy of Great Britain with peculiar clearness.

The old strategy of the British resumed.

The strategy against which Napoleon had to contend on the rupture of the Peace of Amiens comprised, as before, the strict blockade of French ports which had been so effective in the past, and the protection of British commerce by squadrons cruising in all the European waters, as well as on the coasts of the British colonies and India. This resumption of the old policy was made so rapidly, and was so little expected by the French despot, that in the matter of nautical preparations he was all but entirely forestalled. The British navy had been most unwisely reduced by Lord St. Vincent under the Addington administration; but the loss was supplied before it came irreparable, and Nelson in himself was worth more than one fleet, while the French required years to form an efficient navy. The process had as yet scarcely begun; and the efforts necessary to build large ships were vainly expended upon the flotillas of small vessels and flat-bottomed boats which were intended to cover the proposed invasion. The Emperor was forced to use chiefly what fleets he already had, and to add to them those of other nations.

Napoleon's first plan.

Napoleon's first plan was to destroy British commerce in Northern Europe by seizing Hanover, which carried with it the Hanse Towns, and especially Hamburg, and to threaten the Mediterranean and the Indian communications of Great Britain by the seizure of the peninsula of Otranto, from which he expected that he would be able to command Morea, the Ionian Islands, and Egypt. It was this which justified Nelson's alarm for the Levant, an alarm aggravated by his devotion to the Neapolitan Court. In these two directions Napoleon hoped to employ portions of the British fleets while the invasion of England was impending. Though the diversion of these fleets was soon planned upon other lines, the same principle ruled them all. So tremendous, however, were the risks he ran, and so contrary to all probability was his success, that many writers have held that he never had any serious intention to invade; but Captain Mahan (ii. 116, 117) reviews the question, and shows the contrary.

The British fleets were not concentrated in the Channel; but large squadrons of frigates kept constant watch over the boats and vessels assembled in French and Dutch ports, from the Texel to the Channel Islands. The navy had been reduced to that policy by the repeated failures to destroy these vessels which had been made in 1801 by small squadrons under the direction of Nelson himself and Sidney Smith; for their skilful disposition under cover of shore batteries formed an invincible obstacle even to the bravest commanders. This, however, was only a small part of the defence of England. Admiral Cornwallis's large fleet formed the blockade of the French fleet at Brest with the same continuous and unflinching resolution which distinguished that of Hawke before the battle of Quiberon; for it was that Brest fleet which it was necessary at all hazards to prevent from covering the invasion. A few line-of-battle ships at Spithead and at the Downs, and some others cruising

Disposition of British fleets.

M

within reach in the North Sea, formed the nucleus of defence round which Cornwallis was to rally if he were blown off to sea and the Brest fleet should escape in his absence.

Nelson off Toulon.

The Toulon fleet was placed under the direct surveillance of Nelson, whose acquaintance with all the questions concerning the Mediterranean was profound. It was felt that this Toulon fleet was the weapon which Napoleon would use to force the situation, but no one could as yet penetrate his full design. As the seizure of Egypt, with its threatening bearing on India, had been one of Napoleon's original schemes in 1798 for balancing the naval force of his enemy in the Mediterranean, so in Nelson's mind it continued to be one of the chief dangers against which he had to guard, long after the Emperor had relinquished it for a deeper and more unexpected policy. At one time the great admiral believed that the Toulon fleet was to make for Egypt, at another that it would slip out of the Straits to support the invasion of England or Ireland; and it turned out to be true that this last was the work for which it was intended as long as Napoleon had an admiral whom he could trust; and such a man he believed that he had found in Latouche Tréville.

Captain Mahan attributes Nelson's practice of keeping his fleet at anchor in the Maddalena Islands on the north coast of Sardinia, or cruising far out of sight between Spain and Italy, while he watched the French at Toulon with such frigates as he had, to the defective condition in which Lord St. Vincent had left his ships; and Nelson's own despatches seem to intimate as much. On the other hand, the admiral often takes credit to himself for not actually blockading the enemy, but giving them every opportunity to escape, in order that they might be tempted to come out and do battle. The reconciliation of the two different motives may lie in the fact that Nelson found it absolutely impossible to blockade Toulon closely in the existing condition of his squadron, and became so accustomed to the necessity of lying in harbour, and trusting to the look-out kept by his few frigates, that he learnt during his two tedious years of watching to regard that policy as his own choice instead of its being forced on him by necessity as the second best course.

That it was a decidedly defective plan of blockade, or rather not a blockade at all, was proved by the event. Villeneuve, who had succeeded Latouche Tréville in the summer of 1804, got away next spring from Nelson without much difficulty, and even when he returned unobserved to refit his ships which had been battered by a storm, he made a second escape, which enabled Napoleon to work out his final plan, though unsuccessfully. There was only one sure method of checkmating the French, or at least only one which promised all the elements of security which the nature of the case permitted, and that was to blockade both the Brest and Toulon fleets so closely as to be always in touch with them, or, if driven off for the moment, to be instantly before the port again. Even an abundance of frigates or look-out ships must have failed to take the place of the blockading fleet. Even in the steam warfare of the future, ironclads which cannot keep the sea in all weathers will not save England from invasion when the day of trial comes; and to keep up a sufficient

His defective blockade.

relief for these, so as to have a force superior to the enemy always before the blockaded port, will require a second fleet at hand nearly equal to the first. This is the great lesson of the Napoleonic war, which was, after all, only a repetition on a large scale, as far as the sea was concerned, of the Seven Years' War of which Hawke was the hero.

<small>Napoleon's second plan.</small>
Napoleon's new plan in 1805 seems to have been adopted on account of his distrust of Villeneuve, who was yet, in his opinion, the best admiral at his disposal; a well-formed distrust, as his failure at the critical moment showed only too plainly. Was there no junior officer whom he might have discovered and brought to the front at such a moment? He determined, at any rate, under the circumstances, to deprive his Toulon fleet of the importance it had assumed in his earlier plan. It was no longer to make for the British Channel, and, without disturbing the Brest fleet and its blockading force, to cover the landing of his troops; but to take—to use Mahan's expression—"the inferior *rôle* of a diversion." Ganteaume, at the head of the Brest fleet, was to take its place, and escaping Cornwallis in some storm, to cover the invasion, or make for Ireland with a large military force. The Toulon and Rochefort fleets were to sail for the West Indies, and thus, it was hoped, decoy away some thirty British line-of-battle ships to defend their colonies. When some of these colonies had been taken the fleets were to return to Ferrol. In the meantime the invasion would have taken place, and the concentrated French fleets would overpower Cornwallis.

<small>His third plan.</small>
Yet another plan was suggested by the temptation, to which the Emperor yielded, of adding the

Spanish fleet to his navy. Spain was in no condition to resist, and was obliged to incur the hostility of Great Britain, contrary to its ancient maxim, which subsequent events most fully justified, "Peace with England, and war with the rest of the world." The lesson was first taught in the reign of Elizabeth, and was never forgotten with impunity. It is one of the highest tributes to British sea-power. The temptation to reckon Spanish ships, as they were at that period, among the available naval forces, would have had no weight with the British, who knew well that mere size and number are worse than useless unless the equipment, the officers, and the crews are efficient; but Napoleon's ideas on nautical subjects were almost entirely based on the calculations which govern military operations on shore; and though he himself directed his admiral to regard two Spanish as only equivalent to one French ship, their mere presence in line of battle was a serious weakness to a combined force. He hoped also to have received a much more effective addition from Holland; but all his schemes were drowned in the waters of Trafalgar before this part of them could take effect. The Toulon fleet, though still under Villeneuve, was now restored to its first destination, but not before the British had punished the unhappy Spaniards by seizing the treasure-ships which were to have enriched the French, without issuing any Declaration of War. This was held up to reprobation as piracy, but its justice is now generally admitted even by Spanish historians. It must be ranked in the same category with the seizure in 1807 of Danish ships, which were practically the property of France; but no doubt a larger force should have been sent, as in the case of the Danes, so as to excuse the Spanish squadron from making a useless resistance.

The final plan. The final plan of the naval campaign was not absolutely disclosed till Villeneuve, who had evaded Nelson, had been driven back by storms to Toulon. He and Ganteaume received their orders on March 2, 1805, and the campaign now began, which ended, six months later, at Trafalgar. Villeneuve was to sail as soon as possible for Cadiz, picking up the ships in that port, then for Martinique, to wait there forty days for Ganteaume, and if he did not appear, to give him a second rendezvous at the Canary Islands. With the whole forty ships he was then to cover the invasion. But Ganteaume never got away from Brest. He begged to be allowed to fight the blockading squadron when it was reduced for a short period from twenty-one to fifteen ships, but was refused. He never had another chance. It is of course possible that Ganteaume might, even with that superiority of force, have been beaten; and Napoleon's strategy was to avoid all fighting till the critical moment should arrive in the Channel. He afterwards bitterly reproached Villeneuve for not running a necessary risk on the chance of success; but he had himself to blame for not letting Ganteaume fight when he was ready and willing to do so with a substantial majority of ships.

French and British strategy compared. To destroy the enemy if a chance offers without looking farther, is the only true nautical method. The English have for the most part adopted it, the French seldom, if ever. It is thus that their finest officers have so often failed to show the dashing spirit which their land battles have exhibited, and which is inherent in the national character. Being ordered to defend rather than attack, to pursue some ulterior object rather than dispose of their enemy on the spot, they have generally missed their opportunity, and then after all failed in that ulterior object. Even on land this is a demoralising process: at sea it is fatal.

At last, Villeneuve having sailed on March 31st, began that exciting chase which Nelson, in an agony of breathless eagerness, pursued till victory at last crowned his incessant labour, and at the same time put an end to both his glorious life and to the naval war between Great Britain and her enemies. With this last series of guesses and mistakes, of intuitions and successes, we are all so familiar that it may be summed up in a few words. The dramatic interest heightens as we proceed. We follow the hero to Alexandria, fully persuaded as he was that the French, when Villeneuve made his first start, were on their old Egyptian track. The best excuse for Nelson not having as yet discovered Napoleon's intention to make his Toulon fleet the chief instrument of his strategy for the invasion of England, is to be found in the Emperor's well-known opinion that the East was the most vulnerable point of the British Empire,—an opinion which his despatches show he had not even yet relinquished,—and in the skill with which he had blinded friends and enemies by still professing to make Egypt his object. The idea, as we have said, fell in only too well with Nelson's past experiences, and his sentiment concerning the kingdom of Naples.

Villeneuve escapes, 1805.

Villeneuve's second escape on March 31st found Nelson still groping about as blindly as ever, and it was not till April 16th that he discovered that his enemy had made off through the Straits of Gibraltar. On the 13th of May Villeneuve had reached Martinique with a fleet of eighteen line-of-battle ships, made up of different detachments, while Nelson had been fretting under foul winds in the Mediterranean, and did not leave Gibraltar till May 11th. The whole Atlantic lay between them.

Nelson starts in pursuit.

There were, however, no further guesses or mistakes on his part. Finding from English despatches that news of Villeneuve's departure for the West Indies had arrived, he took it on his own responsibility to follow him with perhaps the greatest speed that a fleet of sailing ships has ever attained. That was the one point,—to get at the enemy, or at least divine his further movements, prevent him from conquering the West Indian colonies, and track him to Europe again before the junction, which the hero never knew, but rightly guessed, was designed, could be effected. Napoleon had made another mistake. Attempting too much, he lost all. The conquest of West India islands was a matter of trifling consequence in comparison with the great end of invasion which he had in view. The success of his scheme of decoy, so as to divide the British fleets, was as well provided for by the mere visit of his Toulon, Cadiz, and Rochefort squadrons to the West Indies as by their lingering for the purpose of conquest; and every day was lost during which they lingered. His last chance was to get these squadrons back to Brest, where, along with Ganteaume's Brest fleet, they might have overpowered Cornwallis, and then covered the invasion before any squadron sent in pursuit to the West Indies could arrive. As it was, Nelson, in spite of his enforced delay, was within a hundred miles of Villeneuve before the latter knew of his arrival. Nor would he have failed to dispose of the French at once had he not been grossly misled, by false information, to Trinidad, which gave Villeneuve his chance of slipping away and sailing to Europe according to the orders he had received.

An important link in the progress of the campaign was now supplied by Nelson's foresight in sending the Curieux brig, Captain Bettesworth, to the northward of his own course, in order to obtain news of Villeneuve, whom he rightly guessed to be bound for Ferrol, where a Spanish and French fleet was blockaded by a small British force. He himself made for Gibraltar, whence he had set forth, in order to be on his own station again, ready to defend the Mediterranean if Villeneuve should make for it, and await fresh instructions. But the French fleet sailed slowly, and Bettesworth, having caught sight of it, hurried to England with the news. He was just in time. Pitt had placed at the head of the Admiralty, in succession to his friend Dundas, Sir Charles Middleton, lately created Lord Barham, a veteran of eighty years, who had already shown superior capacity. He now played a great part. With signal promptitude he sent despatches to Cornwallis with orders to strengthen Calder's squadron off Ferrol. Calder was to cruise a hundred miles west of that port in order to intercept Villeneuve; but Brest was to be sealed fast as before, while Nelson's fleet and that of Collingwood, who was blockading Cadiz, were to take care of the south.

His foresight.

These dispositions were successful, except so far

Calder's action.

as that Sir Robert Calder's fleet of fifteen ships was too weak to conquer decisively Villeneuve's twenty. At least he thought so, and after gaining a decided advantage, did not renew the combat. For this error he was tried by court-martial (after Trafalgar) and reprimanded—almost the only case of an officer being punished for gaining a victory. At any rate, he crippled his enemy, who, however, got into Ferrol during his temporary absence, and raised the number of the French ships to twenty-nine. Calder now gave up the blockade and joined Cornwallis off Brest. The failure of Calder was conspicuous in the blaze of such glories as Nelson and Collingwood achieved, but his error was hardly greater than that of the trusty Cornwallis himself, who now tarnished his just reputation for judgment by dividing his fleet off Brest, and sending Calder with eighteen ships to watch Villeneuve at Ferrol. The French had thus the game in their own hands if they had known how to play it. Villeneuve with his twenty-nine ships had nearly double the force of either Calder or Cornwallis, and Napoleon's combinations had worked themselves out, after a chapter of accidents, into an unexpected simplicity. Even a second-rate French admiral would have taken advantage of Calder's inferiority of force, and attacked either him or the fleet off Brest. If successful there, the invasion would have taken place, supposing the weather—a factor on which no one could count—did not interfere.

Villeneuve loses his chance.

But Villeneuve more than justified the Emperor's doubts. He had experienced a run of good fortune in escaping from Nelson, but that had exhausted all his powers. He had also at the critical moment a piece of luck of which he knew nothing, in the departure to England of Nelson himself, sick and weary; but fortune only favours the brave. Villeneuve had personal courage enough, but not moral courage. He retreated to the south instead of advancing to the north, and was caught by the British fleet at Cadiz when making his way again out of that port on October 21st. Collingwood had meanwhile been reinforced; the blockade was effectual; and Villeneuve should not now have left his secure anchorage. But he had received orders to proceed to the Mediterranean for the purpose of supporting the Emperor's Italian campaign. Almost at the same moment Nelson arrived from England to take command of Collingwood's fleet. The French admiral's action was quickened by the discovery that he was no longer to be trusted, but to be superseded by Admiral Rosilly. This meant disgrace; and he put his own honour before his duty, —for Napoleon, when he gave the order, did not know, as he did, that Collingwood had been reinforced. Here was Villeneuve's final blunder, unless we add to it the faulty disposition of his fleet. To draw up his ships in line, for it only accidentally became a crescent, was indeed the scientific form of meeting an enemy who attacked in column; but when his fleet was only a little superior in numbers, to form twelve of his ships into an independent reserve under Gravina, was to give himself away. When his fleet wore and received the British on the port tack, heading for Cadiz, this reserve fell into the rear, and became an easy prey to Collingwood's division.

Nelson's instinctive belief that Napoleon's strategy

Nelson's strategy.

was based on the command of the Mediterranean,—though he had not foreseen, at the beginning of the great naval campaign, that the invasion of England would take the first place in his designs,—was now to bear fruit. We have seen that he made for the Straits of Gibraltar on his arrival from the West Indies. When he joined Collingwood, he still made it his first object to prevent the French fleet from running out of Cadiz into the Mediterranean, and took up his position so as to intercept it. He also pursued his old plan of trying to entice the enemy to come out and fight, by retiring out of sight of the Spanish shores, leaving frigates to convey intelligence; but it was a different thing to be at sea within immediate striking distance, and to be at anchor as of old on the north coast of Sardinia. Cut off from the Straits, and too far off from Cadiz to retreat, Villeneuve had no choice but to fight; and wisely kept Cadiz open in case of the failure which he knew to be imminent. In fact, the French and Spaniards, though they had thirty-three ships to the British twenty-seven, were beaten before they began, and we are left to admire the desperate courage which in many instances they showed when all hope had passed away.

Battle of Trafalgar.

The actual details of the battle are too well known to justify an account which could produce very little in the way of facts and reflections that is not already known, or has not already attracted attention. The interest of a conflict of which the result was a foregone conclusion, and which leads us to pity the doomed allies almost as much as to glory in the victors, pales before the intense passion of the tragedy as it centres in the action of the man who will for ever remain at the head of the British roll of naval heroes. His pregnant sayings before the battle, his idolised position among the noble seamen whom he came to lead—heightened as it was by a presentiment that it was for the last time—his dying words, his last embraces of his friend, his last tribute to the mastering idea of duty which had been his lode-star — combined romance and history in the most exact proportions, and lifted the English Nelsoniad to a level with the epics of Greece and Rome,—with the advantage of being true. The story is dramatic enough without being turned into a poem; but it is surprising that it has never found expression except in prose and in a famous song.

The battle of Trafalgar was a far more marked event and dividing point in the history of the mighty struggle than the Peace of Amiens and its rupture. The Peace had been a mere truce, and its breach a mere continuation of the war, on the same guiding principles and with the same weapons as before. The grand European confederation was again formed and subsidised, the fleets, as we have seen, distributed much as before, so as to guard the Channel and the Mediterranean, and to blockade the French ports; while various squadrons defended British commerce, and the few land forces at command were reinforced by hundreds of thousands of volunteers. The real value in war of that latter force was never tested, because the battle of Trafalgar put an end to the idea of invasion, or indeed to the aggressive action of any French naval force. *A new era in the war.*

Henceforth it was to be a new war, and Napoleon

was the first to perceive it. Without waiting for Villeneuve's destruction of all his hopes and projects by his final retreat to Cadiz, knowing too well what would happen, he broke up his camp at Boulogne some days before the battle; and everything having been secretly prepared by his prescient genius, turned the tide of war upon Austria. The poor relics of the French navy were soon either destroyed or rendered useless, as he foresaw. There remained for him only the subjugation of the British allies— solid and decisive victories by land instead of dreams of victory by sea. Through their subjugation he believed that he should be able to accomplish what his rash Egyptian expedition of 1798 and his passionate plans of invading England had signally and irretrievably failed to achieve. His island enemies had beaten him at every turn. What had supplied their inexhaustible funds? Their manufactures, and their commerce with all the world. These resources should be struck down and rendered powerless by the simple expedient of stopping the access of the British people to their accustomed markets. If the whole coasts of Europe were closed to their ships the change would soon make itself felt. If he could produce this result by the conquest of his immediate neighbours and by treaties with the rest, wrung from their fears, this should be first tried. If that failed, he would conquer all Europe, and then his triumph would at last be complete.

Motives of Napoleon's policy.

This view of Napoleon's conduct has been recently revived—for it was not unfamiliar to former generations of Englishmen—by Captain Mahan, and it may on the whole be accepted; but it must not be supposed that the tremendous drama which it took eight years to work out under this grand, comprehensive plan, was present to the mind of the great strategist from the moment when he turned his back upon Boulogne, and left his vast naval armaments to moulder away. He was no doubt drawn on by events, by the necessity of breaking up the coalition of Austria, Prussia, and Russia with Great Britain, which he well knew that Pitt was once more constructing, by the ever-growing difficulties of the task which he had undertaken, and by the successful defiance of all his precautions on the part of his indefatigable enemy; but if he had any governing principle at all beyond the necessity of making brilliant conquests in order to keep up his imperial supremacy in France, this was his motive. In the indulgence of his policy he knew that he represented the ancient quarrel of centuries, but he did not divine that eventual failure would change the aspect of that enmity, and lead his people to embrace the alliance with Great Britain as their best aid against the nations which they had so terribly injured.

The battle of Austerlitz, which signalised the gigantic character of the new war, occurred, with dramatic promptitude, so immediately after that of Trafalgar, that the gratitude of deliverance from French invasion was almost forgotten by Englishmen in the horror of the new catastrophe. The invincible legions of the conqueror seemed about to lay prostrate all the thrones of the Continent, and to cut off every branch of the alliance by means of which the British Government had hoped to restrain the French within some bounds. There was no longer any room for naval enterprise; there was no Continental State capable of using the subsidies which had hitherto played so great a part in British strategy. What was to be done? It was no wonder that the miserable prospect gave the finishing stroke to the worn-out frame of William Pitt. It was a sad recurrence of the lot which fell to his father. The two greatest and most successful ministers whom their country had ever possessed died, not when the arms of Hawke and Wolfe in one case and of Nelson in the other had raised them each respectively to the highest renown, one as the founder of an empire, the other as the destroyer of the French navies, but from the shock of the American War which broke the heart-strings of Chatham, and from the success of the arch-enemy who had overthrown the allies of Chatham's son. With Pitt, the pilot who had "weathered the storm," and Nelson, who had ruled Britannia's waves like a sea-god, died for the moment the hearts of the British.

Austerlitz and Pitt.

But it must not be supposed that even in the midst of their grief they thought of succumbing to the pressure; not for a moment did the commerce of their merchants cease to be pushed in every channel which presented itself, new and old. The efforts of the French corsairs, manned by seamen who no longer found employment in the men-of-war, were expended in vain against the fleets of convoyed ships "spread like wild swans on their flight," sailing under the protection of the frigates such as Byron described, impatiently waiting for the laggards, "the flapping sail hauled down to wait for logs like these." The master-portrait of an everyday sight which he draws in imperishable verse has never been sur-

British commerce.

passed; but if we wish to see the grand picture of the combined British sea-forces of war and peace, as they presented themselves to the eager gaze of a competent observer at a critical moment of English history, we should turn to the Life of Metternich. The young ambassador to Great Britain in 1793 was taken to a hill in the Isle of Wight, from whence he saw on a summer day the great fleet of Lord Howe at Spithead, anchored in three divisions, with two vast merchant fleets on either side, one stretching along the Solent, the other towards St. Helen's. In admirable language he describes them as they all got under weigh at Lord Howe's signal, the three divisions of men-of-war manœuvring with the precision of land battalions on a field-day, the clouds of convoyed ships making their way and disappearing, one cluster of them up Channel to the North Sea, the other down Channel to the Mediterranean and India, to Africa, the West Indies, and the shores of America.

Such historical pictures as these make more impression than statistics on the ordinary reader; but Captain Mahan has done well to put before us the warfare against British commerce which accompanied the military struggle, in a manner well calculated to show its importance; and he has succeeded in making it intelligible to the careful student who looks below the surface, and who desires to register the lessons taught at that time for future use. He has the advantage of being able to regard it from the point of view of a neutral, and thus to show how the measures which the British found to be necessary with regard to neutrals could not but issue some day in war with the country to which

Captain Mahan's treatment of the subject.

he himself belongs. To make his story clear he has wisely divided the subject chronologically. His first part extends from the opening of the Revolutionary War to 1806, when Napoleon, who had hitherto followed the example of the various French Governments, including the Directory, determined to exclude Great Britain from all the ports of Europe, and for that purpose issued the "Berlin Decree." The second part traces the working of that and the "Milan Decree," their failure, and the final attitude of Great Britain towards neutrals as it issued in the war of 1812 with the United States.

It took six years, counting from the commencement of the Revolutionary War (1793–1799), to obtain, as regards commerce, the full advantage of British naval supremacy, but by the end of that time "the French flag had been swept from the sea." The amount of commerce which fell into the hands of neutrals was at first increasingly great every year. The British carrying trade could not keep up with the demand for British produce, and the vessels of the United States were its main auxiliaries, but the restraints put upon them by the British Government were severe and increasing. The French, on their part, held firmly to the principle that to destroy British commerce was to destroy Britain, and reckoned all neutrals who carried it as enemies. So that the Americans and other neutrals were injured by both parties, nor were their remonstrances attended to during the fury of the struggle. But Great Britain gradually established the principle which Captain Mahan admits was necessary not only for her predominance, but for her "self-preservation," viz., that the United Kingdom should become, for that war,

Hard but necessary fate of neutrals.

the storehouse of the world's commerce. He calls it a "great conception" (ii. 242), "radically sound, and in the end victorious, for upon Great Britain and upon commerce hung the destinies of the world."

Thus at any rate—for she insisted that all provisions carried by neutrals to France should be reckoned as "contraband"—she isolated her enemy, and forced her to rely upon her internal resources. The luxuries of sugar and coffee, and the necessaries of manufactured clothing and various articles of daily use, hitherto derived from the British or from their own colonies, could now alone be obtained by smuggling and by the corruption of officials, which of course immensely raised the prices and profits to the vendors. The depôts for these goods on the Continent were of necessity in neutral territories, first in Holland, then, when that country became French, in the towns at the mouths of the Elbe and the Weser, especially Hamburg. Thus the efforts of the French to exclude British commerce from Europe, for the purpose of destroying it, issued, during the years which preceded the battles of Trafalgar and Austerlitz, in the production of exactly the opposite effect. *Continental depôts for British goods.*

The vast progress which had signalised Pitt's peace administration was only quickened and increased beyond all calculation by the measures of succeeding French Governments. No other manufactories could compete with those of England. She employed larger and larger numbers of workmen, who flocked to her shores from surrounding nations. Her villages expanded into towns, her towns into great cities. Her discoveries of coal within her own limits, and the growth of her canal system, opened *Growth of British resources.*

up ever-new portions of her territory. Her harbours were filled with shipping; her sails covered every sea. An upward rise in the ranks of her society was continually taking place, and the necessary taxes were borne with increasing ease. While all this national prosperity was showing itself, and giving a confident spirit which triumphed over every obstacle, it had also the effect of a longing desire to bring the war to an end, so that the blessings of wealth might be enjoyed without war-taxes, and the numerous reforms which were needed for the lower and middle classes might have some chance of being effected. Hence the joy of the people when the Peace of Amiens was brought about; hence the ovation given by the London populace to the French minister who conveyed the ratification—a mark of degeneracy, as the infuriated Nelson thought, when he cried out against the "scoundrels who dragged a Frenchman's carriage."

Desire for peace.

Again, nothing but the conviction that Napoleon had deliberately left them no alternative but war if they wished to preserve not only their well-being but their lives, bore them up when they tumultuously demanded the rupture of the Peace, when they were depressed by the defeat of their allies and the death of Pitt, and when the Conqueror of Europe issued the fiat which declared the exclusion not only of every British article, but of every British subject from the whole vast circumference of the Continent. Then came to their aid the memories of the past achievements of their race, the inbred confidence, which so many centuries had engrained, in their nautical and commercial enterprise, the resolution to run all risks, even to the offence of

But resolution to fight it out.

those very neutrals to whom they were so much indebted, rather than give way to Napoleon on a single point. One or other must succumb.

In short, the Foreign Policy of Great Britain might be compendiously described at this critical period as war to the death with Napoleon (not with the French people as such) and alliance with the rest of the world, but only just so far as nations would co-operate with her in the mortal struggle. Whatever she might do afterwards, during that war she would hear of no compromise with her ancient rights and privileges. This brought on the war with the United States in 1812; but the northern nations, which had been concerned in the twice-repeated "Armed Neutrality," learnt, speaking generally, to forget their claims for the present in the dangers to which they were exposed in common with the great sea-power, and in the advantage which they gained from the goods which her merchants introduced. As the would-be master of the world extended his ideas of land-blockade from one conquered nation to another, he more and more exhibited himself as the personal enemy of the human race, and the British as its deliverers.

The struggle was with Napoleon, not with French people.

CHAPTER X.

BRITISH FOREIGN POLICY DURING THE NAPOLEONIC WAR (*continued*)—1807–1808.

It did not suit either the British Government or the people to rest satisfied with the mere conquests of commerce, however sure they might be in the long run to prevail. The nation which had lowered the pride of Philip II. of Spain and Louis XIV. of France was by no means willing to believe that she could not assist the Continental Powers to make head against the new Emperor of the West. The difficulty was where to find a fulcrum on which the lever might rest which was to move the world. The year 1806 had witnessed the strange spectacle of ancient thrones tumbled down one after another by this extraordinary man. Austria and Prussia licked the dust. Russian troops had been beaten at Austerlitz when combined with those of Austria; and the French victories over Russia at Eylau and Friedland lowered the Czar to the level of his fellow-monarchs. The "Confederation of the Rhine" practically extended the limits of France into the centre of Europe, and British subsidies to conquered States were by the terms of the case impossible. There were no independent States. The victorious British fleets could find no enemy to employ their energies, nor was there any question as to the safety of India.

The system of subsidies broken up.

All over that vast peninsula the British rule was making progress under the able hands of the Marquis Wellesley and of his brother, Sir Arthur, who had already served his great apprenticeship in preparation for the work which no one yet guessed was in store for him.

But how to check the conqueror of Europe? This was the vital question which the Ministry of Fox and Grenville, the feeble successors of Pitt, found themselves called upon to answer. A new direction for the old British Foreign Policy was required, but it was not forthcoming. Fox hoped to shape it in an impossible way. He was bound by his antecedents to see if the Peace which he had been so often demanding from Pitt could not be obtained by himself, now that he could treat directly with Napoleon. He soon found himself mistaken. The Emperor's circumstances were too prosperous for such a step, and his negotiations were consequently a mere mockery. Fox's efforts for peace had thus only added one last failure to those which had attended him throughout his political career. *How to supply its place?*

Nor could the "Ministry of all the Talents" make the least head against the tide of misfortunes which flowed from the hands of Napoleon. Ill-conceived and ill-managed expeditions in South America, in Egypt, and in Turkey proclaimed their incapacity. Almost unobserved, however, a Dutch colony was at this very time appropriated by the British, from which vast and quite unexpected consequences have resulted. It was the Cape of Good Hope, which seemed at first to be only useful as commanding the highway to India, but which has led to the extension of British power and influence over a large *Failure of Pitt's successors.*

portion of the African continent. In the very same year was carried at last the Abolition of the Slave-trade, to which Clarkson, Wilberforce, and others had devoted their lives in a noble crusade against received opinions, prejudice of the fiercest kind, and the most dense ignorance. Thus the gradual freedom of the negro corresponded with the development of British settlements on the Continent from which the race had come,—settlements which had as yet been only feebly represented on the western coast. The unwonted pause in an active Foreign Policy presented an opportunity which Pitt looked for in vain. The credit for the great act of Abolition must never be separated from the names of Fox and Grenville.

Abolition of the slave-trade.

And here it may be proper to take advantage of this pause to set the historic course pursued by Great Britain in a light which is too much obscured. No one would think of defending her ancient patronage of the slave-trade, but we have no business to judge the agents or the statesmen of those times by modern standards. The best of men did not at first perceive the inherent vice of slavery. In our own days we have been called upon to witness the long and painful process by which public opinion has been formed amongst our kinsmen in the United States. The trade in negroes with Africa had, as we all know, been established with the benevolent idea of saving the feebler races of Mexico and the West Indies from extinction; so that the moral sense of Europe was for a very long time wholly unshocked by its continuance. The *Assiento* or contract for the exclusive right of importing negroes from Africa to the Spanish colonies was granted to Great Britain at the Peace of Utrecht as a compensation for her

Responsibilities of the English for slavery.

many sacrifices in the cause of peace. No one remonstrated on the ground of its cruelty or wickedness. It was thought to be a simple commercial transaction with a particular Company. About that very time we have the strongest proof that the form of slavery brought about by the slave-trade was not in itself considered reprehensible. The Society for the Propagation of the Gospel received from the brilliant Christopher Codrington for missionary purposes a portion of his West India estates, with its contingent of negro slaves; but its records show that the notion of emancipating them never struck the excellent bishops and other dignitaries who formed its Committee, though they undertook their education and conversion as a primary duty.

It became, in short, a received doctrine that negroes were better off as slaves than amongst their own savage kindred, and no doubt there were many cases in which this was true. Naval officers who had served in the West Indies imbibed the views of the planters, and helped to propagate the illusion. Nor were the horrors of the Middle Passage so shocking in its early stages. It was one of the evils accompanying the working of the Act that the difficulties of transport greatly multiplied the sufferings of the slaves. Those who delight in minimising the good fame of their country may well be reminded that it was Great Britain after all which steadily put down this foul practice as carried on by its own offspring, and, by the force of a strenuous and constant pressure upon other nations, has gradually abolished the trade all over the civilised world. Her ability to do so sprang from her Foreign Policy, which, guided by the commercial instinct, tended to make and keep her mistress of the seas. Still more, when did any nation make a greater sacrifice than that which formed the corollary of the Abolition Act, when Great Britain paid down twenty millions sterling as compensation to her own planters for the emancipation of all slaves within her dominions?

The New Ministry.

Fox's death in 1806, and the incapacity of the Ministry of which he had been the main strength, brought on the ministerial stage the remains of Pitt's party, along with the Pittite Whigs—a junction which by no means inspired the confidence that the Government had enjoyed while the great minister was its guiding spirit and all-powerful champion. In the new ministry the Duke of Portland was the nominal head, but it included Canning and Sir Arthur Wellesley—the first as Foreign Secretary, the last as Secretary for Ireland; and in observing the course of these two great men we are for our present purpose absolved from noticing the rest. The future was in their hands.

The name of the former, though it was many years before he became Prime Minister, connects British Foreign Policy with the course it had pursued under Pitt. Canning was his pupil and friend, his enthusiastic supporter in speech, in verse, in prose. His 'Anti-Jacobin' had already in some degree taken the place of Burke's more solemn appeals to the nation.

Canning's special merit.

It was his especial merit that he knew how to enlist the sympathies of the British people in a cause which he made his own, the cause of Spain, or rather of the Spaniards; and its adoption placed the British on the track of which they were in search. It gave them a foremost place in the direct and active pursuit of the conflict with Napoleon, and was perhaps, by drawing off his forces to Spain, the chief agency in bringing about his fall. We must dwell a little longer on the circumstances which turned British Foreign Policy in this direction, and on the statesman whose preparation seemed to have peculiarly fitted him to take advantage of them.

When the successful, all-victorious "Emperor of the West" had laid the great monarchs of Europe at his feet, it was natural that he should think it only a small thing to imitate his assumed prototype Charlemagne in the Spanish Peninsula. But that was an imperfect model. No Saracens were at hand to keep him north of the Ebro. He would realise the dreams of Louis XIV., and "abolish the Pyrenees." It required but a word to direct a sufficient force into the midst of a people who would not dare to resist, and to cajole into his power an effete royal family, whom he would replace by his own brother Joseph. Unfortunately for himself and his plausible scheme, he had to reckon in this matter with George Canning. *[margin: Napoleon and Spain.]*

The great conqueror now found himself for the first time, and just at the moment when he had arrived at the summit of his career, face to face with his destiny. Kings, armies, and alliances had been shattered to pieces by his hands. He had set on foot a policy by which the British people would soon be reduced, as he believed, to harmlessness. All Europe should learn what it was to be directed by one beneficent will, and nations which had stained the pages of history by their mutual contentions were to be harmonious co-operators in the work of progress. He was about to be disillusioned. He was to learn what strength there lay in the weakness of a people, feeble, disunited, contemptible from a military point of view, and ruined as a nation by years of misgovernment, when the people themselves were aroused to a desperate patriotism, and assisted by a competent military force of some other nation round which they could rally. This was to be the "Spanish ulcer," as he termed it, which almost from the moment when he commenced his nefarious attempt to enslave the country began to eat away his overweighted system.

<small>The "Spanish ulcer."</small>

Canning, in more respects than one, was peculiarly fitted to extend his great master's Foreign Policy by the method which unexpectedly offered itself for acceptance. His political position was the same. Like Pitt and like Burke, he had been rather anti-Foxite than one of the so-called orthodox Tories,—who, however, it must be remembered, followed each of these men in turn as their natural leader, and deserve to share their glories. It is remarkable that it should have fallen to these three men, who were in the strict sense of the word above party, to lead the nation through its perils. It is an example of the sterling patriotism which rises to the surface in all British emergencies, leading the large majority to forget on such occasions their party ties, and consigning the dregs to factious insignificance.

It is scarcely too much to say that Canning's adoption of the Peninsular policy was a greater stroke of genius than any for which his predecessors could be credited. The old English policy of subsidies to the allied Powers of the Continent, the only one open to Pitt, had collapsed at Austerlitz, and seemed to be buried in his grave. Canning saw that not only must a limit be put, for the time at least, to a system of loans which had become useless, but that British gold and British troops must be freely used in support of some country where those troops, aided by the navy, might hold their own. The Low Countries were no longer available as of old. Was it possible that the Spanish Peninsula had offered at last the true base of operations? It was a question of exceeding difficulty; for nothing was known about the state of Spain. The wisest statesmen freely expressed their doubts.[1] Large bodies of the Tories entirely distrusted a popular insurrection, and they had only too just cause for hesitation. From another point of view, in spite of the popular support which carried Canning over every obstacle, the organs of the Whigs discouraged any further opposition to the invincible Napoleon. With some of them he was even yet an idol.

Adoption of Spain by Canning.

It was no doubt a dangerous experiment, as the course of events proved. How often was the cause all but shipwrecked! Yet it was Canning's own infectious enthusiasm which made him dash into the fray while he had the power to lead the country; and the British were soon too far committed to draw back. That enthusiasm was supplied by his popular sympathies. His confidence in the desperate resolution of the Spanish people turned out at last, after many a bitter trial, to be well founded. The truth

[1] It is a wonderful proof of Pitt's foresight that he remarked to Lord Wellesley, the last visitor he saw before his death, "Only a war of peoples could save Europe, and this war would begin in Spain." It was one of those prophecies which help to fulfil themselves. Canning and the Wellesleys no doubt shared that opinion, and treasured up the saying. See "Talleyrand," ii. 105, by Lady Blennerhasset (English edition).

The outcome of his popular sympathies. is, if we examine Canning's career, we shall find that, with all his contempt of the arts of the demagogue, and all his horror of the French Revolution and its English supporters, there was a side of his character which led him to believe from the bottom of his heart that the people of England would be with him if they were only properly led. Instead of leaving them out of his calculations, as was too much the fashion of an ancient aristocratic society, he would write for them, legislate in their favour, use them for the public service, attract and guide them into patriotism. These ingrained ideas as to his own people helped him to believe in the people of Spain and Portugal.

But before Canning engaged in this congenial field for his talents he became responsible for one of the boldest strokes of British war-policy which had yet been made. The Czar Alexander, staggered by the unexpected success of Napoleon, and offended with the British, whose opposition to the Armed Neutrality had prevented them from making common cause with Russia as entirely as they had with Austria and Prussia, showed a disposition to come to terms with the conqueror. Of this Napoleon well knew how to take advantage. "Let us divide the world," said he. "Great Britain will soon be harmless, and you shall have Turkey as far as the Balkans, Finland, and the rest of Poland." The Emperor of the West would treat with the "Emperor of the East" on equal terms. On a raft moored in the river Niemen the Treaty of Tilsit (July 7, 1807) was concluded between the two despots. There were also secret Articles, but they were not secret to Canning, whose information was excellent; and one of them provided for the use of the Danish fleet by the French against Great Britain. The minister was equal to the occasion, and instantly replied to the Treaty by seizing the fleet at Copenhagen. It was only a question of days and hours whether the two allies should use this fleet against his country, or be prevented from doing so by the menaced State. There was no hesitation. Not an hour was lost. To the amazement of the Emperors of the East and West, while they were still paying compliments to one another, the thing was done. Lords Gambier and Cathcart, with a force against which resistance was hopeless, carried off the fleet to England, the Danes having refused the offered terms of surrendering it as a deposit till a general peace. This was a most dexterous stroke; but few things gave a greater shock to the opinion still entertained of British honour. "No expedition," says Lord Malmesbury, "was ever better planned or better executed, and none ever occasioned more clamour."[1] *Seizure of the Danish fleet.*

It was too successful, too barefaced a robbery,— so the world said. Here was the nation which professed such philanthropical sentiments, in which Wilberforce, after a struggle of twenty years, had just carried the Abolition of the Slave-trade,—a nation which, from a pinnacle of moral elevation, was never weary of denouncing the crimes of its enemies, condescending to an act which deserved to be classed with the violent defiances of elementary law so often committed by the French. This was the language of friends and foes upon the Continent, and of not a few in the country by which the blow was struck. Even Heeren, an historian of the times, *Defence of the policy.*

[1] Malmesbury Diaries, iv. 391.

who, writing a generation afterwards, most plainly perceived the true relations between Great Britain and Napoleon during the deadly struggle, passes over the seizure of the fleet with the dry remark that "it gave England an accession of security but not of renown."

Since those days, however, historical opinion has decidedly settled down in favour of the course which Canning pursued. Even at the time, Wilberforce, statesman and philanthropist, declared the "policy might be doubtful, but our right clear if self-defence is clear"; and again, "After much reflection, I am convinced that, under all the circumstances of the case, the Danish expedition was just." The fact is that the issue has been absurdly confused and distorted by the bitter hostilities of the times. The arguments against the British action towards a Power with which she was not at war, assumed as a premiss the independence of the gallant Danes; whereas their independence, like that of the Low Countries, could only be a reality when collective Europe guaranteed it. When the Continent was parcelled out between France and Russia, the Danish fleet belonged to one or other of those nations. Denmark was grievously to be pitied for finding herself in such a dilemma; but what country did not suffer in that fearful conflict? It would have been well if she could have accepted the conditions offered her; but she not unnaturally preferred to throw herself into the arms of the enemies of Great Britain, and took the consequences. The seizure of these ships was neither better nor worse than a thousand other acts which occur in war, and which pass unheeded from the simple necessity of the case in hand.

It must also be remembered—and it is part of our general subject—that Denmark had its own policy in reference to Sweden and Norway, which cannot be severed from these transactions. It is indeed the key to them. Sweden was at this moment the one ally in the north which elected to stand by the hard-pressed British; and yet it was an impotent ally, for its king was to all practical purposes insane. When Canning sent Sir John Moore with a small but efficient army to support Gustavus IV., he was obliged to return as he went; for no common action was possible. Great Britain then, it is plain, could not let the Baltic take care of itself. Necessity was laid upon her. The policy of Denmark was naturally opposed to that of the ally of Sweden, its deadly enemy. Under such circumstances there could be no basis of support for Great Britain in the friendliness of either the people of Denmark or their rulers, even if they had not the excuse that they were acting under pressure. It was precisely that action under pressure which the British could not afford to permit. It had no choice.[1]

The state of the Baltic.

This high-handed act—for such, however justifiable, it was—had removed one danger. It was a sort of corollary to Trafalgar. There should be no revival of the threat of invasion, no interference with the steady progress of British manufactures or

[1] The paragraphs on this subject are taken from "Imperial England," published in 1880. It is satisfactory to be able to quote in confirmation of them Captain Mahan's mature judgment recently delivered: "The transaction has been visited with the most severe, yet uncalled for, condemnation. . . . To have receded before the obstinacy of the Danish Government would have been utter weakness."—Mahan, ii. 277.

commerce. But what a spectacle presented itself to the new Foreign Minister, face to face with the new "Continental System," formulated by the Berlin Decree of December 21, 1806, and the Milan Decree of November 17, 1807, and forced upon the nations of the Continent! The arbiter of Europe, building on the foundation laid by the preceding French Revolutionary Governments, and extending the platform of the old "Armed Neutrality" of the northern nations, threatened the absolute destruction of his inveterate foe. Baffled in Egypt and Syria, baffled on the coast of Boulogne, his naval forces absolutely destroyed, he had taken his revenge. He had by these Decrees at last succeeded in sealing up the whole of the coasts of Europe, as he supposed, from the commerce of Great Britain. He had only to deprive her of the coast of Portugal, the one friendly strip of territory left through which the "nation of shopkeepers" could pour their goods into Europe. This last ally, the most ancient of England's allies, was forced to declare war with her friends in August 1807. Her fleet was to be seized in the Tagus by the army which poured into the country; and then Great Britain would die of inanition, then the world would be at rest. These calculations were falsified; the first by a British naval force on the spot; the second by the inherent difficulty of the scheme which appeared so feasible on paper. Canning, who had seized the Danish, was not likely to allow the Portuguese fleet to be absorbed by French land-forces. He encouraged the royal family to seek refuge in Brazil rather than submit, and a British fleet convoyed them on their way; while the vanguard of Junot's army arrived only in time to obtain a distant view of the last ship of the Portuguese naval service clearing out of the Tagus.

The final object, the annihilation of British commerce by the "Continental System," was a more complicated matter, and was decided against Napoleon by two main agencies—the resolute measures taken by the British Government, and the spontaneous working of the universal law of supply and demand. Both of these were altogether beyond the Emperor's power to control. But it could not be expected that the wisest statesmen would be able to forecast this future. The present was dismal enough. The "Continental System" declared the British Isles to be in a state of blockade, and every British subject found on the Continent a prisoner of war. It prohibited all trade in British or colonial merchandise, and it forbade all vessels sailing from British harbours or colonies to touch the shores of the Continent. Against these Decrees the outraged British Government issued the famous "Orders in Council," which retaliated by prohibiting neutrals from entering any port which was under French influence, by an actual blockade of the mouths of the Elbe and Weser, by a declaration of blockade against all ports which excluded the British flag, and by the capture of all ships whatever which proceeded to the said ports without having first touched at a British port and paid duty.

<small>British "Orders in Council."</small>

These all-embracing measures on both sides destroyed for a time the whole trade of neutral nations. They were particularly resented by the United States, which stood outside the circumference of the struggle, and were prepared to reap, if possible, the full harvest of commerce to which they considered they had a right. On the other hand, both belligerents, believing their own policy to be a matter of life and death, refused to listen to the remonstrances of the neutral Powers. Both in their desperation resorted to the principle of a "paper blockade"; but the difference between them was that the ships of Great Britain, forced by their foe into an unwonted severity, were in a position to carry it out more or less effectually by the capture of offenders at sea; while not even Napoleon could prevent the organised smuggling which will always exist where the wants of a people rise to a certain point and pass beyond control.

<small>British concentration of trade.</small> The British were thus able to concentrate the trade of the world in their own hands. They did not, as we have seen, prevent neutrals from carrying goods to Continental ports so long as they first touched on British shores and paid duty; the object of the Government was to enrich their country so that it might be able to rely upon its own resources in the mortal conflict, and thus to assist the Continental States to enfranchise themselves when the time should arrive. Those who were the universal paymasters, and were drawing by hundreds of millions on posterity for this purpose, should at least have the power of paying interest to the national creditors.

It is well that we should remember how matters appeared to that generation. On the other hand, we observe what that generation could hardly perceive till events disclosed the fact, that the great general and statesman who was now bestriding the world like a Colossus, was marching straight on to his own destruction by means of his "Continental System." He was shutting up Europe in one vast prison, isolating the Continent while he thought he was isolating Great Britain, and driving the despairing populations to rebellion while he pretended to be their deliverer. Surrounded by an army of spies, what could these oppressed people do but darkly conspire and grimly watch for the signal of insurrection? As each port used for the landing of British goods was closed, one after another, in the Baltic and in the Mediterranean and on the Atlantic coasts of the Peninsula, its place was taken by individual enterprise which it was the common interest to keep secret, just as in the previous century British merchandise made its way in spite of all obstacles to the coast of Spanish America. *Effect of French policy on the Continent.*

Smuggling thus became so universal that in 1810 the great gaoler himself was obliged to legalise it by means of licences. Even before that his own regiments had been clothed in British broadcloth. The consequences of this system were not only disastrous to himself, but beneficial to his enemy in other ways than by the wealth it brought them. The professed liberator became odious, not only as a cruel conqueror, but as a confessed tyrant, forcing the sense of misery upon nations, families, and individuals by interfering with the first law of civilisation, the free interchange of all useful and familiar commodities. On the other hand, his own acts presented Great Britain before the Continent as the liberator and benefactor of the human race. The envy which had attended her nautical triumphs, the spectacle of her prosperity, the arrogance and selfishness with which she was charged, the highhanded though justifiable seizure of the Danish fleet, were all forgotten in the indignant desire for what Napoleon would not allow men to have, or only at prices for a licence which none could afford but the wealthy,—prices enhanced by the unavoidable risks of smuggling.

Under these circumstances Heligoland, close off the German coast, was seized by the British as an emporium for the contraband goods of their merchants; Malta was used for the same purpose in relation to the coasts of Italy; and neutrals found their way freely into Russian and other Baltic ports under British licences, granted on their having paid duty in England. The climax of the Emperor's despotic and reckless policy was reached when, exasperated by the success of the methods which had been pursued for the evasion of his futile decrees, he ordered that all British manufactured goods, wherever found within his empire or in countries under his power, should be publicly burned; and this was done. It has been justly called a "frantic" act. The sentiments of disgust and resentment on the part of cowering Europe were now exchanged for despair and conspiracy. Russia was sullenly verging on war, and every other nation was looking for an opportunity to throw off the yoke which it detested.

The natural working of these principles and counter-principles took effect gradually; the impulse to his own destruction was given by Napoleon himself in 1807, at a time when it seemed that no weapon forged by man could reach to his towering and impregnable height. Having handed over the Empire of the East to Russia, and obtained her compliance with his schemes for rounding off the Empire of the West, he made up his mind to realise his dream of absorbing the Spanish Peninsula, and in such a way as to prevent, as he thought, all possibility of resistance. The "Continental System" could then be perfected in the south, as he intended that it should be in the north of Europe.

We need not dwell on the details of the opening of the Peninsular War. The story of the shameful seizure of the Spanish royal family, the apparently mad insurrection of the Spanish people, the unexpected glories of Saragossa, the still more extraordinary capture of Dupont's army, and then, in painful contrast, the failures of Spain, the crushing defeats, the treacheries, the surprises of all sorts which marked the progress of the struggle, all these are familiar enough. But it is not easy, now that we know the result, to measure the weight of the arguments which decided the course of the great Foreign Minister on whom lay the chief responsibility of accepting the challenge. *Napoleon seizes Spain.*

Canning's merits in this respect have been obscured by the errors into which he was led through the inexperience of his agents, especially through the influence of the poetical but unpractical Frere. How bitter, and yet how well deserved, is Napier's scathing exposure of the waste of British subsidies poured into the coffers of those who had not the smallest idea how to use them, of the corruption and incapacity of the Spanish upper and middle classes, the mountain upon mountain of obstacles which they piled up against the British enterprise. And yet it could hardly have been otherwise. It is a terrible thing for a nation which has once been great to learn, under the torture of bitter experience, that it is perfectly incapable of obtaining its own freedom, and must depend for it on another nation which *Canning accepts the challenge.*

it has little reason to love, and could hardly help suspecting of selfish ends. It is easy to turn into ridicule the bombastic pretensions, the absurd ebullitions of national vanity, the feeble combinations, the childish strategy of a people who had been subject for centuries to every political and social disadvantage. All that might be forgotten if it did not live in an immortal work. Napier's "Peninsular War" has never been, nor is it ever likely to be, superseded. There we have the winged words of an eye-witness, brave, capable, exact, industrious, eloquent. His Whig admiration of Napoleon is itself an advantage, since his keen appreciation of the "Iron Duke" acquires force from the evident signs of impartiality.

Reasons for Canning's policy. To those who have followed the preceding sketch of British Foreign Policy, the arguments which weighed with Canning against those above mentioned will readily suggest themselves. From a military point of view there were advantages which the Revolution-War had never yet afforded. The Peninsula could be reached both from the Atlantic and from the Mediterranean. Its distance from England was not too great; it cut asunder the home resources of France; it had fine harbours for British fleets. The moral advantage was also great; for this support of an oppressed people, rising, regardless of odds, against the common enemy, called forth the more generous and noble element in the British character, and raised the strife above the level of the usual political combinations so unintelligible to the masses.

It was this which made the difference between the present enterprise and the war of the Spanish

Succession in Queen Anne's time. The military advantages were much the same, though greater now than before, since on that occasion the war in Flanders and Germany starved the war in Spain; but the Spanish people did not then feel any general desire to throw off the French yoke, and looked upon English and Germans as greedy foreigners bent on their own aggrandisement, while the ancient jealousies between Castile and Aragon, and the diverging interests of Germany and Great Britain, formed special features which really controlled the situation. The hopes of a successful issue were in this case much better grounded. The people of a whole nation, proud and brave though disorganised, were sure to feel the iron of this later, more undisguised, French tyranny enter into their soul; and in that corner of Europe not only might French armies be detained from trampling upon other nations, but fresh heart might be given to the whole mass of the down-trodden populations of Europe. These might learn in time to follow the example of Spain. At the very least Portugal might be saved, the old ally and valuable friend of the British.

All this entered into the calculations of Canning and his friends. All this came to pass, and much more. It is high time also that we took a large and generous view of the conduct of the Peninsular nations. It will be to all time the glory of Spain and Portugal that the terrific sufferings they endured at the hands of the Emperor placed them in the front rank with Great Britain in the liberation of the world.

Lastly, in reviewing Canning's direction of British

Foreign Policy we are to remember, not only his irrevocable seizure of the Peninsula as the British battle-ground, but his courage in resisting Napoleon's overtures at the Congress of Erfurt (1808). With proper spirit he refused to listen to them unless the Spanish nation, recently overrun by French armies, were included in the negotiations. To have listened at that moment would have been high treason to Europe. He, in fact, represented the indomitable spirit of Pitt, his mighty gift for ruling senates, his power of infusing his own enthusiasm into others, his reliance upon elevated principles which were not shared by the ordinary run of statesmen.

The secret of Canning's power.

These are the qualities, tried in a time of sore need, which oblige us to forget how much longer Canning persisted in leaning upon the independent efforts of the Spaniards than experience justified, and how inferior he showed himself to the Marquis Wellesley in the political ability necessary for dealing with the complicated questions which were always arising between the British and their allies. He was unfortunate in having to leave office before he had the opportunity of retrieving those errors. We shall come across him again as the director of British Foreign Policy at a later date, and we shall understand him better for having fairly assigned him his place during his first administration. Even if he had not effectively championed the cause of liberty in Greece and elsewhere at the close of his career, his relation to the Peninsular War must yet for ever place him in the first rank of British statesmen.

CHAPTER XI.

BRITISH FOREIGN POLICY DURING THE NAPOLEONIC WAR (*continued*)—1808-1814.

THE other great agent in British Foreign Policy besides Canning was Arthur Wellesley, soon to become Duke of Wellington—the man who made, we might almost say, no mistakes, the destined man whose ample shadow had already been dimly projected before his country from the plains of India. Trained in the schools of adversity and prosperity; having learned many valuable lessons in the disastrous campaigns for which the Duke of York was responsible in the Low Countries; in India, thrown upon his own responsibility at the critical age when a man may make or mar his fortunes; always enjoying the advantage of contact with the leading minds of the day, such as his great brother the Marquis and the members of the Cabinet which he served as Secretary for Ireland, from first to last we detect in him nothing small. His standard was lofty; his acquired qualities were so exactly complementary to those which he possessed by nature, that nothing was wanting for such a man but a fair field.

The British public, with every disposition to follow Canning's lead as a statesman, felt deeply the need of a military leader. They had a choice

Sir Arthur Wellesley.

of seamen, men of the Nelson type, formed in his school; but they were of no use for this enterprise. Not many were observant enough to perceive that the instrument had been already formed; nor did even these really understand their good fortune till the voice of all Europe shouted his name in their ears.

Wellesley succeeds Canning as the national representative. It might seem at first sight questionable whether it is right to treat the great Duke, who was the agent and servant of the Government during the Peninsular War, as the representative of British Foreign Policy in succession to Canning, who resigned office in 1809 on account of his quarrel and duel with Lord Castlereagh. Strictly speaking, of course, this cannot be affirmed. Mr. Perceval, and, after he was assassinated, Lord Liverpool, were the Prime Ministers responsible for the war which we specially associate with Canning as Foreign Secretary; but the Duke, soon after the war began, was in reality master of the situation. The Governments under which he commanded were those of second-rate men; and the difficulties under which they laboured were stupendous.

Popular enthusiasm is a grand impulsive force, but it soon evaporates under trial unless it is fanned by the corresponding enthusiasm of the highest class of leaders; and even they must have some supply of success and triumph to feed the flame. A sagacious judgment might perceive in the first victories of Moore and Wellesley, though they bore little immediate fruit, in the temper of the Spanish people as distinguished from their leaders, and in the stirrings of impatient patriotism which were thus kindled in the other conquered nations of

Europe, sufficient and more than sufficient encouragement to persevere. But when it seemed that the British were entirely overmatched by the immense armies which Napoleon, after the first successes of the Spaniards, poured into Spain under his best marshals, when the mismanaged and disastrous Walcheren Expedition had drained off so large a portion of the British resources, when tidings of the entire unpreparedness and unwillingness of the Spaniards to be helped came with every mail, when all attempts to support Wellesley from the east of the Peninsula were found to be futile—these things were too much for the average Briton. Even though the great battle of Talavera proved to demonstration that the British, led by their undaunted chief, could conquer, though almost desperately hampered by their Spanish allies, a far superior force of the French, it scarcely affected the British discontent.

These murmurs at the waste of money, wrung from taxpayers whose enthusiasm had cooled under so many disappointments, and at the losses sustained by so many families in a war which seemed to display unusual recklessness of life, could not but have an effect on feeble ministries. They might have been brushed aside by Pitt. Canning had for the time retired from his great position. A most short-sighted policy prevailed at headquarters. Ministers would and they would not. They dared not give up the war. They would starve it. Yet nothing availed to sour the temper of the great general. Over and over again it was his right arm which, humanly speaking, alone supported the Government. Over and over again, when, fainting

British murmurs.

under the pressure of factious and turbulent opposition, those at the helm refused their general the necessary supplies, or almost crippled his strategy by untimely interference, or in despair threw the whole responsibility for continuing the war upon his shoulders, it was his magnificent courage, patience, sagacity, all-comprehending foresight, which carried the vessel of the State over the tumultuous waves. Nothing but the conviction which he, and he alone, infused by degrees into the nation, that it was at last reaping the fruits of so many years of bitter trial and heroic sacrifice, could have turned the tide. If we had to fix upon the particular part of that noble roll of great deeds which chiefly produced this effect, we could not but select the events which gathered round the Lines of Torres Vedras in 1810. This was generally acknowledged by the generation which witnessed the struggle,—for it was obvious enough,—but perhaps is not so clearly perceived now that the famous battles which followed it have intervened with more brilliant effect in the pages of history.

Torres Vedras.

It is enough here to remind the reader that the defences, secretly prepared with consummate foresight and skill, were used with equal judgment on the advance of Masséna's army, which was driven to an ignominious retreat with the loss of 30,000 men, while the British were rested and refreshed, reinforced and enthusiastic. Portugal was thus set free, and the victor ready to invade Spain. The consequences were soon apparent. The unworthy opposition in England to the Peninsular War sank and slunk away; the crushed peoples of the Continent took heart. All through the year 1811 preparations for a united struggle which should be to the death were in progress, and, as usual, Great Britain was quite understood to be the one independent Power whose inexhaustible resources would, when the day came, be distributed throughout the mass. Once more, then, the British stood in the way of the Emperor of the West, just as they had barred his progress so often before. His wisest plan, had it been possible, would have been to take command of his Spanish armies and attempt to dispose of Wellington at once. But he held too many threads in his hand, and felt that enslaved Europe might rise while he was shut up in Spain. It was too great a risk. He could not be sure that it would be a short campaign, and unless it were short he was lost. So he resolved to deal first with Russia, and settle afterwards with Great Britain. It turned out that he was rushing to ruin. <small>Revival of European spirit.</small>

By this time the cup of misery which Napoleon had forced Europe to drink was full, while at the same time his own France was exhausted by the incessant drain of men and money, and quite unable to meet his immense expenses by trade or commerce. Great Britain was also bitterly suffering, but her Government at least continued to fight the commercial battle with success. Her "Orders in Council" met, as we have seen, her enemy at every turn, and forced the trade of all neutrals into her own ports; while the Emperor ruled his subject States by military force alone, and to supply his needs was obliged to anticipate his stock of French soldiers from a generation which ought not yet to have been taken from boys' schools. Thus he found the service not unnaturally becoming unpopular, <small>Gloomy prospects of the French.</small>

and wholesale evasions of military duty a standing difficulty. All this time he was attempting to make war support war, and wherever he was put to expense, to recoup himself from the subject nation which caused it. In Spain he was gradually arousing the whole people to fury by the exactions necessary to support his armies; and though of little or no use as regular troops, the guerilla warfare, which they organised in a more or less scientific form, exactly suited their genius, and forced the French to detach such immense military convoys to carry in provisions and escort despatches that for the last two years of the war this formed a sensible diversion in favour of the British. To this was added the drain of French troops, which began as soon as ever the Emperor discovered that Russia was meditating hostilities, and became serious at the end of the year 1811. We are brought, then, to the opening of the final act of the drama, and observe that two main causes operated to bring it on.

Causes of Russian resistance. The revolt of Russia was at bottom no doubt due to the rising sense of indignation at the treatment she had received, along with her allies, at the hands of one whom she could not but regard as a contemptible upstart of mushroom growth. The Czar, remembering the fate of his father, perceived that there must be some change from the false position which he had assumed on the raft at Tilsit, as joint-Emperor of Europe with Napoleon. His subjects might be loyal enough if he represented their convictions, but only on that condition. They were now disgusted by the effects of the "Continental System," which had been forced upon them with ever-fresh importunity. Napoleon, intent on his one main object of striking down Great Britain through the exclusion of her commerce, and finding that his system was rendered to a great extent nugatory by the passive resistance of the German and Scandinavian peoples, grew more and more determined to persevere at all costs. Having practically incorporated the Low Countries, and made himself master of the German and Danish coasts, in order that he might put down smuggling with severe completeness, he conceived himself to be approaching a successful result of so many efforts. But he offended the pride and independence of Russia beyond all bearing when he insisted on the same severity in the case of that great country.

The Czar, in pursuance of the principles of the Armed Neutrality, had already taken a line of his own with respect to neutrals, though it was impossible to deny that under the pretence of neutrality they imported British goods. From Russia these goods had been conveyed to the great Fair of Leipsic, and the Czar positively refused to rescind the decrees which thus frustrated the Emperor's policy. The peremptory and offensive language of Napoleon coincided with his reckless seizure of Oldenburg, the Duke of which State was related to the Czar; and both sides prepared for the war which had become inevitable. This was the main cause of the war. Its connection with Great Britain was direct in so far as Napoleon's proceedings were grounded on the Russian refusal to join him against his deadly enemy, but the action of the Czar was not taken in concert with the British, though they soon made common cause.

Injured by the Continental System.

The other operative motive of the Russian Policy

P

Tempted by the employment of French troops in Spain. was the detention of so large a French force in Spain. This was a strategic circumstance of great weight. Only a portion of the vast French army could be brought against Russia, and thus, what was of inestimable value in such a case, the enemy would be divided into two halves by a diversion which was not created by Russia herself. The consequence was not so apparent at first, because the consummate skill of the Emperor made a more efficient force out of the troops marshalled under his banner from the conquered nations than could have been expected; but it was foreseen by the wiser of the Czar's counsellors, and when the trial came, it was soon evident that these auxiliaries could not be relied upon. Here again the impulse towards resistance proceeded from the movement in Spain which the British had initiated. The example of an invading force lured to its destruction by the opening out of the Spanish people to receive it, and then, led by British troops, closing in upon its rear, was certainly not lost upon the much larger population of stubborn Russia. That great country taught the world for all time that any sacrifice, even of the greatest and most cherished national possessions, such as "Holy Moscow," was not to be named in comparison with national freedom.

Position of Austria and Prussia. Austria and Prussia were no less impressed with the spectacle presented by Spain and the leadership of Wellington, and they were far more affected by the rigour of the "Continental System"; but crushing defeats had rendered them powerless for the time, and Austria had been forced to consent to the ignominy of marrying her Emperor's daughter to the conqueror in the room of the divorced Josephine.

She had to provide 30,000 troops, who formed the main strength of the right wing of the great army of invasion. Prussia had to supply a contingent of 20,000, who formed the main strength of the left wing, and also vast munitions of war. To that brave nation the disgrace of thus slavishly serving the tyrant of Europe was the more terrible, as it had already begun to adopt, under Stein, Hardenberg, and Scharnhorst, the reforms which were to bear fruit in a just retaliation and eventually in empire. The political freedom and military education organised by these great men may be summed up in a sentence or two. The antiquated feudal system of land and of personal servitude was abolished, the serfs emancipated; the peasant farmers became free tenants, and the towns were enfranchised; while the system of short service and regular drafting into the reserves soon turned the people into a nation of soldiers. Within the compass of these few words lies the secret of national strength; but at the crisis of 1812 Prussia was not ready to take an independent part; and Napoleon had practically surrounded it by his organisation of the German States, of Poland, and of West Galicia. It had not long to wait.

The main army was composed of French, Italians, Poles, Swiss, Rhenish Germans, Illyrians, and others. Some twenty nations in all followed the standards of the modern Xerxes, some half-million of soldiers, with every requisite for war—"all but their hearts were there";—and when the truth leaked out that this unwieldy mass had been driven headlong into a trap, rewards and punishments ceased to take effect. *The Invasion of Russia.*

Step for step with Napoleon's march to destruction advanced the sure and steady battalions of the *Wellington's advance.*

British army under Lord Wellington. Not till 1812, indeed, was he ready to make the long-desired advance upon Spain itself, which was the reward of Torres Vedras. The possession of the great frontier fortresses of Ciudad Rodrigo on the north of the frontier, and Badajos on the south, was a necessary preliminary for this advance; and though for their siege the British General had no proper guns nor engineering implements, nevertheless, in the early months of 1812, by dint of skilful manœuvres and a terrible loss of life, chiefly at Badajos, both were captured, and the way to Madrid lay open from whatever point he chose to invade. Such storming of fortified towns recalls the ruder warfare of the Middle Ages, but it was this or nothing. No corresponding energy was shown in England, and the bare bodies of soldiers had to do the duty of war material. Even in the Middle Ages there would have been more assistance from the science appropriate to the warfare of the times; but the result justified the so-called recklessness of life, which was really a calculated venture. Officers and men could by this time undertake the most hazardous enterprises, and gloried in the opportunity.

The invasion of Spain from the northern frontiers of Portugal now took place, and the decisive battle of Salamanca on July 12, 1812, issued in a great British victory over Marshal Marmont at the very moment when Napoleon was in full career on the way to Russia. That fatal march, the noble resolution of Russia that no terms should be listened to while an enemy remained within the Empire, the storm of Smolensk, the continued retreat of Kutusoff and his army, the battle of the Borodino, where

The Russian strategy.

each side lost some 40,000 men, the advance upon Moscow, the rejoicing of the wearied invaders when they had once settled in comfortable quarters, with the general himself lodged in the Kremlin; and then, the sudden bursting forth of the flames from a hundred quarters, the despair which seized the invaders when they found the fire inextinguishable, their hoped-for supplies destroyed, their sheltering roofs burnt over their heads; and when the truth flashed upon them that there was nothing for them but to retreat by the way they came—all this is such history as few can forget. When the premature winter set in, and this almost countless multitude, shortly before so glorious in "battle's magnificently stern array," was destroyed by the prolonged agony of a merciless frost, a relentless enemy, and an absolute disorganisation, the imagination requires the help of a Dante to realise the facts, and the illustrations of a Doré to present them. *The French catastrophe.*

This was not a mere rebuff to an ambitious soldier who desired to conquer the world for conquest's sake, nor was it the outcome of long-pent-up national hatred. What was the cause of Napoleon's quarrel with the Czar? We repeat that it was his fixed determination to force Europe into the formation of one uniform barrier against British commerce. The policy was all-embracing, admitting of no exception. If any potentate showed reluctance or connivance with the enemy—still more if he resisted—his country must be subdued. Thus whole nations and peoples, outraged beyond endurance, were aroused to fury, and after this fatal retreat, taking courage from one another, declared war with him to the death. Imperialism was no longer possible in Europe; nations *General rising of Europe.*

with such a history as those of the Continent possessed could never be treated as if nationalism had ceased to be the rule of their existence. In order to carry out the theory adopted by one nation, it could not be that others should be made to bend by force. The ancient world had afforded lessons of the same sort, which had been forgotten.

It was still, however, necessary to put an end to the rule of the man who had so misled his own long-suffering people and trodden down the rest of the world. Both sides prepared for the final struggle. With masterly skill and courage the common enemy once more gathered his legions together to resist the united tide of avenging nations. The year 1813 opened with the forward march of the irresistible Russians, with the enthusiastic rising of the Prussians, already turned into a nation of freemen and soldiers, and with alliances between Great Britain and these patriotic peoples, to whom she promised a great subsidy over and above the diversion hitherto made by her in the Peninsula. Bernadotte also brought over the Swedes. Napoleon indeed still found friends in Saxony, in Italy, and in Denmark; and the Rhenish provinces still provided their contingents; while Austria, which had hitherto suffered most, remained uncertain what to do. The Elbe divided the defeated invaders from the avengers.

The War of Liberation.

The War of Liberation actually began on March 27, 1813, and the hesitation of those who had not yet thrown in their lot with Russia and Prussia soon stiffened into patriotic action under the enthusiastic impulse of the Liberators. Napoleon, after his usual manner, gave them little time to decide; and if he had only been able to provide artillery and cavalry—

trained forces which cannot be raised in a moment—as rapidly as he collected men, he might yet have turned the scale. But though he won the battles of Lützen and Bautzen, he could make no decided impression upon the masses whom he saw gathering around him on every side, and hoped that a two months' truce might enable him to act with better results. *The fatal Truce for France.*

This was another of the errors which this great master of the art of war found himself forced to commit, or perhaps we should say one of the inevitable consequences of an ambition which had "o'erleaped itself." He could hardly have failed to foresee the inevitable consequence. During these two months the waverers were plied from every side. They began to feel that there was something solid to fall back upon; and all the while Napoleon showed himself as resolute as ever to rivet the chains on the nations which he still held in subjection. This determined the long lingering resolution of Austria, alarmed though it had been at the liberal principles of the Prussian liberators. She now threw herself into line with them and Russia, and from that moment steadfastly worked for the overthrow of the tyrant.

The three great armies under Schwartzenberg, Blücher, and Bernadotte converged upon Dresden, the headquarters of Napoleon, and the finest spirit prevailed. It was all one army, one great united force, of which Austria, out of regard for its old Imperial position, was acknowledged as the chief. The three sovereigns accompanied their armies, not as generals, but to be at hand for mutual support. When had such a thing been seen before since the first settlement of the Teutons in Europe? When, *The Allies defeated at Dresden.*

since Attila, had such an enemy been seen? But the absence of any really great general in this vast force is too plainly to be perceived in all the accounts of the campaign. Partly from this cause, but still more from the immense difficulty of combining the unwieldy levies of different nations, the attack of the Allies upon Dresden failed. Moreau, the victor of Hohenlinden, did his best as general, and was killed in the battle.

Napoleon defeated at Leipsic.

Happily the forces opposed to Napoleon were too numerous, and animated with too vehement a spirit. to make the defeat of much consequence. Happily also there was a Prussian general of cavalry who, though not of the first rank, possessed the impassioned, all-defying temper which makes up for many deficiencies. Old Marshal Blücher—"Marshal Forwards," as the soldiers loved to call him—was the representative of all the patriotic elements which were combined in the Army of Liberation. Napoleon had intended to follow up in person his victory at Dresden, but was obliged to leave Marshal Macdonald in his place. Blücher annihilated Macdonald's army at Katzbach; Bernadotte defeated Oudinot at Gross-Beeren; and Ney was routed by Bülow and Bernadotte. Finding himself by this time too weak to hold Dresden, Napoleon concentrated all his forces at Leipsic, and here the great three days' "battle of the nations" was fought, the greatest of that or perhaps any other war,—fought by half a million of combatants, and resulting in the ruin of the overpressed and overmatched Emperor. The Allies were in a decided superiority of numbers, and Napoleon had to retreat on October 18.

The Allies had also recently become more closely

compacted than ever by the Treaty of Töplitz (September 9, 1813), in which the views of Metternich, representing Austria, prevailed to keep the princes of the Rhenish Confederation on their thrones, instead of deposing them, when the protection of their late conqueror and ruler should be finally removed. This was a wise provision. It saved the institution of monarchy for Europe, and left it for the coming age to apply the checks upon that form of Government necessary for political growth and personal freedom,—those controlling popular influences which had been displayed by Great Britain during the war, and adopted by Prussia in the recent moment of her agony. The opposite policy, advocated by Russia and Prussia in the white heat of their fury against all the adherents of the tyrant, would have split up many millions of Germans into hostile divisions at a critical moment, and left a legacy of civil war for the immediate future.

Though Schwartzenberg was the general in command of the allied army at Leipsic, Blücher carried off the chief glory of this decisive battle, and it was he who gave no rest to the defeated French, reduced to a third of their numbers, till they had crossed the Rhine. Now arose the cry for freedom and vengeance from the whole of the West German peoples, who, from being broken up into small States, had hitherto been forced to march at the heels of a conqueror. A popular rising, in which even women took part as soldiers, proclaimed that the power of France over the provinces on the right bank of the Rhine—a power which began in the sixteenth century, and was bred out of the religious conflicts of those times—was gone for ever. Nothing was

Rising of the West Germans.

left of the French conquests east of the Rhine but the garrisons of a few great cities, which were soon reduced. Holland now joined the victors, and the assistance rendered by Bernadotte was rewarded by the exchange of Pomerania for Norway, the former being passed over, though not for long, to Denmark. The Danish adherence to France, almost throughout the war, told heavily against that gallant people when the tide of conquest turned. Italy and Illyria were defended for a time by Eugène Beauharnais and Murat. The former had to retire before superior force; the latter played fast and loose with the Allies, and ended by being shot as a traitor.

Diplomatic difficulties. We can easily survey this furious struggle, spread over half a continent, by selecting a few salient points such as the foregoing. But it is not so easy to place ourselves in the midst of the shifting policy of the Allies when they had once put the Rhine between themselves and the dangerous fugitive. Concentrating their forces at Frankfort, the differences which had been suppressed for the moment began to show themselves. The Emperor of Austria remembered his daughter, and was unwilling to reduce her husband too low. The surpassing reputation of Napoleon, defeated with such difficulty, hung like lead over the counsels of the Allies; he might, if followed to his lair, break through the nets and undo all that had been accomplished at such a sacrifice. Some argued that he would have learnt a lesson, and henceforth confine himself to France. Let him, said they, have his "natural boundary," the Rhine, and be received into the ranks of the royal families on equal terms. It can hardly now be believed that such ideas prevailed; and it is almost equally incredible that Napoleon declined to accept the proposal, which was now definitely put before him. Yet, happily for the world, so it was. The opportunity did not recur. Warned of the desperate tenacity of the man by this refusal, spurred by the successes of Wellington in Spain, and pushed by the energetic zeal of Stein and Blücher, the great inert mass of the Allies once more resolved to move without delay. By so doing they disconcerted all the plans of Napoleon, which were based on the belief that he would have the winter before him. By giving him no time to recover from exhaustion they hunted him down. *Allies resolve to press on.*

And here we may observe, since they so seriously affected the general issue, the corresponding dates of the British advance in Spain during the eventful year 1813. We left Wellington making his forward movement, after the battle of Salamanca, just when the Emperor was in full march to Russia; and for the second time he drove the French out of Madrid, which he entered on August 12, 1812. Again, however, the impotence of the Spanish troops, to whom he had assigned an inferior part in the movement, obliged him to retreat; but it was for the last time; and the difficulties of Napoleon's situation after the failure of his rash invasion of Russia, brought at last both sides to something like equality in Spain. Wellington was now strong enough to threaten the communications of King Joseph with France, and by a series of masterly manœuvres he stopped at Vittoria the retreat from Madrid which the French with nervous haste commenced. This famous battle (June 21, 1813) was decisive; the French occupation of Spain was at an end. It would have been *Correspondence of Wellington's victories with the movements of the Allies.*

a more crushing defeat still if Wellington's disposition of his forces had been properly carried out by all his subordinates. As it was, however, the rout was complete. Some 2000 prisoners, the whole of the artillery, the military chest, and the accumulated treasures amassed from the spoils of Spain, along with the despatches and papers which had passed between King Joseph and his brother, rewarded the victors, from whom King Joseph himself only escaped with difficulty. Further resistance was speedily put down. Pampelona was soon surrendered; San Sebastian, which held out three months, was stormed; and Soult, who gallantly defended the frontier, was beaten in the three furious battles of the Pyrenees. On October 7, 1813, Wellington crossed the Bidassoa, which divides France from Spain.

The South French campaign. The struggle now took the form of a contest for South France, defended by the only one of Napoleon's marshals who proved himself worthy to face the only first-rate general of whom the Allies could boast. It will then be observed that this invasion of France was almost exactly contemporaneous with the battle of Leipsic, and that the fury of the struggle, marked by the numerous engagements which followed, resounded throughout Western Europe, and could not but affect the decision of the Allies to march forward upon North France in correspondence with the British movement upon the South. As soon as the rains allowed Wellington to cross the numerous rivers which flow from the Pyrenees through Gascony, the forward progress of the Allies was cheered by the news of battle after battle, each ending victoriously for their cause: those of the Nive and of the Nivelle, following upon that of Orthez, the evacuation of Bayonne, and the occupation of Bordeaux. Just at the moment when Napoleon had been forced to abdicate, the struggle ended with the crowning victory of Toulouse, which prevented the indefatigable Soult from joining hands with Suchet, who still commanded the army of Catalonia, now recalled for the defence of France.

It was deplorable that the news of the abdication had not reached the armies before this last sanguinary battle, but it had at least the effect of enabling the Allies to dictate terms of peace, which were not hampered by any claim on the part of the French to hold the southern provinces by military force. These coincidences have been insisted upon here because neither French nor German writers seem to remember much about them in modern times. They were quite understood and appreciated in the earlier part of the century.

It was not till the year 1814 had commenced that the allied armies found themselves able to open a winter campaign and cross the Rhine. This they did in three great divisions, the Austrians across the Upper Rhine and Switzerland under Schwarzenberg, the Prussians across the Middle Rhine under Blücher, the mixed army of the Netherlands across the Lower Rhine under Bülow and Bernadotte. This wide distribution of forces gave Napoleon the opportunity of which he well knew how to take advantage. His inferior numbers might be compensated by their concentration in Champagne, for they would at least be handled by a master of the art of war; and his genius did indeed effect as much as could be expected; but, on the other hand, the Allies could afford to lose something, and they pressed

The Allies cross the Rhine.

on without intermission. The Congress of Chatillon (February 3 to March 15, 1814) kept the various ministers in touch with one another, and by the Treaty of Chaumont, on March 1, the four Powers, Great Britain, Russia, Austria, and Prusssia, formed a quadruple alliance for twenty years.

<small>Importance of the Congresses of the Allies.</small> These common links between the Powers are of the highest importance, since they formed an epoch in European history. They lead up to the Treaty of Vienna in the following year, when France, being finally freed from the presence of Napoleon, entered the general Council of Europe as a fifth Power, and the system of concerted action upon international questions began to take the place of the armed interference of particular States. Much yet remained to be done. The storm still left a tumultuous swell upon the ocean of European life; but throughout the present century, which is now drawing towards its end, the principle has been conserved, has been sometimes operative, and has led to beneficial results. It is another form of the Balance of Power, which did good in its day though sometimes abused, but when outraged, as by Charles V., Philip II., Louis XIV., and Napoleon, in each case banded the oppressed nations together; and in each case, when the common enemy had been overthrown, a vigilant watchfulness against the recurrence of the danger has been more and more firmly maintained.

CHAPTER XII.

BRITISH FOREIGN POLICY FROM 1814 TO 1827.

EVEN in the spring of 1814 illusions had not disappeared at the Congress of Chatillon. The Allies still thought Napoleon could be left on the throne, with France reduced to its old limits; and Napoleon still believed he could stand out for the Rhine frontier, and for Italy, with Eugène Beauharnais as king. Fortunate it was that he had so erroneously measured the strength of the Allies, who once more marched forward, and would now listen to nothing short of abdication. They met with reverses, natural enough with so many masters, but recovered themselves by the masterly retreat of Blücher and the advent on the scene of Bernadotte. In vain the great strategist pushed his army round the hosts, and appeared in their rear. The Allies were numerous enough to cover his diminished forces and push on to Paris, where they fought a great battle; and Blücher, always to the front, stormed the heights of Montmartre. On March 31 the Allies entered Paris to the joy of the people, to whom they had long previously proclaimed themselves as deliverers from a tyrant. The marshals, finding the case desperate, insisted on their chief's abdication, and on April 4, 1814, Napoleon signed the instrument at Fontainebleau. The terms were generous. He was still to

Napoleon still resists.

His abdication.

be "Emperor," but his empire was the island of Elba, with a sufficient income for that position. He could expect no more.

But who was to succeed? It soon became palpable that, exhausted with the struggles of twenty-five years, the idea of tradition, of security arising out of the idea of right, had resumed its long-forgotten sway. *The Bourbons.* The Bourbons alone offered any promise of stability; and if they could have grasped the situation, they might have ruled France, wearied with war and ripe for permanent reforms, much longer than they did; but it was soon discovered that they had "learnt nothing and forgotten nothing." Not quite yet, however, were they at full liberty to disclose their incompetence. Their first year of sovereignty was almost nominal, their restored kingdom being in the hands of the Allies; nor was it till 1818 that it was thought safe to leave them entirely to themselves. Not that the victorious Allies for a moment trusted the Bourbons with the unlimited power which had led to the misfortunes of the French and the dangers to which Europe had been exposed. It is a remarkable tribute to the example which had been set by Great Britain that her peculiar inheritance of Constitutionalism formed the model on which the restored Government of France was established. *The new Charter.* Louis XVIII. had to accept a Charter which provided not only for a new House of Peers and a representative body, with powers of taxation, but also for civil and religious freedom, for Trial by Jury, and for the Liberty of the Press. The old feudal privileges were not restored, and equality before the law was proclaimed. Thus the Constitution was laid down on a basis which was quite as liberal as the country at that time required; and the open interference of the Crown with the two Assemblies was as carefully guarded against as it had been in England itself after centuries of struggle.

To Talleyrand belongs the honour of being the chief agent in pushing these ideas. From the moment when he began, along with Mirabeau, to take the lead in the French Revolution, he kept the English Constitution before his eyes. Tortuous and contemptible as his political course often, and shameful as his private life always was, he was a patriot, and used his wonderful talents for his country's good. No Government could do without him. He remarked that when they misused him they had the bad luck to come to grief; and this was true. When Napoleon was just keeping his head above water in the Hundred Days, he said he would rather hear of Talleyrand coming in than all the rest together. But the clever diplomatist was better employed, for he was then using his immense influence with the allied sovereigns and their ministers to save France in its supreme hour of distress; and he succeeded. He had no favourable feeling for the Bourbons, but he respected their traditional claim, and believed that if tied by a Charter of Liberties, they might at least form a stage in the regeneration of France. The English Revolution, he said, had lasted fifty years: the world must have patience with the French. To Talleyrand also was due the acceptance of the Charter by Louis XVIII. It was the last thing the king desired, but he had no choice. On the Continent it was a new experiment. Both Houses, the Senate through Talleyrand, and the

margin: Talleyrand.

Q

House of Representatives through Fouché, openly and categorically demanded that France should be ruled like Great Britain.

The credit for the Charter of Constitution imposed on France must be shared with Russia, a circumstance due very largely to the peculiar sentiments of the Czar, Alexander I. Though at the head of an absolute monarchy, he had imbibed, partly from his old tutor La Harpe, partly from English sources, a generous love of liberty, not unconnected with the Western ideas of religion which had found an entrance into a remarkably open and enthusiastic mind. But the political ideas of his country also found in him a true national representative. The outrages and insults inflicted by the French were too fresh to be put aside; and, mingled with the fury suggested by the ruins of Moscow and Smolensk, was the desire for aggrandisement, not only as a simple inheritance from Peter and Catherine, but by way of precaution and compensation. All this was more than shared by Prussia, whose wrongs were of a still more private and harrowing nature. The Emperor of Austria, on the other hand, though his country had been even yet more desperately mangled by the hand of Napoleon, could not forget that his daughter was Napoleon's wife; and when Great Britain insisted on withstanding the dismemberment of France, Austria ranged herself on her side.

The Czar, Alexander I.

Britain and Austria prevent the dismemberment of France.

In becoming the champion of this policy, Great Britain acted consistently with her whole past history. As Burke more than once asserts in his sonorous phrases, she had been the guardian and administrator of the Balance of Power for many ages. It was essential to that system that France should be strong; and though after what had taken place she could not be allowed to retain the Rhine boundary at the expense of the Teutonic peoples to whom the left bank belonged, she should not be deprived of the territory which she possessed before the war. This settlement indeed excluded her from the other countries which she had occupied—Spain, Italy, Switzerland, Holland, and Belgium; but she had previously performed her part well without these conquests, and it was necessary that she should be able to do so again. It cost no little friction—not very far from a war—between the conquerors to obtain the admission of France, restored to her old limits, into the circle of the Great Powers. But a new representative of Great Britain now appeared on the scene. The Duke of Wellington, fresh from his conquest of the Peninsula and of South France, arrived at Vienna early in 1815. No defeats had deprived him of the halo of his victories; the British people recognised in him their virtual king; and his statesmanlike grasp of the situation at once impressed itself on the allied sovereigns and their ministers.

The rude and sudden interruption of the Congress of Vienna on March 7, 1815, by the startling news of Napoleon's escape from Elba, has been discussed from every point of view. Perhaps the most extraordinary thing about it is the ignorance of his character which the Allies had displayed when they supposed he would be bound by promises or treaties to remain in an island which was within sight of the Continent, and where he was practically free. It was at any rate a generous confidence, if mis- *[Napoleon's escape.]*

placed. It was shared by the British military officer placed in charge of him, and by the naval officers who were supposed to watch his proceedings. But this was to run the risk of having to do the work of a quarter of a century all over again, and the Allies were not wrong in attributing the escape to British carelessness. The armies had been for the most part scattered and reduced. Napoleon was not the man to lose a moment in taking advantage of such a state of things. There was not indeed an hour to lose.

His advance from Cannes. The advance from Cannes on March 1, 1815, showed plainly that the new *régime* had no resisting power of its own. The very people who had cursed the cause of their misfortunes a few weeks before, threw themselves at his feet as he rushed to Paris,—anything to get rid of the foreign occupation. The Bourbons fled at once. Many of the old marshals, many of the old troops, came again to the front; and though the army, so hastily collected, was far below the force required to match that of the Allies when they should once have formed their ranks, Napoleon knew very well that if he could only secure exact obedience to his orders, he could balance that superiority by rapidity of movement, as he had often done before. He knew the advantage of a single will, and he had no reason to think that his His strategy. enemies could secure any such advantage. Indeed he left Elba with a full belief that they were hopelessly disunited. Blücher and Wellington were nearest the frontier, and with them he would have to deal; but the first was rash, and the second was cautious. They were sure not to pull together. He would get between them and destroy each in succession.

Large bodies of the British army, and especially the Dutch and the Belgians, had fought under his banner. They would be sure to swell his numbers after, if not before, victory, and he could then hurl them upon the Russians and Austrians, who were still at a great distance from their allies.

It was a fine conception, but the conditions of success were wanting. Grouchy and D'Erlon were inferior generals. Soult, though brave and able, had never before been chief of the staff, and Ney was more a soldier than a general. Napoleon himself was overwhelmed with the labours of the previous days, and delays occurred owing to his illness. The crisis required his old generals, his own old, unclouded powers, and an amount of time which the Allies were not foolish enough to grant. But on the other side were quite equal disadvantages, especially on the part of the British. No preparations whatever had been made in England for such a contingency. Recruits had to be raised from all parts of the country at a moment's notice, and there was no time for efficient drill; but these country lads were placed under charge of experienced officers, and the best was made of the Belgian and Dutch troops who were on the spot. Not more than one-half of Wellington's army was composed of superior fighting men. There was, however, an absolute confidence in the Duke, and an unflinching resolution amongst the British, which, when the trial came, told on the recruits quite as much as on the veterans. *Disadvantages on both sides.*

Both sides made mistakes, but the British the fewest. It has been loudly asserted that Wellington's concentration on his right wing was one of these; we now know that it was for the purpose of keeping *The British made fewest mistakes.*

open his retreat to the sea in case of defeat. But he seems to have underrated the rapidity of his enemy's movements, and to have been more or less surprised by Napoleon's attack upon the Prussians, who were beaten at Ligny. Here, however, came in his foresight as to the battle-field itself, and his knowledge of Blücher. He was certain that if he could only stand long enough on the ground he had previously examined, Blücher would not fail him, even though he had to make a very difficult march in order to act as a reserve force at the last. Nor was he disappointed. "He saw what he foresaw." Napoleon, on the contrary, had overrated the talents of Marshal Grouchy, and he had underrated the valour and energy of the Prussians. He was completely deceived throughout the day. When evening was closing in, he had convinced himself that he was about to be supported by Grouchy; but in fact he was in the presence of the terrible Blücher, and had practically no reserves. What a moment for him!

Battle of Waterloo.

Then came the decisive stroke. The magnificent patience shown by Wellington's army during the whole day won the battle. Mown down by thousands under the superior artillery of the French, but remaining immovable against their cavalry charges, and defending their outposts to the last gasp, it was a waiting game such as was perhaps never played before. "We must all stand and die here," said the Duke, and that was perfectly understood by all. At last, when the Prussians were unmistakably engaged with the French flank and rear, the word was given, and the whole remnant of Wellington's army rushing forward, swept the French off the field in headlong rout. The Prussians, comparatively fresh, took up the pursuit. The French were annihilated. Napoleon had again to abdicate, and for the last time. There could be no more playing with the question, no more Elbas; St. Helena was the best choice that could be made. It is a pity that the officer selected to keep this dangerous prisoner in charge was not a more suitable man than Sir Hudson Lowe. *The final abdication.*

We may conclude this brief notice of Wellington's victory by quoting the remark made by Lord Roberts in his " Rise of Wellington." "The place I should assign to Wellington as a general would be one in the very first rank—equal, if not superior, to that given to Napoleon." He then gives his reasons— the reasons of a great soldier and general—and concludes: "For a brief period the military genius of Napoleon revolutionised Continental Europe; that of Wellington enabled him to lead his British soldiers, few in number, but incomparable in quality, from victory to victory, to march triumphant from Lisbon to Toulouse, and from Waterloo to Paris, to overthrow his great opponent, and to establish a peace which lasted for nearly forty years" (p. 190). *Lord Roberts' estimate of the two generals.*

To return to the Congress. We have noticed the critical character of the arrangements by which the Congress of Vienna secured as best it could the Balance of the Continental nations. The Powers were now vitally concerned in checking the aggrandisement of each other, and their wholesome vigilance illustrates our subject. The compensation assigned by the treaties of this time to the country which had raised her national debt from 200 millions of pounds to 800 millions in the great cause, which had destroyed the French marine, caused the mis- *The Congress of Vienna.*

carriage of Napoleon in his designs upon Turkey and the East, and contributed no small share to his final overthrow by the hand of the Duke of Wellington, could not be said to have been in any sense commensurate with her victorious career. Of all that she had taken from France and her allies, she retained only the necessary posts for her commerce in India, the Mediterranean, the West Indies, and the German Ocean. The Isle of France, Malacca, the Cape of Good Hope (then a small district adjoining the Cape), Malta, Heligoland (a mere speck in the sea), Tobago, and St. Lucia, along with some of the Dutch possessions in Guiana, formed the whole of her gains. Ceylon and Trinidad had been acquired at the Peace of Amiens. But this disproportion passed almost unnoticed. It was reckoned upon as a matter of course; and indeed she could scarcely have expected to succeed in impressing moderation upon her allies unless she had herself set the example.

Moderation of the Allies.

This spirit had found remarkable expression in other ways at the first Treaty of Paris, made by the Congress on May 30, 1814. Even the spoils which France had captured from the capitals of the world were left in her possession, though at the second Treaty of Paris, November 20, 1815, the clause was cancelled by the Powers, whose exasperation at the renewal of the war by the escape of Napoleon could not be restrained from doing what was only an act of justice. Even two-thirds of the war-ships at Antwerp were returned to France, while the remainder were handed over to the King of Holland.

In accordance with the previous settlements of Europe, the Low Countries were now once more rendered independent of France, but in the form of which then seemed best fitted to secure them, the union of Belgium and Holland. It was a well-meant experiment, in which England was chiefly concerned, made under the belief that the friendly Power which guarded the opposite side of the Channel could not be too strong; but the arrangement ignored the essential differences which had grown up in the course of ages between the Dutch and the Flemish portions of the Low Countries; and so what had really become the natural division into two distinct kingdoms took once more in 1830 the place of the attempted union. The relations of Poland, Saxony, and Italy to the great Powers were settled on as sound a basis as the circumstances of the moment permitted; not, indeed, as satisfactorily as might have been wished, but very differently from what such settlement would have been except for the determined attitude assumed by the Duke of Wellington as the British plenipotentiary, and for the assistance rendered him by Talleyrand.

The Kingdom of the Netherlands.

As Great Britain took so prominent a part in these arrangements, this is the place to remark that to load the Treaties of Paris and Vienna with obloquy, because they disregarded the wishes of certain populations, is in the abstract laudable; but it is to mistake wishes and theories for facts and realities. It is an anachronism, not unlike the complaints made on previous occasions, when prolonged wars were brought to an end by unpopular treaties. It was not to be expected that the great military Powers, which had felt the iron heel of the conqueror, and were hardly restrained from tearing France to pieces in their vengeful wrath, could

True view of the Treaty of Vienna.

cordially accept modern ideas which would have had the effect of materially reducing the compensations for losses to which they naturally looked. It was necessary to make the best of the situation, and to leave, as at the Peace of Utrecht (1713)—the last great settlement previously made by a combination of European Powers—the minor arrangements to the action of time.

Europe could by no means afford to have any more wars; the very memory of these dreadful times would suffice to influence the nations towards a future policy of pacific compromises. So, indeed, it turned out. If some of the mistakes into which the Congress was forced, especially as regards Italy, have not been set right without wars, it is but fair to remember that the general peace has not been seriously disturbed till of late years, and that sudden changes might not have turned out so well as did the action and reaction of despotic and constitutional ideas, which we shall presently trace. The lesson taught by the active operation of extreme principles on both sides is not seldom the prelude to satisfactory settlements.

Continuity of British Foreign Policy.

It may once more be observed in reviewing the action of Great Britain, both in the process and conclusion of this the greatest struggle in which she has ever been engaged, that it was exactly consistent with the whole of her previous Foreign Policy. What she now contended for and carried may be described in the simple words already familiar to us—viz., the safety of her shores, her commerce, and her dependencies, the balance of European States, the concert of the European Powers. The last, indeed, had been a policy of more recent date than the rest; but some glimmerings of the principle are to be found in the time of Elizabeth, and when Europe gradually emerged from the barbaric turbulence of the Religious Wars, it found its most definite expression in the diplomacy of Great Britain. She had also proved in these struggles her perfect comprehension of the fundamental political truth, that the nation which is not ready at a great crisis to make every sacrifice demanded by the occasion is doomed to the loss of its influence, and then of its independence.

This is not to claim superhuman virtues for the British race. The policy was forced upon it by circumstances similar to those which accompany the action of human beings in every stage of national life. As each generation received its inheritance from its predecessors, it followed the law of nature in attending to the preservation of that inheritance. To preserve it demanded alliances, for which in the last century the possession of Hanover gave great advantages. Each alliance contributed towards the support of the definite Foreign Policy which was required by the very nature of the Empire. When Europe was invaded by the aggressive enthusiasm of the Republican French, and then conquered by the genius of Napoleon, the time had come to do one of two things—either to relinquish what previous generations had established, with the certainty of having after all to fight at last on British shores, or else to do precisely what was done—engage in the struggle and fight to the last. There was no middle course. It had not escaped the observation of statesmen that Great Britain could no longer depend on the cultivation of her soil, or on the

The British forced into the path they adopted.

exchange of her produce with her colonies, but must support herself by her foreign commerce, extending over every part of the world. The issue could not be evaded. The whole past history of the nation, as well as its growing necessities, demanded the course it took, and it is difficult to see what considerable step was really wrong in the entire series of transactions. As the Empire was gained, so must it be defended.

The American War of 1812. Our notices of this period must include, though in the merest sketch, the American War of 1812. We have seen that it was the inevitable result of the British policy with respect to neutrals, maintained with dogged resolution, whatever might be the consequences, as the only means of dealing with Napoleon's "Continental System." We have also seen that Captain Mahan admits this policy towards neutrals to have been necessary not only for her predominance at sea, but for her self-preservation. But he not unnaturally blames the Government of the United States for having too tamely submitted to the indignities which accompanied the process, and appears to think that the war of 1812 was justified.

Its causes. The fact seems to be that the patience of the great Transatlantic people had been too long and too severely taxed, and that such sympathy as there had been with the British cause was gradually destroyed under the pressure of British aggression. On the other hand, the British Government, having no further employment for such great numbers of men as were required before the battle of Trafalgar, looked with horror and aversion at the employment of these trained seamen by the States, and the evasion of the British laws as to neutrals. So they relaxed no portion of their continuous efforts to search for them in neutral ships and detain them as prisoners. Some of these had originally been Americans, pressed into the British service in England or the colonies, and glad to revert to their original status.

Nor had the idea that the States might suddenly turn into a naval Power, and dispute the predominance of the recognised mistress of the seas, once crossed the minds of the British, who were totally unprepared for the emergency of an American war. The Admiralty were absolutely unaware that the American navy, though extremely small, had with great sagacity been supplied with a few ships capable of meeting the British frigates on their shores with a greatly superior force. Nor could the Government, fully occupied at that moment with the Peninsular War and Napoleon's invasion of Russia, bring themselves to believe that the Americans were in earnest. Five days after the American Declaration of War, some time before it reached England, the Government did what ought to have been done long previously, and suspended the Orders of Council as regarded the States. It was too late. The American War party had been growing in strength, and were by no means conciliated by so tardy a proceeding; and thus the war of brothers once more commenced. *Foresight of the American Government.*

The only way in which this ill-conducted and ill-omened war can range itself under the heading of British Foreign Policy, is to regard it as a mark of the resolute determination of the mother country to defend her loyal colonies, and to submit to no limitation of her nautical rights at the hand of violence. In both these objects she succeeded. After many fluctuations she maintained her hold on Canada, and when peace was made in 1815 was able to retain the two safeguards of her ancient policy, the Right of Search, and the liability to seizure of enemy's cargoes borne under neutral flags. The disparity of the frigates belonging to the two nations gave the British a rude awakening and a much-needed lesson; but Broke's victory in the Shannon over the Chesapeake, a ship of equal force, put an end to the panic, and on the whole success and defeat were fairly balanced between the combatants.

Results. What really turned the scale was the stoppage of American trade by the Power which had command of the sea, and the collapse of American credit, which threatened universal distress if it should continue. Some of the New England States had foreseen these results from the first; for the commercial portion of the population had already been severely crippled by the anti-neutral policy with which Great Britain had fought out the Napoleonic war. The terms of the Peace of Ghent were also not a little influenced by the fact that the Continental war was over, and Great Britain free to act in a much more energetic manner than heretofore. But the people of the States gained as much fame, or more, by their defence of New Orleans against the veterans of the Peninsula as they lost by the capture of Washington, their capital. The success of that defence had been almost unexpected, and to a young nation the inspiration of hope and confidence in the future is far more valuable than material gains.

This fratricidal war has been an episode in the

history of our subject. We are now to trace British Foreign Policy in the circumstances which could not but accompany the close of the mighty struggle, and which required the guidance of diplomatic statecraft rather than arms. The Great Powers had combined for the purpose of putting an end to Napoleon's tyranny, but it was inevitable that they should regard from different points of view the settling down of the nations which they had liberated. The principles of despotism were too deeply engrained in the sovereigns and ruling classes of Russia, Austria, and Prussia to admit of their leaving the newly-freed nations to go their own way. Those three Powers had already, in 1815, agreed to what was called the "Holy Alliance," by which they undertook to support one another in using their influence to promote "justice, Christian charity, and peace."

The "Holy Alliance."

Such noble sentiments, sincere enough no doubt, depended for their value upon the interpretation put upon them by acts, and were soon found to be open to a very objectionable application. To support despotic governments by force against constitutional parties in various States appeared to the Allies just and charitable, if not peaceful; and it soon became plain that another spirit, the spirit of aggrandisement, which had been peremptorily checked at Paris and Vienna, was incorporated with this policy, France, or rather the Bourbon family, was, when left to itself, on the side of the Holy Alliance, and the problems thus presented to British ministers were exceedingly troublesome and inconvenient. Lord Castlereagh had dissatisfied the British public by failing to offer any efficient resistance to what was so profoundly repugnant to their ideas. And as the

British people were clamouring for liberal reforms which had been too long withheld, and indeed impracticable during the war, the feeling towards these absolute Powers almost entirely changed. The friendly enthusiasm with which the Czar and the King of Prussia had been received when they visited England in 1814 was succeeded by dislike and distrust.

Canning's return to office.

It fell once more to Canning to guide his country through the difficulties of peace, as he had previously guided them in making the Peninsula the theatre of war. When he came into power in 1822, the necessity for some decided action on the part of the British had become evident, nor was the country in a condition to trifle with the subject. The party of reform had been gathering force, and the dislike entertained to the character of George IV. had added to the discredit of Toryism. The state of his relations with his Queen had rendered him exceedingly unpopular, though a more unfortunate standard round which to rally a political party was never set up. Canning had kept himself clear of the general excitement, and when Castlereagh committed suicide in 1822, it was plain that the man to supply his place as Foreign Secretary was his old opponent. The popular wave of discontent with the despotism which animated the Great Powers had also overflowed Italy and Spain, dissatisfied as they were with the condition in which they had been left at the Peace. The Austrians had acted with vigour in Italy, putting down with ease all tumultuous risings, and riveting the chains which Europe had placed in her hands. France was interfering in a similar way with Spain, Turkey with Greece, and Prussia with Poland.

Oppression of Italy, Spain, Greece, and Poland.

All these movements were, in fact, the inevitable results of the great Revolution-War. The armies which had been combating one another for more than twenty years could only, in the existing state of Europe, be wielded by sovereigns, and those of the old absolute type. Of course these sovereigns and their advisers considered the questions which arose at the Peace mainly from a military point of view. On the other hand, the peoples of the different States, though scarcely represented in the various Governments, beheld themselves delivered from one tyranny only to fall under the rule of another, and had as yet no way of remedy except by tumultuous and irregular risings. Such constitutional privileges as had been given to France and Spain were as yet of too feeble a character to be of use. Kings had quickly put in practice the old methods of dealing with such disturbing forces. In the case of Spain, there was a special danger to Great Britain. Its large and powerful colonies had been seized with the universal desire for freedom, and if France were to obtain possession of these colonies by the annexation of Spain, all the work of the last century would have to be done again by the British. The place which Canning had formerly occupied as Pitt's lieutenant, and afterwards as the saviour of the Spanish Peninsula, and very much by that means, of Europe, exactly fitted him to deal with these multiplied difficulties.

Against the will both of George IV. and of the most bigoted of the Tories, Canning was forced into power by the leading Tory ministers, who were themselves satisfied with his general principles, knew well the public feeling, and saw that he alone could repre-

Reactionary Congresses. sent the country at this crisis. For a crisis it was, as was proved by the Congresses of Troppau and Laybach in 1820 and 1821—Congresses to be distinguished from those already mentioned, since only Russia, Austria, and Prussia met. At these gatherings they decided to assist each other in carrying out the Absolutist policy. All movements towards constitutional measures which proceeded from the people were to be repressed by force, in whatever country they might arise. It was thus reserved for Great Britain to throw her weight into the scale of freedom, and at the same time to do so without once more plunging Europe into war; and this was the difficult task undertaken by Canning.

It was indeed found impossible to exercise any direct interference with Austria in her despotic treatment of Italy. That had to be left to the next *Canning deals with Spain and Portugal,* generation; but with Spain and Portugal Canning took effectual measures. The latter country was at once taken under British protection. The former was deprived of the power of doing an injury to the general peace by the countenance which the British afforded to her revolted colonies in South America. In 1825 this was followed by a distinct recognition of the independence of those States, and has ever since been famous as the occasion when Canning declared that he had called "a new world into existence in order to redress the balance of the old." In Spain itself the Constitutionalists entered into that struggle with the Absolutists, who were assisted by France, which lingered on through another generation.

and then with Greece. But the case of Greece gave Canning much more trouble, and excited the British people to a far higher degree. The popular risings which immediately after the Peace occurred in the Spanish Peninsula extended to the country which at this time was specially interesting to the British. The classical enthusiasm of the upper classes had been more and more diffused with the growth of education all through the previous half-century, and found a devoted representative in Lord Byron, now at the very height of his popularity. The Greeks, scarcely counting the cost, rose in arms against the Turks in 1821, and were the more patronised by Englishmen since they were specially distinguished for their nautical prowess. A glamour of romance and poetry surrounded the insurrection, and the Turks applied the principles of repression, to which they had no doubt full claim, in the ferocious and barbarous manner which has at different times lent such force to the cause of their opponents. Byron's "Childe Harold," with its famous song, "The Isles of Greece," was in every one's mouth.

So complicated and dangerous was the state of Eastern Europe under these circumstances, that a Congress of all Europe was agreed upon by the Five Powers, to be held at Verona. Great Britain was to have been represented by Lord Castlereagh, but on his suicide the Duke of Wellington took his place. The situation was almost ludicrous; for Russia was acting in opposition to the principles of the Holy Alliance in supporting the Greek insurrection against Turkey, while encouraging the French in their invasion of Spain for the alleged purpose of putting down the Constitutionalists. Great Britain alone held aloft, under Canning's instructions, the principle of internal independence in the different States; but the principle landed him in a serious difficulty

The Congress of Verona, 1822.

as regarded Turkey. It was one thing to discourage the ambition of Russia, which had abetted Greece; it was another to curb the tyranny of Turkey. But circumstances came to the support of his policy, though not till after his own death.

One effect of the European complication may be briefly stated at once. It thoroughly discredited Congresses; and this almost immediately after they had achieved their grand triumph in the settlement of Europe. But they have been brought into useful operation in later days; and all that can be said against them is, that such a delicate machinery should not be used except when it is impossible to dispense with it.

Battle of Navarino.
As the battle of Navarino brought matters to a crisis so soon after Canning's death in 1827, it must be noticed here in connection with his policy. The reluctance of the British Government to interfere openly in favour of Greece, while at the same time a direct impulse was given to the insurgents by the British press and the assistance of British volunteers, betrayed the Turks into a complete recklessness as to European opinion; and this speedily settled the question against them. The naval ardour of Admiral Sir Edward Codrington was inflamed by the cruelties which were proceeding in the immediate neighbourhood of his fleet, and a decisive battle, which destroyed the Turkish force, took place, one might almost say, of itself. The British seaman, representing the sentiments of the people, forced the hand of British statesmen at Navarino. To the Duke of Wellington, who spoke the mind of Canning, it was an "untoward event"; but nothing else could have solved the difficulty.

CHAPTER XIII.

BRITISH FOREIGN POLICY AFTER 1827.

THE Turks were, and always have been, in a false position. By right of conquest, they had in the fifteenth century come into full possession of the vast territories of the Byzantine empire; and they successfully defied all Europe to turn them out. They were then the leading military power of the day, and seemed at one time about to make the Mediterranean their own. But, as it happened, their conquered subjects were not only Christians, but determined to remain so. As the military prowess of the conquerors decayed, the oppressed people experienced sympathy from the surrounding Christian nations, which could not indeed find much expression during the sixteenth and seventeenth centuries; but the eighteenth century had seen the gradual advance of Russia, which was in religion and politics at the head of these nations, and which, declaring itself to be the Protector of the Christian subjects of the Porte, pursued a continuous course of interference. This led to conquest, and the consequent disintegration of the Ottoman empire. The Peace of Kainardji in 1774 produced a change, and Great Britain gradually and imperceptibly succeeded to the place of Protector.

It was the commerce of the Levant, and the

<small>Virtual Protectorate of Great Britain.</small>

necessity to the British of defending the highway to India, which naturally drew the two Powers together by the cords of mutual interest. As to the Christian population, British influence would, it was hoped, supersede the rougher methods of Russia in their defence; but the Turks, taking courage from the Holy Alliance, soon found out that they had relied too much upon European forbearance. They argued thus. If the Christian Powers had laid down rules for the mutual support of Absolutist governments against revolutionary reforms, was the Ottoman Empire to be excluded from the benefit of such rules? What portion of the empire which they had formed so long ago would survive if the desire for independence was to be indulged irrespective of the rights which came in the train of conquest?

This was a question of life and death to the Turks, and the case might have been debated by diplomatists for ever. But the battle of Navarino taught the Porte a rough lesson. The Turks now began to discover that their Empire was to be protected, but only on condition that it took its place amongst the nations as responsible to the public opinion of Europe. Nevertheless they plainly perceived that the mutual jealousy of the leading nations would itself act as a defence, and were not sorry to find that Europe was willing to believe in the power of time to introduce improvements upon the barbaric spirit of Mohammedan government.

<small>The Eastern Question.</small>

Such was the situation as the course of events interpreted it, and just in that way British Foreign Policy shaped itself in relation to what had come to be called the "Eastern Question." Up to his death in 1852 the influence of the Duke of Wellington on the successive Czars, Alexander I. and Nicholas I., was very great; and it was much to the credit of their powerful Empire, which not unnaturally considered its career of Turkish conquest and Russian protectorate only suspended during the convulsions of Europe, that it followed so long in the track of the European Concert. When at a later date the impatience of Russia could no longer be restrained, and broke out in the Crimean War of 1854, it was under the belief that the French had delivered a challenge which could not be declined, and that Great Britain would not interfere; but on the revolt of Greece, which we are now considering, it was content to send an efficient naval force under the leadership of the English for the purpose of watching the Turks; and in 1840 Russia, Austria, and Prussia joined Great Britain against Mehemet Ali and the Egyptians, who had revolted from Turkey and were threatening Constantinople.

Thus from 1815 to 1854—a period of nearly forty years—the memory of the French Revolution-War had sufficed to keep the Peace, though not without troubles with which the Great Powers had to deal as best they might. The independence of Greece being achieved, and Turkey having subsided into conformity with the general policy of Europe, the Eastern Question was more or less settled for a time; and the subject Christian nations were familiarised with the prospect of gradual enfranchisement, with or without the preservation of Turkish suzerainty.

The Peninsulas of Spain (including Portugal) and of Italy had to be dealt with by Canning's successors. The troubles arose partly out of the action of the *Troubles in the Peninsula.*

Holy Alliance already mentioned, and partly from the activity of the growing forces of "Constitutionalism." Those latter forces would have probably prevailed in the long run, just as they had in the case of England herself in her resistance to the Stuart despotism and her acceptance of William III. at the bloodless English "Revolution." But the popular fermentation which was working in Spain and Portugal was greatly encouraged by the profound sympathy of the mass of both the French and English people. The Second French Revolution of 1830 showed that the Bourbon reaction had spent its force.

This new Revolution was the emphatic protest of the French people against the blind reactionary policy of the restored Bourbons; at the same time the English rising in favour of the Reform Bill proclaimed the advent of political reform and the close of the Tory era. The two movements were simultaneous. *Separation of Belgium and Holland.* The cry for the separation of Belgium and Holland was the first result, and was speedily effected by the five Great Powers, acting in concert, with scarcely any bloodshed. Both France and Great Britain found their account in this new arrangement of the Low Countries, which indeed was a monument of political good sense. The French were glad to get rid of a too powerful neighbour, forced upon them in a time of weakness; and the British hereditary policy of keeping the opposite shore of the Channel in friendly hands was satisfied by the belief that the barrier she required against France was really the stronger for having been divided into two parts. So it has turned out.

The monarchical and constitutional principles were

in this case happily blended. Holland was left to be governed by the old House which had so often fought by the side of England; Belgium was placed under the excellent Leopold of Saxe-Coburg, who became both English and French by his marriage with the Princess Charlotte and his subsequent marriage with the daughter of Louis Philippe. The freedom of both countries had been insured by the liberal Constitutions which had now become the rule in Western Europe; and both peoples—too far different in race and religion to be voluntarily one nation —started on a career which has been on the whole prosperous, with very little interruption from external sources. Talleyrand again must have most of the credit due to the actors in this arrangement. He was the coadjutor of Canning till his death, and of Wellington before and after that event. When Lord Londonderry in the House of Lords attacked the veteran ambassador for his shifting politics, the Duke said he had always found him as loyal and honourable towards foreign Powers as he was steadfast and enlightened with regard to the interests of his own country. *Final services of Talleyrand.*

The history of British interference in the Spanish Peninsula is of a different kind. The opposite principles which agitated Europe and issued in the independence of Greece, the Revolution of July in France, and the separation of Belgium from Holland, were in both Spain and Portugal represented by different branches of the royal family in each country. Was this a question which Europe should suffer to be fought out by the nations themselves? That was no doubt the logical sequence of the European policy which had been laid down at the settlement of Europe after the great war. The Duke of Wellington, as representing the settlement, understood it to mean that and nothing else. But he had himself been present at the Congress of Verona, where he found out that the "Holy Alliance" was still in full force; and it became plain to many thoughtful observers that as external influence had been used in one direction, that of Absolutism, nothing could fairly be said against the application of external influence on the side of the Constitutionalists. A very large proportion of the British people, who were so deeply engaged in the same struggle, took the side of the latter, and their representative in Foreign Policy was Lord Palmerston.

<small>Palmerston pursues Canning's policy.</small>

Palmerston had become Secretary of State for Foreign Affairs under the Reform Ministry of Lord Grey in 1830, and a new era for Great Britain, both at home and abroad, may be said to have begun at this time, under the new king, William IV. The sailor-king was favourable to the new and prevailing opinions, though alarmed lest they should take the form of revolution,—not, in short, a Radical, a term which came into use about this time, but a Whig. Palmerston had been the friend of Canning and his fellow-worker. His foreign policy was substantially the same, but he went much farther, and deliberately set himself to work in favour of the Liberal cause in the Peninsula. It might well be believed that Canning would have done so if he had lived a little longer and been more free to act. But how to interfere without once more stirring up a European war? That was the question.

<small>Question of intervention.</small>

The policy of intervention could not have been carried into effect if the tide had not completely turned in France. It was no longer possible for French kings, even if they had wished it, to send military aid to the Absolutist party in the Peninsula. The Orleanist dynasty, the Whigs of France, were bound to favour the Liberal cause, with which their own success had been identified; but they could not afford a war for their allies any more than could Great Britain. Both countries therefore resorted to the methods by which Queen Elizabeth reaped, in France and the Low Countries, both glory and safety in her own perilous times,—methods which could not be defended by strict International Law, but which were justified under the circumstances, and eventually answered their purpose. A Quadruple Alliance was formed in 1834 between Great Britain and France, Spain and Portugal, in direct opposition to Don Carlos and the Legitimists in Spain, and Don Miguel in Portugal. This gave at once a decided preponderance to the Constitutionalist party in both countries; but the struggle was obstinate, and it was agreed that permanent assistance supplied from outside the Peninsula should take the form of a voluntary " Legion " from France and from Great Britain. *The Spanish Legion.*

In both countries there was available an abundance of skilled officers and men, as well as of enthusiasm for the two young queens, Christina of Spain and Maria of Portugal. General Sir De Lacy Evans, who commanded the British Legion in Spain, was the best known of these officers, and his old Peninsular experience came to the aid of his advanced Liberalism. The services of the Legion were conspicuous and decisive; but, as might be expected, they were not performed without many a passage of arms between the officers and men of the different nationalities, loosely bound together in the Legion. Portugal was efficiently aided by a volunteer squadron under Sir Charles Napier, and the struggle upon land was of far less consequence than in Spain. The result has been that both countries, like Greece, Belgium, and Holland, were unreservedly admitted into the fellowship of European States, and the marks of the cruel processes by which they had marched to freedom were almost obliterated.

<small>Triumph of Constitutionalism.</small>

It was not Palmerston's fault that these countries did not keep step with the British in the matter of slave-dealing; but it was the persistent influence which Great Britain had earned a right to use which at last wiped out the stain. Brazil, severed by the Atlantic, took a longer time still to yield to the growing opinion of the European public on this point. So determined was the attitude of successive British ministers in imposing the Abolition of the Slave-trade, by all means short of war, upon every nation subject to its influence, that it may properly take rank as one of the leading features of British Foreign Policy in the nineteenth century. It was right that it should be so. Though not the first offenders, the English and their colonists had been most eager and extensive abettors of the iniquitous traffic, and it was therefore fitting that they should take the lead in putting it down.

<small>The slave-trade put down at last.</small>

There was one European country which had not yet been able to follow in the track of the liberated nations. Italy did indeed benefit largely by the influence and goodwill of the British people, but the British Government could not take the lead, as it had in the liberations already effected, owing to the

<small>The state of Italy.</small>

attitude of the Great Powers which had concurred with the British in the settlement of Europe. These Powers, finding that the Holy Alliance had virtually come to an end by the death of Alexander I. of Russia in 1825, clung the more closely to the system of popular repression both in the German and the Italian States. They were well aware that the spirit of Constitutionalism and of national patriotism had been let loose, and that the German States were themselves greatly affected thereby. While there was time, they would stave off peril at home by vigorous action in the country which had now for many ages been under German influences. Metternich, who had taken so great a part in the European settlement, represented these principles with the decision and ability which might have been expected from his past career.

The famous saying of that statesman, that "Italy" was only a "geographical expression," was founded on patent historical facts. The great struggle for Italian dominion between France and Germany, which the French began in 1494, had destroyed the political vitality of the country. Its essential feebleness had invited the attack, and soon left it a prey to the foreigners. Of these, Austria came to be the most important State, and had in the eighteenth century been supported by Great Britain as a counterpoise to the French influence exercised over the "Two Sicilies" by the Spanish Bourbons. Nor, whatever might be desired, could any change be made at the Congresses which settled Europe after the great war. Family relationship existed between the Austrian House and many of the petty Italian States. Indeed, the rule of Austria virtually

Austrian influence in Italy.

extended throughout the Peninsula. Savoy had caught the infection of popular repression, and its restored king out-Bourboned the restored Bourbons of France.

But Metternich, and the German Powers in general, failed, in the righteous enthusiasm of their anti-Napoleonic rising, to observe that, with all the palpable faults of his government, the French conqueror had ruled the enslaved States of Europe in a spirit of justice, order, and popular sympathy, or at least with a parade of these qualities, which was his best inheritance from the French Revolution. These ideas had had time to take root, and nothing could extinguish them. Europe was in great need of some such sharp and bitter incitement before it could direct its course by what Heeren called the "bright Polar Star across the British Channel." Perhaps the lessons it received from Napoleon were, after all, less terrible than the long periods of civil war which might have taken their place.

As the influence of Austria over Italy was so powerful and ubiquitous, the movements of the patriots were necessarily driven into channels which were objectionable in themselves, and gave handle enough to their enemies. The Secret Societies were formed and flourished: while the sufferings of men like Silvio Pellico, much in the same way as those of Poerio at a later date, inflamed the minds of the British people, for whom Byron had revived the touching story of Bonivard, the Prisoner of Chillon, and the wrongs he had received from the former princes of Savoy. The popular enthusiasm previously felt for the Greeks was transferred to Italy; and when in 1846 Palmerston became Foreign

Secret Societies.

Secretary for the third time, he knew that in fostering the Liberationists he had the British people at his back. It was not, indeed, till that year that any real progress was made in the liberation of Italy. In 1830 the Second French Revolution, commonly called the "Revolution of July," blew the sparks of political agitation into a momentary flame, but Austria was still sufficiently powerful to prevent any general conflagration. The principles of self-government, though in the most violent form, made some progress under the auspices of Mazzini, whose insurrectionary efforts found support both in and out of Italy, but plainly proved by their repeated failure that the liberation of Italy could not be effected without the intervention of external aid. *The Second French Revolution.*

What seemed almost a hopeless cause was guided to victory by means which the wildest dreamers could never have guessed, much less expected. But those agencies could have attained no permanent success unless the ground had been prepared by the events of the previous half-century. Every one of the premature movements, every cruel stroke of repression, had been required to prevent the formation of feeble and short-lived establishments, and to give the character of moderation and permanency to the United Italy which was to take its place among the nations for the first time in the history of the world.[1] For such a birth no previous labour might seem too great or too prolonged. These agencies were found in two persons—in Pio Nono, the newly elected Pope of 1846, and in Garibaldi, an adventurous seaman of the old heroic type; *Pio Nono and Garibaldi.*

---

[1] One can hardly reckon the transient governments of the Early Middle Ages as exceptions to this statement.

but the final success could not have been achieved unless the little kingdom of Sardinia had been gradually prepared for its future by Cavour and his king.

The popular progress must have been extending widely beneath the surface when a Pope deemed it expedient to hoist the colours of Constitutionalism; and when he

> "back recoiled,
> E'en at the sound himself had made,"

he discovered that he had gone too far, and that encouragement of this sort from a Pope could not be as if it had never been. The example not only affected every Italian State, but gave an impulse to the rest of Europe which powerfully assisted the wide movement set afoot by the Third French Revolution in 1848. The smaller States of Italy followed suit, and not far behind them marched the greater States in the north and south, Sardinia and the two Sicilies. The spread of the flame to Lombardy warned Austria that she must interfere by arms if she wished to save her Italian possessions; and in 1848 war broke out between her and King Charles Albert of Sardinia. The issue went at first against Radetzky, the veteran Austrian general; but he soon recovered his position by the victory obtained under Archduke Albert at Custozza. Yet the hopes of Italy still survived in the beaten but courageous, and now steadfast, friend of liberty, the kingdom of Sardinia. Victor Emmanuel had succeeded his father, who abdicated after his defeat at Novara in 1849, and the new king inspired a confidence which was fully justified in the result; but

Victor Emmanuel.

he was scarcely Italian, and his time had not yet come. He had to wait ten years.

Two other forces appeared on the stage in 1848. Rome, during the absence of the Pope, had under Garibaldi's auspices pronounced for a Republic, and his romantic and reckless valour began to point him out as the active agent round whom the bolder spirits might be rallied, however long the necessities of diplomacy might hamper Sardinia. And secondly, Louis Napoleon, the first President of the new French Republic, correctly interpreting the desire of the French to interpose in Italian affairs, as they had done time out of mind, sent a French army to recover Rome for the Pope, and eject Garibaldi and the Republicans. Thus the old ambitions which had ruined Italy at the close of the Middle Ages, appeared once more to be dominant. Austria was, it is true, checked for the moment by the intervention of France, but the liberation of Italy seemed to be rather farther off than ever. Two of the Great Powers were crushing it instead of one.

A third, Great Britain, was also intervening in Italian affairs, but in a very different way. Lord Palmerston, the Foreign Secretary, was using his lengthened experience of British Foreign Policy in the direction of liberty with a skill scarcely acknowledged at the time; while he avoided serious offence to either Austria or France, whose place in the European polity he was far from wishing to disturb. Lord Minto was the agent through whom he advised the Pope at Rome, the Court of Sardinia at Turin, and that of Tuscany at Florence; while he plied every argument that could be used to convince Austria that the time had come when she ought

Marginal note: Louis Napoleon.

to recognise her own danger in defying Italian opinion. Cavour was now coming to the front, and in 1852 found himself in the full exercise of his wonderful diplomatic abilities as Victor Emmanuel's Prime Minister. Never were patience, good sense, and foresight more required. The general policy which the Sardinian State began to pursue was struck out in these conferences with the British envoys. The confidence of the Italian patriots was gradually won, and the little kingdom was prepared to take advantage of every favourable wind that blew.

<small>Palmerston and Cavour.</small>

The Russian War of 1854 gave Cavour an excellent opportunity of strengthening his position by offering to act with Great Britain and France in the Crimea. The acceptance of his offer, and the good service of the Sardinian army, had the effect of enlisting both the French and British people on the Italian side. It also opened the way for that conflict between France and Austria which had been long impending. Nothing short of force could remove the dead weight of the Austrian dominion, which however, it must be remembered, had been sanctioned by Europe at a time when the services of Austria against Napoleon had been invaluable. In 1859 the French supplied that force, and, in conjunction with Sardinia, by this time strong and well-governed, brought Austria to terms. The motives of Louis Napoleon in forming this alliance were so complex that it adds only one more to the unexpected order of events which in the end produced equilibrium; but he was quite aware that "war for an idea" was not likely to satisfy the French people. The annexation of Savoy and Nice

<small>French intervention in Italy.</small>

was to be the condition of his aid, and the Austrians having been defeated at Magenta and Solferino, the price was paid. But here the French Emperor stopped. The Peace of Villafranca (1859) did indeed give Lombardy to Sardinia, but Austria still kept Venetia and the Quadrilateral, as well as her old position in Central Italy. The two Sicilies remained as before. *They annex Savoy and Nice.*

This was by no means a united Italy; and so, as far as we can see, it would have remained—a mere "geographical expression." That it emerged from such a perilous condition was the work of Garibaldi. The hero of the Italian patriots astonished Europe by bursting into Sicily with a handful of followers, and in less than four months he had virtually conquered the Bourbon kingdom on both sides of the Straits of Messina. He then had the courage to conquer himself. Finding that the Sardinian army had begun to assert dominion over Central Italy and the Papal forces, and was marching upon Gaeta to besiege the King of Naples, whom Garibaldi himself had driven from his capital, he resigned all claims to power, and handed over the work to the one sovereign who was prepared to complete it. In 1862 the task was completed, and Victor Emmanuel reaped his reward in the assembly of a Parliament at Turin from all parts of Italy except Venetia and Rome, and in the title then conferred of "King of Italy." In this same year Garibaldi and his volunteers emerged once more, determined to give Italy her ancient capital; but the royal forces were, in consequence of the complicated relations of the Papal power with European sovereigns, under the melancholy necessity of putting him down. His work was done. *Garibaldi in Sicily and Naples. Victor Emmanuel, "King of Italy."*

The kingdom of Italy has now long ranked among the Great Powers. When Austria succumbed to Prussia in 1866, Italy acquired Venetia; and at last, in 1871, Rome became its capital—for the great wars of that year left the King of Italy free to act. The plaintive lines of Byron—

> "Italia! O Italia! that thou wert
> Less lovely or more strong,"

were at last exchanged for the jubilant phrase, "Italy is free from the Alps to the Adriatic."

<small>Palmerston promotes Constitutional freedom, not Republicanism.</small> The best, perhaps the only, available source from which a just idea can be gained of the part played by Great Britain in this half-century of Italian struggle to be free, is to be found in the letters and despatches of Lord Palmerston. A sufficient number of them for that purpose are quoted by Mr. Evelyn Ashley, the biographer of his later years. We have seen that there were overpowering reasons why neither the Government of Great Britain nor of any other Great Power could deal with the Italian question as they had with those of Greece, Spain, and Portugal. The progress of the various movements above noticed was therefore all the more anxiously watched by the British. We have also seen how vital to British interests the Mediterranean had become, and how much of the British warfare of the eighteenth century had arisen from the conviction that Italy must not be allowed to fall into the hands of hostile Powers.

Further, it is not too much to say that, besides the difficulties connected with the singular position of Austria, the spirit which Mazzini represented was more feared than approved. There was indeed more sympathy with the object than was publicly avowed; but the wilder revolutionists drew from the movement an encouragement to assassination, and that excited horror. The bitter anti-clerical spirit, which could hardly but be formed by the opponents of the Papacy and of its princely and imperial agents, also went far to stifle sympathy, even amongst Protestants. Lord Palmerston felt deeply these repellent influences. His efforts were in all cases directed towards the attainment of constitutional freedom, not of republicanism; and thus it was that he fostered by every means in his power the growth and development of the little kingdom in north-western Italy, which alone offered a prospect of leadership and progress towards the goal which he set before himself.

It may be well to consider the action of this influential minister a little further. When he became Foreign Secretary in 1846 the circumstances invited, as we have seen, the co-operation of Great Britain, and he became at once the adviser and guide of the great men who brought about the freedom of Italy. His instructions to Lord Minto directed that statesman to encourage the different States which had commenced a "system of progressive improvement," and to proclaim publicly the British disapproval of all attempts at restraint on the part of Foreign Governments. His agent was thus publicly identified with the cause of Italian independence; but Palmerston held out no prospect of direct interposition by force of arms, and remonstrated as time went on in the strongest language with Austria for doing so. When the general movement of 1848 swept over Italy, the British Minister went further, and denied the right of Austria to hold any portion of the latter country. Austria, he contended, had broken the Treaty of Vienna by its recent seizure of Cracow (1846), and had repudiated its engagement to give national institutions to Poland. He tried, therefore, to persuade her to give up Lombardy for a sum of money, contenting herself with Venetia; and he joined the French in demanding from Austria an armistice when Radetzky had conquered Sardinia.

He represented British Foreign Policy.

In all this he fairly represented his country, as was sufficiently proved by the failure of extreme politicians on both sides to make good any charge against his policy. There was no disposition in England to proceed as far as war for Italy; and the British people had to wait till the moral influence of their Government could be brought to bear. France, on the contrary, and especially her Emperor, had her own reasons for rushing into the war with Austria, and Palmerston laboured in vain to prevent it. No one could then foresee that out of the clash of French and Austrian arms was to come the rise of a German empire, whose interest it would be to keep Italy strong, and give her the repose which she had earned by the discipline of prolonged suffering, by the political wisdom she had displayed, by her persistent effort, and by a patience unequalled in the history of the world.

Defence of that position.

This rapid sketch of Italian affairs has been necessary in order to show the true bearing of British Foreign Policy during the generations which immediately succeeded the great French Revolution-War. During the subsidence of the dangerous elements which had been stirred to fury for a period of more than twenty years, no rash experiments were to be made. It was the business of the nation which had taken the lead in the stress of the storm to adopt a system of policy which might utilise for the benefit of mankind all that had been gained, and at the same time to impede, if it was not possible to prevent, a recurrence of the dreadful experience through which Europe had passed. This was not to be effected by simply declining to take notice of the interference of the Great Powers in concert with which the settlement had been made. The machine would not work without being cleaned from time to time, but it was not to be taken to pieces, with everything to begin again. It was to be a policy of authoritative influence, with war in the background as the last resort, but only as the last resort. The authoritative influence, the counter-interferences, if such should be necessary, were to be regulated on the principles of popular freedom and self-government, under the checks and balances of recognised constitutions. Progress and security could only be maintained by a middle course between despotic authority and anarchical revolution.

It would be a gross error to suppose that even the most benevolent theory of Foreign Policy could support the doctrine that a country like Great Britain, suffering under the debt she had incurred both for her own safety and the peace of the world, and without any considerable army at her disposal, should rush into war on every occasion when her influence was set at nought. We rightly call such a policy Quixotic. The people of Great Britain have always demanded, and had a right to demand, that such

Not a Quixotic policy.

wars should only be undertaken where their interests were directly concerned; and, as we have seen in the earlier parts of this review of Foreign Policy, commerce and national safety have been the leading features of those interests. Palmerston was often accused of encouraging hopes which he knew he was unable to aid in fulfilling, and it would be untrue to say that his interferences were always wise; but they were always justifiable, and they were always successful in the end. The case of Poland is hardly in point. The British people were vehemently sympathetic with the Poles, but the three Great Powers which had partitioned it unopposed in the eighteenth century could not be reached in the nineteenth either by diplomacy or war, and nothing could be done. It was different with Switzerland, where sound diplomatic advice took effect; as it did also in Portugal, when, long after its settlement under Donna Maria, attempts were made to unite it to Spain under Republican government.

<small>Poland, Switzerland, Portugal.</small>

With France herself and Russia the British relations have been far more difficult. With the first, war has been more than once imminent; with the second it actually took place. Both affairs arose out of the "Eastern Question." We have seen that the course of events had deprived Russia of the sole "Protectorship" of Turkey, and that the French policy under Napoleon I. was openly directed towards its conquest. "Constantinople must be either French or Cossack," said Napoleon I. But, as a matter of fact, it had fallen to Great Britain to take the place which her commercial and political interests would not allow to be taken by either Russia or France.

She had conquered the Mediterranean at the battle of the Nile; and every day made it more apparent to statesmen that India could not be retained if a hostile Power occupied the Levant. Each year also the enormous responsibility which the possession of India involved was brought more and more home to the British nation by dangerous wars and insurrections.

The ties of honour were stronger still. The victory of Navarino had imposed a corresponding duty on the victors. The destruction of the Turkish fleet had given an opportunity for the revolt of Egypt; and Mehemet Ali, a powerful and ambitious ruler, knew how to utilise it. He had been encouraged by the French, who also saw their opportunity. Thus it was high time to summon Europe to council; for Syria had already been overrun (1840), and the Turkish admiral had been bribed. France alone, under the guidance of M. Thiers, refused to join the concert of Europe, and stood aside. It was a critical moment; but Palmerston resolved to run the risk of a French war, and without much difficulty the British Mediterranean fleet drove the Egyptians out of Syria, and established Mehemet Ali's dynasty on its present footing in relation to Turkey. The experienced Louis Philippe controlled his indignant minister; and when he had resigned, the French perceived that war on such a question would have been an anachronism. It was an essential part of British Foreign Policy that the *entente cordiale* between the two nations should be preserved, and no small part in the process was taken by the Queen and Prince Albert in relation to Louis Philippe and Louis Napoleon successively.

<small>The Egyptian invasion of Turkey.</small>

<small>Action of the French and British towards Turkey.</small>

This had an important bearing on affairs. Much was said about revenge for Waterloo; but, speaking generally, the French remembered that the contest had not been with their nation, but with Napoleon, and that the one firm friend they had at the settlement of Europe was the British nation.

The Crimean War. Those friendly feelings prevailed when the other great test of British Foreign Policy, the Crimean War, stained, through a series of blunders, the history of Europe. It was the Eastern Question again; but Palmerston was not Prime Minister nor even Foreign Secretary in the Government of Lord Aberdeen, which took office at the end of the year 1852. It was a ministry of divided counsels, and he was Home Secretary. Not that he is thus relieved from a share of responsibility; and he would have been wise if he had disengaged himself from it earlier than he did. The difficulties were no doubt enormous, and they have lately been presented in an able manner by Sir Arthur Gordon, now Lord Stanmore; but whatever Lord Aberdeen's merits, he was not the man for the crisis, and no terms can be too strong to express the disgrace which rested both on British diplomacy and British administration. The country called on Lord Palmerston to retrieve its credit, and found him once more equal to the situation.

Present state of the Eastern Question. It was impossible at the Treaty of Paris in 1856, which concluded the war, to effect any decided reform of the relations between the Ottoman Porte and its Christian subjects; but the public opinion of Europe has been ripening ever since, and the principles of Canning and Palmerston have made great progress under their successors. Several Christian

States, once conquered and enslaved, are now substantially free, and yet the Turkish power, with its centre at Constantinople, has not been broken up. The Eastern Question is always threatening, but there is no reason for despair, still less for a relaxation of vigilance.

It is no part of the present undertaking to trace in detail the events which have influenced British Foreign Policy during the last generation, nor to show how, after some tendency to vacillation, it has reverted to a patriotic continuity; nor yet to examine minutely the attitude of the Court of St. James's to each Foreign Power and each "burning question" throughout the world; still less to forecast the future and attempt to lay down the lines of the Foreign Policy which Great Britain will, or might, or should adopt. These questions, though a natural sequel to the subject in hand, are the province of the diplomatist and the politician rather than of the historian. The briefest summary will therefore suffice.

Later Foreign Policy.

The later Foreign Policy of Great Britain, so far as it has been called into activity, has been concerned with the preservation and extension of her Empire in the continents of Asia, Africa, and America. In dealing with the great European nations and with the United States, it has been one of absolute non-interference, and possesses, therefore, no spark of the vital interest which characterised the mighty struggles through which the path of empire has been traced in the preceding pages. This policy has been identical with that of former times, and has found its proper application in a strict adherence to the old principle of strengthening, as occasion seemed to

Non-Intervention in Europe.

require, the defences of the British Isles and their dependencies, and in a scrupulous care lest British interests should be endangered by the changes which were taking place amongst the nations.

And in the United States. In the war between the Northern and Southern States of America (1860–66) the temper of the British people was sorely tried by the serious difficulties which could not but affect them. The "Trent affair" fell like a fiery spark upon inflammable matter; but Palmerston, by his prompt action, accompanied by a conciliatory treatment of the question, in which the Queen and Prince Consort took a decisive part, brought out the good sense and statesmanship of both Governments. War was happily averted, and the hard-won triumph of the Northern States renewed the cordial relations of the kindred peoples on either side of the Atlantic.

In the European wars which led up to the present position of Germany (1865-71) the temptation to interfere was not nearly so great. The strife of the combatants arose out of mutual quarrels and ambitions which did not concern British interests, nor lead to a despotism which required a forcible readjustment of the Balance of Power. Russia indeed, reckoning on the continuance of the British policy of non-interference, took advantage of these wars to repudiate the Treaty of Paris by which the Crimean War had been concluded; but her invasion of Turkey in 1877, which ensued upon that repudiation, was rendered harmless, and even beneficial, by the interposition at the critical moment of Great Britain, *Lord Beaconsfield and the Eastern Question.* This was the act of Lord Beaconsfield, who did not even hesitate to summon troops from India to support the fleet which he had sent to the Bosphorus.

The Berlin Conference of 1878—the last great event of the kind—restrained Russia from assuming the "Protectorate" of the enfranchised States of the Ottoman empire; and as Lord Beaconsfield had previously bought up the greater part of the Suez Canal shares, and obtained Cyprus for a British station in the Levant, he left his mark upon the "Eastern Question" as only second to that of Palmerston.

In India the rivalry of Asiatic Russia, or the fear of it, has directly or indirectly connected itself with nearly all the little wars which have been waged there since the middle of the century. As in Great Britain itself, the first duty has been to consolidate the power of the British rulers. The Afghan, Belooch, and Sikh wars, the various annexations, the measures taken after the Sepoy Mutiny, the Burmese, and the recent frontier wars, have each contributed to the building up of a united and self-supporting empire, which might be dangerous to any Power which should venture to attack it. Nor has the same feeling about Asiatic Russia been altogether absent from the policy pursued by Great Britain in China and Japan. In these countries, however, the efforts necessary to defend British commerce have mostly ruled the situation; and though it has been sometimes necessary to employ force, the practical tutorship of able men such as Sir Harry Parkes has been much more effectual than force. Time will show whether the policy of isolation from the other European Powers was the right course to pursue when, after the war between China and Japan, some of these Powers had decided upon intervention.

Russia and Great Britain in the East.

In Africa the Foreign Policy of Great Britain,

Pacific rivalry of the Powers in Africa.

after having for more than a century confined itself to the development of British Settlements, and to such wars in their behalf as those of Abyssinia, Ashanti, and South Africa, has in recent years taken the direction of pacific rivalry with other European nations in building up vast territorial acquisitions on the basis of modern enterprise and discovery. The future of these various empires who can guess? Every resource of modern diplomacy, mutual consideration, and arbitration will be required in order to preserve harmony and co-operation. They at least open up more markets for the countries which can make use of them; but they offer a far nobler prospect in the civilisation and future happiness of races whose wrongs lie at the door of Europe and America.

British Colonies.

To speak of a Foreign Policy in reference to the numerous and important Colonies of Great Britain would be a misuse of words. Every year is adding to the gathered wisdom acquired by alternate success and misfortune with respect to their treatment. The errors of the last century are not at all likely to recur; and the easy relations which at present exist between them and the mother-country still retain them in a wholesome connection which the first whisper of European war would instantly ripen into an intimate union for offence and defence. They are the "Greater Britain."

The British in Egypt.

Egypt still proves the truth of the ancient view which refused to consider it a country belonging to either Europe, Asia, or Africa. From the earliest ages it has occupied a separate position of its own, and it shares with Constantinople the claim to hold the key of the mysterious "Eastern Question."

It is only necessary to say here that the recent interference of Great Britain in Egypt, when the Khedive's government of the country had been overthrown by the insurrection of his army under Arabi, is the final outcome of a Mediterranean policy which has been in principle continuous for a century and a half. The lines laid down on this and all other points by Pitt, Canning, Palmerston, and Beaconsfield—themselves a practical continuation of the policy of former ages—have been, and are still, those upon which modern British Foreign Policy has been built. No change can be made in it without the greatest danger to the country, first of all to its commerce, next to the sustenance of its teeming millions, next to its possessions, and finally to the safety of its own shores.

This is perfectly understood by statesmen of all parties, and is perhaps not much less firmly founded in the national mind. Education has already vastly enlarged the sphere of popular knowledge on these vital points, and it is not too much to say that history has played no small part in the process. Its study is no longer regarded as a mere exploration of antiquaries in the domain of facts, interesting to intelligent persons, but of little practical value. It is more and more understood that its province is to act as an interpreter, as a light to illuminate the onward path of national life, and to point out by the examples of the past what future course is most free from danger, and most likely to lead to honourable peace and wholesome prosperity. Conclusion.

INDEX.

Abercromby, Sir Ralph, 146—conquers the French army at Alexandria, 167.
Aberdeen, Earl of, 282.
Abolition Act, 202. See also Slave-trade.
Aboukir, French fleet destroyed at, 161.
Absolutists in Spain, their struggle with the Constitutionalists, 258.
Abyssinian war, the, 286.
Acre, Sidney Smith's defence of, 161—Napoleon's designs on Constantinople frustrated by it, *ib.*
Act of Settlement, 37.
Addington, Henry, afterwards Lord Sidmouth, 172—his administration, 176.
Afghan war, the, 285.
Africa, 193, 285—British commerce with, 49—attempts to colonise, 109—rivalry of the Powers in, 286—negroes imported from, 200—settlements in South Africa, 53—wars in the same, 286.
Aix-la-Chapelle, Peace of, 84, 108.
Albemarle, William Anne, 2nd Earl, 111.
Alberoni, Cardinal, Prime Minister of Spain, 51
Albert, Archduke of Austria, his victory at Custozza, 272.
Albert, Prince Consort of England, 231, 234.
Alexander I., Czar of Russia, 168, 206, 225, 242, 256, 263, 269—cause of Napoleon's quarrel with, 229.
Alexandria, 183—French army defeated at, 167.

Algiers, 22.
Allies, the, combine against Napoleon, 230—concentrate their forces at Frankfort, 234—cross the Rhine, 237—congresses of, 238—France in the hands of, 239—moderation of, 248.
Alsace, 40.
Amboyna, 20.
America, 93, 95, 127, 147, 149, 193, 194, 283.
——, discovery of, 8.
——, British colonies in, 53, 55—their relations to the mother-country, 54 — attack on them, 108, 109—government of, 113—discontent with the Home Government, 116 — European allies of, 117—their revolt, 117, 118, 119.
——, the French in America, 108-114.
——, American war of 1812 and its causes, 252—the American navy, 253 — American Government, foresight of the, 253—war between the Northern and Southern States, 284.
America, North, formation of forts in rear of the English colonies, 61.
——, settlers of North American coasts, 62.
America, South, 199 — revolted Spanish colonies in, 258.
America, Spanish, 213—war of empire arose out of commercial struggle in, Chapters IV. and V. *passim.*
Amherst, General Jeffrey, Lord, 93, 102.

INDEX.

Amiens, Peace of, 163, 164, 165, 167, 169, 174, 189, 196, 248—
rupture of, 172, 176.
Anglo-Saxons, the, 2, 53.
Anne, Princess, afterwards Queen, 31, 37, 48, 62, 66, 85, 88, 98, 127, 130, 217.
Anson, Lord, 91, 94, 102, 111.
Antwerp, warships there returned to France, 248.
Aquitaine, 4, 8.
Arabi, insurrection of the Khedive's army under, 287.
Aragon, 6, 46, 217.
Arcola, battle of, 167.
Armada, the, 13.
Armed neutrality, the, 123-125, 127, 131, 144, 151, 167, 168.
Army, the English, state of, 93—
improvement of, 146.
Army of Liberation (1813), 232. See Allies.
Ashanti war, the, 286.
Asia, Russia and Great Britain in, 285.
Assiento, the, 66, 67.
Atlantic Ocean, the, 119.
Atterbury, Bishop Francis, 81.
Attila, 173, 232.
Augsburg, the League of, 26.
Austerlitz, battle of, 191, 195, 198, 204—Russian troops beaten at, 198.
Australia, settlements in, 53.
Austria, 15, 19, 38, 96, 128, 151, 157, 159, 167, 190, 191, 226, 230, 231, 255, 258, 263, 269, 270, 272, 273, 274, 275, 276, 277, 278.
——, its defeat at Austerlitz, 198.
——, the Austrian Succession, 46.
——, effect on Austria and Prussia of affairs in Spain, 226.
——, Emperor of, 234, 242.

Badajos, capture of, 228.
Balance of Power, policy of, 5-13, loses its dominant religious character, 39—its usefulness, 41—mentioned, 87, 107, 112, 129, 140.
Balearic Isles, the, 46.
Baltic, state of the (1809), 209—
mentioned, 127, 167, 213.
Bar, France secures the reversion of, 61.
Barbary, the States of, 56.
——, Barbary pirates, immunity enjoyed by, in 16th and 17th centuries, 21—temporary suppression of their piracy, 21.
Barcelona, taken by Lord Peterborough, 47.
Barnard, Sir John, 74, 77, 79.
Bath, Earl of. See Pulteney, William.
Bautzen, battle of, 231.
Bavaria, 15, 39, 127, 162—the Electoral Prince of, 34.
Bayonne, evacuation of, 237.
Beachy Head, battle of, 32.
Beaconsfield, Lord, 284, 285, 287.
Beauharnais, Eugène, 234, 239.
Belfast, Jacobin Clubs at, 149.
Belgium, 40, 97, 243, 249, 268.
——, the Belgian and Dutch troops, 245.
——, separation of Belgium from Holland, 264.
Belooch war, the, 285.
Benbow, Admiral, 46, 63.
Berlin Conference, the, 285.
Berlin Decree, the (Nov. 1806), 194, 210.
Bernadotte, Marshal, 230, 231, 232, 234, 237, 239.
Berwick, James, Duke of, victory of, 48.
Berwick, the, commanded by Hawke, 94.
Bettesworth, Captain, 185.
Bidassoa, the river, 236.
Biscay, the Bay of, 138.
Blake, Admiral, 20, 22, 55, 144, 174.
Blenheim, battle of, 45, 47.
Blücher, Marshal, 231, 232-235, 237, 239, 244-246.
Bolingbroke, Lord, 48, 79.
Bonaparte, Joseph, 203, 236.
Bonaparte, Napoleon. See Napoleon, Emperor.
Bonn, capture of, 44.
Bordeaux, occupation of, by the Allies, 237.
Borodino, battle of the, 228.
Boscawen, Admiral the Hon. Edward, 94, 103, 104.

Bosphorus, the, troops from India sent to support the fleet in, 284.
Boulogne, 190, 191 — Napoleon baffled on the coast of, 210.
Bourbon, Philip of. See Philip V. of Spain.
Bourbon kings, the, 60, 77, 91, 97, 240, 244, 255, 275.
Braddock, General, in America, 93.
Brandenburg, Electorate of, 41, 177, 184, 185, 186.
Brazil, 268.
Brest, 177, 178, 182, 184, 185, 186.
Bridport, Admiral Viscount, 143.
Bristol merchants, 62.
Britain, Great, Allies of, under William III., 40—danger besetting it and its colonies, 89—gloomy prospects for, 97—a "nation of shopkeepers," 105—effects of the American war upon, 121—its relations with Turkey, 125, 126—position of, before the great war, 132 —summoned to administer the International Law of Europe, 133 —union with Ireland, 149—its coalition with Austria, Prussia, and Russia, 191—its commercial supremacy, 195—issues Orders in Council against neutrals, 211.
——, the British Empire founded by the aristocracy, 105.
——, the unity of the British Isles recovered by William III., 29. See also England.
British, the, and the Barbary pirates, 21 — Louis XIV. attempts to ruin the British, 23— outwitted by the French, 111.
British Allies, the, conquest of, by Napoleon, 157 — subjugation of, 190.
British Channel. See English Channel.
British colonies, the, remaining after the great Revolt, 150.
British commerce, 45, 46, 192— effect of the capture of Gibraltar on, 49, 50—Capt. Mahan's views on, 193 — British credit, 141 — complaints of British merchants, 72 — British concentration of trade, 212.
British goods, Continental depôts for, 195 — ordered by Napoleon to be burned, 214—British goods and subjects excluded from the Continent, 196—growth of British manufactories, 195.
British defence on shore, 173, 174.
British Foreign Policy, the principles of, before and during the reign of Elizabeth, 1-13,—under the Stuarts and Cromwell, 14-24, —under William III., 25-41—in the earlier part of the 18th century, 42-57—during the events which led to the war with Spain (in 1739), 58-86—during the wars which founded the Empire (1739-1763), 87-114 — from 1763-1789, 115-135 — during the French Revolution-war (1793-1800), 136-164—during the Napoleonic war (1798-1807), 165-197 — (1807-1808), 198-218 — (1808-1814), 219-238 — from 1814 to 1827, 239-260—after 1827, 261-287.
British Foreign Policy, attacks on, 134—continuity of, 250—represented by Lord Palmerston, 278 —not a Quixotic policy, 279— later foreign policy, 283 *et seq.*
British Mediterranean fleet drives the Egyptians out of Syria, 281.
British salt-fleet, the, convoyed by Durell, escape from two Spanish line-of-battle ships, 72.
British ships, capture and detention of, by the Spaniards, 71, 73— Walpole's conduct concerning the same, 74-81.
British strategy against Napoleon, 176 *et seq.*
Brittany, 4-6, 7.
Broke, Captain Philip, his victory in the Shannon, 254.
Brooke, Henry, his "Gustavus Vasa," 80.
Bruces, the, of Scotland, mischief caused by, in Ireland, 29.
Buckingham, George, Duke of, 18.
Bülow, General, 232, 237.
Burgundy, 40.
Burke, Edmund, his statements concerning the war of 1739 ac-

counted for, 83—his "Thoughts on a Regicide Peace," 156.
Burke, Edmund, mentioned, 27, 57, 79, 80, 83, 97, 117, 137, 140, 150, 172, 202, 204, 242.
Burmese war, the, 285.
Bute, John, Earl of, 115.
Byng, Admiral John, 102, 104, 112.
Byron, Lord, 192, 259, 270, 276.
Byzantine Empire, the, 261.

Cabot, Sebastian, and his father, 52.
Cadiz, 49, 182, 184, 187, 190.
Calais, 7.
Calder, Sir Robert, 185—his battle with Villeneuve and trial by court-martial, 186.
Calvin, John, 12.
Campbell, Thomas, the poet, 168.
Campeachy, Bay of, 72.
Camperdown, battle of, 158.
Canada, 53, 254—effects of the American war upon, 122, 123—French colony of, 109, 114.
Cannes, Napoleon at, 244.
Canning, Rt. Hon. George, 172, 215, 256, 257, 258, 259, 260, 265, 282, 287.
———, his training under Pitt, 202—his policy in the Peninsular War, 203-207—defence of the policy, 207-208—seizes the Danish fleet, 207—accepts Napoleon's challenge in Spain, 215—his duel with Lord Castlereagh, 220—in retirement, 221—his return to office, 256—deals with Spain and Portugal, 258—and with Greece, 258.
Cape Breton, island of, its fortifications strengthened, 109.
Cape of Good Hope, 199, 248.
Caribbean Seas, Governor-Generals of the, 62.
Carlos, Don, of Spain, 267.
Carteret, John, Lord Granville, 70, 79.
Castile, 6, 46, 47.
Castile and Aragon, feud between, 46, 217.
Castlereagh, Lord (1809), 220, 255—suicide of, 259.
Catalonia, 47, 237.

Cathcart, Lord, 207.
Catherine of Aragon, 10.
Catherine of Braganza, 130.
Catherine, Empress of Russia, 123, 125, 127, 167.
———, plots of, and Joseph II., Emperor, 127.
Cavour, Count de, 272, 274.
Ceylon, 170—acquired at the Peace of Amiens, 248.
Champagne, 237.
Charles I., of England, 17, 18, 55—adopts his father's mistaken foreign policy, 18.
Charles II., of England, 23, 24, 28, 55, 65, 130.
Charles V., Emperor, 7, 9, 238.
Charles VI., Emperor, 34, 46.
"Charles III.," of Spain, 46.
Charles the Bold, or the Rash, of Burgundy, 40.
Charles Albert, King of Sardinia, 272.
Charlotte, Princess, of England, 265.
Chatham, Earl of (William Pitt, the elder), 43, 83, 91, 93, 94, 95, 96, 98, 101-105, 111, 115, 116, 119, 120, 123, 125, 126.
———, offers to exchange Gibraltar for Minorca, 52—his policy touching the navy, 102-105—resumes power, 115. See also Pitt, William, the younger.
Chatillon, Congress of, 238, 239.
Chaumont, Treaty of, 238.
Chesapeake, the, Broke's victory over, 254.
Chesterfield, Lord, 99, 100.
China, 285.
Christian IV., King of Denmark, 18.
Christina, Queen of Spain, 267.
Cinque Ports, fleet of the, 4.
———, Volunteers, 173.
Ciudad Rodrigo, capture of, 228.
Civil War, the English, or Great Rebellion, 144.
Clarendon, Edward Hyde, Earl of, 23.
Clarkson, Thomas, 200.
Claverhouse, Lord, 31.
Clive, Lord, 93, 111.
Codrington, Christopher, 62, 201.

INDEX. 293

Codrington, Admiral Sir Edward, 260.
Collingwood, Admiral Lord, 143, 185–188.
Constantinople, 159, 160, 283, 286.
Constitutional freedom promoted by Lord Palmerston, 276.
Constitutionalism, 264 — triumph of, 267, 268, 277.
Constitutionalists in Spain, their struggle with the Absolutists, 258.
Continent, the, state of, at William III.'s death, 37, 38.
Continental Powers, English alliances with, continued necessity of, 3.
"Continental System," the, and British commerce, 210–212.
Coote, Sir Eyre, 93.
Copenhagen, the battle of, 168, 169.
Cornwallis, Charles, Marquis of, 95, 119, 123, 149, 160.
Cornwallis, Admiral, 177, 178, 180, 184, 186.
Cortes, Ferdinand, 53.
Cracow, seizure of, by Austria, 278.
'Craftsman,' the, 69.
Crimean war, the, 128, 263, 274, 282, 284.
Cromwell, Oliver, 18–21, 23, 55, 100, 130—in his foreign policy supports France instead of Spain, 18—the "Cromwellian Settlement," 30.
Crown, address to the (1738), 78.
Culloden, battle of, 93.
Cumberland, William Augustus, Duke of, 93.
Curieux, the brig, her great service, 185.
Custozza, victory under Archduke Albert at, 272.
Cyprus, obtained for a British station by Lord Beaconsfield, 285.

Danube, the, Marlborough at, 43, 47.
Darien Expedition, William III.'s discouragement of the, 43.
"Declaration to the Nations" by the French Republic, 139.
Denmark, 16, 43, 123, 128, 167, 168, 169, 209 and note, 230, 234.

Denmark, seizure of the Danish fleet by Canning (1807), 181, 207–209.
D'Erlon, General, 245.
Dettingen, battle of, 94.
Directory, French Government called the, 160, 194.
Drake, Sir Francis, 12, 55, 174.
Dresden, the Allies defeated at, 231–232.
Dublin, Jacobin clubs at, 149.
Dunbar, in Scotland, Cromwell's victory of, 31.
Duncan, Adam, Lord, 143.
Dundas, Henry, Viscount, 185.
Dunkirk, 19, 80.
Dupleix, General, 109, 117.
Dupont, General, capture of his army, 215.
Durell, Captain Thomas, R.N., 72.
Dutch, the. See Holland.

East India Company, the, 89, 117.
Eastern Question, the, 262, 263, 280, 282, 285, 286—Lord Beaconsfield and, 284.
Ecclesiastical States, the, 157.
Edward III. and the Sovereignty of the Seas, 5.
Edward VI., King, 10, 52.
Egypt, 167, 178, 281—Napoleon's descent on, 159–161—the British in, 286.
Elba, island of, 171, 240, 243, 244.
Elbe, the river, 195, 211, 230.
Elizabeth, Queen, 2, 6, 8, 9, 14, 15, 28, 29, 52, 53, 55, 87, 125, 251, 267.
——, adopts the policy of Balance of Power, 9—a necessary policy for, 11, 12—her motives and means of action, 12—effects of her policy, 13—the Stuarts reverse her policy, 14—the causes of this, 15.
Elliott, General, Lord Heathfield, 120.
Emmet's rebellion in Ireland, 171.
England, the early kings Continental potentates, 3—the Flemish alliance with, 5—becomes a consolidated State, 6—claims the

sovereignty of the Narrow Seas, 20—the English retain the "honour of the flag" in the Dutch wars, 21. See also Britain, Great.

English or British Channel, the, 21, 127, 138, 147, 156.

Erfurt, Congress of (1808), 218.

Eugene, Prince of Savoy, 43, 48.

Europe—the "Concert of Europe," 7, 16, 129, 238—condition of, under Walpole, 64—scourged by Napoleon, 173—her coasts sealed against British commerce, 210—general rising of, 229.

———, low condition of European States in the Napoleonic war, 153.

Evans, General Sir De Lacy, 267.

Eylau, battle of, 198.

Falkland Islands, 132.
Faversham, 28.
Ferdinand I., Emperor, 10.
Ferdinand, Prince of Brunswick, 103.
Ferrol, 180, 185, 186.
Finland, 127.
Fitzgerald, Lord Edward, 149.
Flanders, 4, 5, 7, 8, 16, 40, 217.
Fleury, Cardinal, France under him, 61.
Flodden Field, battle of, 31.
Florence, Court of Tuscany at, 273.
Floridas, the, given up to France, 171.
Fouché, Joseph, 242.
Fox, Charles James, 126, 134, 135, 150, 171, 200.
———, failure of his India Bill, 123—Ministry of, 199—death of (1806), 202.
France, 4–11, 13, 16–19, 21, 22, 25, 30, 36, 38, 40, 45, 49, 50, 60, 61, 106, 108, 109, 112, 121, 123–133, 138–148, 151, 152, 155, 157, 165, 166, 171, 195, 198, 208, 233, 255–258, 264, 267, 269, 273, 274, 281.
———, unification of, 8 — Balance of Power held by, 17—the Restored Stuarts pensioned by, 22—the French attempts to ruin the Dutch and British, 23–24 — France under Cardinal Fleury, 61—secret treaty between France and Spain, 60—provocation to war on the part of France, 85—assists the revolt of the American colonies, 105—descents upon, 140—military eminence of, 145—effect of Napoleon's policy on the Continent, 213 — exhausted by the drain of men and money, 223, 224—the South French campaign, 236, 243—Government of Louis XVIII. formed, 240—charter of Constitution, 242 — saved by Talleyrand, 241 — Britain and Austria prevent the dismemberment of France, 242.

France, Revolution-war, 146–164.
———, the House of Representatives and the Senate demand the British Constitution, 242.
———, kings of, 3—Regent Orleans of, 97. See also French.
France, Isle of, 248.
Francis I., King of France, 9, 38, 41.
Frankfort, the Allies concentrate their forces at, 234.
Franks, the, 3.
Frederick the Great of Prussia, 101, 103, 125, 127—his extraordinary victories, 103.
Frederick, Prince of Wales, his death, 101.
French, the, gloomy prospects of, in 1811, 223.
———, separate action of the French and British in 1840, 281.
French and British strategy compared, 182.
French corsairs, the, after Trafalgar, 192.
French navy, the, demoralisation of, 143.
French Revolution, the, 132, 133, 145, 148, 270—Pitt's views on, 136, 137.
———, the second French Revolution, 264, 265, 271.
———, the third French Revolution, 272.
Frere, Right Hon. John Hookham, 215.
Friedland, battle of, 198.

INDEX. 295

Gaeta, Garibaldi marches upon, 275.
Galicia, West, 227.
Galisonière, 109.
Gallican liberties, the, 38, 166.
Galway, Lord, 48.
Gambier, Admiral Lord, 207.
Ganteaume, Admiral, 180, 182, 184.
Garibaldi, General, 271—in Sicily and Naples, 273, 275.
Gascony, 6, 53, 236.
George I., 37, 50, 51.
George II., 94, 101.
George III., 43, 115, 129, 173—his views on the revolt of the British colonists in America, 118, 119, 120.
George IV., 256, 257.
German States near the Rhine, 39.
Germany, 5, 6, 8, 11, 16, 17, 34, 45, 101, 151, 217, 227—National Assemblies of, 153—Protestant Powers of, 33, 38—rising of the West Germans, 233.
Ghent, Peace of, 254.
Gibraltar, 60, 67, 92, 106, 120, 122, 185.
——, capture of, 47—its importance, 48—its loss seriously felt by France and Spain, 49, 50—George I. offers to restore it, 51—Spanish siege of, 51—expense of, 51.
——, Straits of, 184, 188.
Glover, Richard, 79—his ballad of "Hosier's Ghost," 60, 80.
Gondomar, Spanish ambassador, 15, 17—reports that the English are a nation of shopkeepers, 15.
Gordon, Sir Arthur, afterwards Lord Stanmore, 282.
Granville, Lord. See Carteret.
Grattan's Parliament, 30.
Gravina, Admiral, 187.
Great Britain. See Britain.
"Greater Britain," 53, 286.
Greece, 53, 218, 268.
——, the ancient States of, 6.
——, is oppressed by Turkey, 256.
——, Greek insurrection against Turkey, 258, 259, 260—its independence, 263.
Grenville, George, 116.

Grenville, William, Lord, 199, 200.
Grey, Earl, the Reform Ministry of, 266.
Gross-Beeren, battle of, 232.
Grotius, Hugo, 63.
Grouchy, Marshal, 245, 246.
Guipuscoa, province of, 34.
Guise family, the, 22.
Gustavus Adolphus, King of Sweden, 18.
Gustavus IV., King of Sweden, 209.

Halifax, colony of, 110.
Hamburg, 176, 195.
Hanover, 43, 96, 101, 106, 114, 176, 251—its relation to Holland, 96, 97.
Hanse Towns, 176.
Hardenberg, Charles Augustus, Prince of, 227.
Hawke, Edward, Lord, 91, 94, 102, 104, 143, 174, 177, 180, 192.
Hawkins, Sir John, 12, 55.
Heligoland, 214, 248.
Henri IV., King of France, 13, 15, 17, 38—his position towards the Balance of Power, 15, 17.
Henry II. of England, 29.
Henry VII., 2, 6-9, 11, 52—his daughter Margaret, 31—adopts the policy of Balance of Power, 8-9.
Henry VIII., 2, 6, 9, 11, 52—promotes the policy of Balance of Power, 9.
Herbert, Admiral, Lord Torrington, 32.
Hesse, troops of, 43.
Highlanders, Scottish, 93.
Hohenlinden, battle of, 162, 167, 168.
Holland, 16, 19, 25, 33, 35, 37, 40, 61, 97, 105, 117, 123, 127, 130, 137, 140, 148, 158, 181, 195, 234, 243, 248, 249, 268.
——, the Dutch, 23, 24, 56, 108, 245.
——, the Dutch wars an episode, 19—the French attempts to ruin the Dutch, 23, 24—Holland ceases to be a great Power, 24—British alliance with, under William III.,

95—its relation to Hanover, 96—
failures in Holland, 144—Dutch
fleet at Camperdown, 158.
Holland, the Dutch garrisons in
frontier towns, 36.
———, the Dutch wars, 23, 24.
Holland, King of, 248.
"Holy Alliance," the, 255, 256,
259, 262, 264, 266, 269.
Home policy, basis of foreign, 13,
29, 42, 100, 149.
Hood, Admiral Lord, 143.
Hosier, Admiral, 58, 59, 60—catastrophe of his fleet, 59.
Howe, Admiral Earl, 91, 103, 143,
174, 193.
Huguenots, the, 18, 38.
Hungary, 43.
Huy, 44.

Illyria, defended by Beauharnais,
234.
"Imperial Federation," 150.
India, 122, 123, 149, 159, 160, 193,
199, 219, 248, 281, 285.
———, the three presidencies of, 89,
90—French attack on the colonists in, 109—effects of the war
upon, 122, 123—organisation of,
149.
Indian Ocean, the, 108.
International Law, 7, 106, 128, 129,
133.
Intervention, exceptional policy of,
266.
Ionian Islands, 177.
Ireland, 1, 5, 11, 13, 29, 30, 35, 42,
99, 163, 171, 178.
———, historical relations with England, 29—its state under Lord
Chesterfield, 99—after American
war torn by factions, 100—Rebellion of, 148—Orange lodges, 148,
149.
Italy, 6, 8, 16, 22, 34, 39, 43, 46,
60, 122, 159, 162, 167, 230,
234, 239, 243, 249, 250, 268-
278.
———, British commerce with, 49.
———, oppressed by Austria, 256.
———, the state of, after 1815, 268—
Austrian influence in, 269—liberation of, 272-278.

Jacobites, the, 36.
Jacobitism, 142, 148.
Jamaica, 59, 72.
———, capture of, 55.
James I., King of England, 17, 18,
20, 30, 31, 53, 55.
———, (as James VI., King of Scots),
14, 15, 31.
James II., 23, 26, 28-30, 35, 42,
100—as Duke of York, 23—his
son James Edward, 36 — his
daughter Mary, 25.
James IV., King of Scotland, his
marriage, 31.
Japan, 285.
Jenkins, Captain, 57, 58, 64.
Jesuits, the, 27, 38.
———, expelled from Portugal, 131.
———, Jesuit missionaries, the,
110.
Jonquière, M., 109.
Joseph II., Emperor, 127.
Joseph Bonaparte, King of Spain,
235, 236.
Josephine, Empress, 226.
Junot, Marshal, army of, 210.
Jutes, the 53.

Kainardji, Peace of, 126, 261.
Katzbach, battle of, 232.
Keene, Benjamin, British ambassador in Spain, 70.
Keppel, Viscount, Admiral, 91, 103.
Khedive, the, and Arabi's rebellion,
287.
Kremlin, the, at Moscow, 229.
Kutusoff, General, retreat of his
army, 228.

La Harpe, John Francis de, 242.
Lally, Count de, 109.
Landen, battle of, 33.
Laybach, Congress of, 258.
Leake, Admiral Sir John, 48.
Legitimists in Spain, the, 267.
Leipsic, the battle of, 232, 233, 236.
———, the fair of, 225.
Leopold of Saxe-Coburg, Prince,
265.
Leslie, Alexander, Earl of Leven,
Cromwell's victory over him
(1653), 31.
Lestock, Admiral, 91.

INDEX.

Levant, the, 88, 171, 261, 281—British commerce with, 49, 106.
Liége, capture of, 44.
Ligny, Prussians beaten at, 246.
Limbourg, capture of, 44.
Lisbon, 47, 130, 247—earthquake at, 131.
Liverpool, Earl of, 220.
Livonia, 17, 41.
Lodi, victory of, 167.
Lombardy, 34, 275, 278.
London, the people's ovation to the French minister in, 196.
London merchants, 62.
Londonderry, Marquess of, 265.
Lorraine, 40, 97—France secures the reversion of, 61.
Louis, Prince Royal of France, 4.
Louis XIV., King, 19, 22-26, 32-36, 38, 39, 44, 45, 55, 61, 88, 108, 155, 170, 198, 203, 238.
———, grasps at the Spanish and British Empires, 35—and thereby ruins France, 36—makes Toulon a fortified naval arsenal, 49.
Louis XV., 108.
Louis XVIII., forced to accept a charter, 240.
Louis Napoleon, Emperor of the French, 273, 274, 281.
Louis Philippe, King of France, 265, 281.
Louisbourg, 109.
Louisiana, 109—given up to France, 171.
Low Countries, 4, 5, 8, 13, 93, 95, 138, 155, 157, 159, 164, 171, 205, 219, 225, 248, 249, 264, 267. See Netherlands and Holland.
Lowe, Sir Hudson, 247.
Lunéville, Treaty of, 167.
Lützen, battle of, 231.
Luxemburg, 40.
Lyons, Gulf of, 138.

Macaulay, Lord, 146, 171.
Macdonald, Marshal, 232.
Maddalena Islands, 178.
Madrid, 73, 228, 235.
Magenta, battle of, 275.
Mahan, Captain (on Sea-Power), 32, 92, 169 note, 175, 177, 178, 180, 190, 193, 194, 209 note, 252.

Mahratta Princes, the, 160.
Malacca, 248.
Malmesbury, 1st Earl of, 207.
Malta, 92, 122, 162, 167, 169 note, 170, 214, 248.
Malta, Knights of, 22, 167.
Manufactories, growth of British, 195.
Marengo, victory at, 162, 167.
Margaret, daughter of Henry VII., wife to James IV. of Scotland, 31.
Maria, Queen of Portugal, 267, 280.
Maria Theresa, Empress, 112.
Marlborough, John, Duke of, 35-37, 43, 47, 51, 83, 93.
———, at the head of the Allies, 43—success of his campaigns, 45, 48.
Marmont, Marshal, 228.
Martinique, island of, 182—Villeneuve at, 184.
Mary Stuart, wife of Francis II., King of France, afterwards Queen of Scots, 10, 22, 23.
Mary I., Queen of England, 10.
Mary II., daughter of James II., 25.
Masséna, Marshal, 222.
Mathews, Admiral, 84, 91—his battle off Toulon, 94.
Maximilian, Emperor, 6, 9.
Mazzini, 271, 276.
Mediterranean, the, 8, 22, 34, 88, 91, 92, 97, 106, 108, 112, 114, 128, 130, 141, 159, 162, 167, 178, 184, 185, 187, 188, 193, 213, 248, 261, 276.
———, English commerce in, 46—defence of, 46—its control, 52—attempt to close it, 112—effects of the war upon, 122—British supremacy in, 122, 162, 281.
Mehemet Ali, of Egypt, 263, 281.
Messina, Straits of, 275.
Methuen Treaty (Portugal), 46, 130, 131.
Metternich, Prince, 193, 233, 269, 270.
Mexico, 200—the Gulf of, 53, 54, 59, 63.
Middleton, Sir Charles, afterwards Lord Barham, First Lord of the Admiralty, 185.
Miguel, Don, of Spain, 267.
Milan Decree, the, 194, 210.

Militia, the, organisation of, 100, 101 note.
Ministry, the Fox and Grenville, 199.
Minorca, island of, 48, 52, 60, 67, 92, 106—loss of, 122
Minto, Gilbert, Earl of, 273, 277.
Mirabeau, 241.
Mississippi, the, 109.
Monk, George, Duke of Albemarle, 21, 23, 31, 144.
Monmouth, Duke of, rebellion of, 26.
Montagu, Earl of Sandwich, Admiral, 21, 23.
Montmartre, storming of, 239.
Moore, General Sir John, 146, 220 —in Sweden, 209.
Moors, the, in Spain and Portugal, 8, 130.
Morea, 177.
Moreau, General, 162, 167—at the battle of Dresden, 232.
Mornington, Earl of, 160.
Moscow, 226, 229, 242.
Munster, Treaty of, 56.
Murat, Prince, 234.
Muscovy, 17. See Russia.

Namur, victory of, 33.
Napier, Admiral Sir Charles, 268.
Napier's "Peninsular War," 215, 216.
Naples, 60, 123, 151, 170, 275.
Napoleon I., Emperor of the French, 135, 139, 146, 157, 158, 160, 184, 187, 189, 194, 221, 247, 251, 252, 270, 274, 280.
Napoleon, his descent on Egypt, 159 —his *coup d'état*, 161—turns on Austria and Russia, 161 — becomes First Consul, 165—reforms and victories of, 166, 167 — his acts during Peace of Amiens, 170 — prepares to invade England, 171—his strategy, 175—plans to invade England, 176—motives of his policy, 180-182, 190—forces Britain to continue the war, 196 — the struggle with Napoleon, not with the French people, 197 —Fox negotiates with him, 199 —attempts to conquer Spain, 203 — concludes with Russia the Peace of Tilsit, 206—hopes by the new Continental system to ruin British commerce, 210, 211 — unable to prevent organised smuggling, 212 — orders all British goods to be burned, 214 —he seizes Spain, 215—his overtures to Canning, 218—resolves to fight Russia before driving the British out of Spain, 223—finds difficulty in obtaining soldiers, 223—his exactions in Spain, 224 —incorporates the Low Countries, 225—mixed nationalities of his army, 227 — his fatal march to Moscow, 229 — the cause of his quarrel with the Czar, 229 — general rising in Europe against him, 230—defeats Allies at Dresden, 231, 232 — is defeated at Leipzic, 232—Allies press their advantage on, 235—he abdicates, 237—escapes from Elba, 243— advances from Cannes, 244—defeated at Waterloo, 245, 246— final abdication of, 247—banished to St. Helena, 247.
Narborough, Admiral Sir John, 22.
Narrow Seas, the, 63, 64.
National Debt, the, 116, 134, 142.
Navarino, battle of, 260, 262, 281.
Navy, the Royal, necessity of a standing navy, 3 — the "Royal Navy of the Cinque Ports," 4— better than that of other nations, *ib.*—deplorable state of, 90—reform of the Navy the keystone of the national success, 91—Pitt's policy concerning the navy, 102 —supremacy of, 105, 114, 140—at its height of efficiency, 143, 144 —mutinies in, 157—efficiency of naval defence, 174 — disposition of the British fleets against Napoleon, 177.
Negroes, African, 67. See also Slavery.
Nelson, Horatio, Lord, 89, 93, 143, 158, 160, 168, 174-179, 182-189, 192, 196, 220.
———, and the Nile, 160-162, 281— his fleet off Toulon, 178 — his

blockade of Toulon, 179—pursues Villeneuve, 184—his foresight, 185—his strategy, 188.
Nelson, see Trafalgar.
Netherlands, the, 25, 34, 43, 91, 127, 138, 156, 249.
New England States, the, 254.
New Orleans, defence of, 254.
Ney, Marshal, 232, 245.
Nicholas I., Czar, 263.
Niemen, the river, 206.
Nimeguen, Peace of, 170.
Nive, the battle of the, 236.
Nivelle, the battle of the, 236.
Nootka Sound, 132.
Nore, Mutiny of the, 157.
Norman Conquest, the, 1, 20, 155.
Normandy and the Normans, 2–6.
North, Lord, 117, 119, 120.
Norway, 209, 234.
Novara, battle of, 272.
Nova Scotia, the French in, 110, 111.
Nugent, the poet, 80.

Oczakoff, capture of, 126.
Oldenburg, seizure of, 225.
Onslow, Speaker, 78.
"Orange Lodges" formed by the Irish Protestants, 148.
Orleanists, the, 267.
Orthez, battle of, 236.
Otranto, peninsula of, 176.
Ottoman Empire, the, 38, 41, 126, 261, 262, 285. See also Turkey.
Oudinot, Marshal, 232.

Palatine, the Elector and the Electress, 17.
Palmerston, Lord, 266, 268, 273, 278, 280–282, 284, 285, 287— pursues Canning's policy, 266— becomes Foreign Secretary, 266, 270—Palmerston and Cavour, 274 — promotes constitutional freedom, 277.
Pampelona, surrender of, 236.
Panama, the fair of, 68.
Papacy, the, and Papists, 14, 17, 147, 277.
Papal States, the, 6, 15.
Pardo, Convention of, 79, 83.
Paris, 45, 239, 244, 247.

Paris, Treaties of, 106, 115, 248, 249, 284.
Parker, Admiral Sir Hyde, 168.
Parkes, Sir Harry, 285.
Parliament, petitions to, on the seizure of British ships, 73—the Long Parliament, 130—the "Pension Parliament," 23.
Parliamentary debates, quoted, 72, 76–79.
Partition Treaties, the, 46—made for the sake of the Mediterranean policy, 33, 34.
"Patriots," the, 72.
Paul, Czar of Russia, 162, 167, 168.
Peace, policy of, under James I., 14, 15, 55.
Pelham, Thomas, Duke of Newcastle, Administration of, 111–112.
Pellico, Silvio, 270.
Penal laws against Papists, 147.
Peninsular war, the, 155, 215–236 —later troubles in Spain and Portugal, 263–268.
Perceval, Spencer, assassinated (1812), 220.
Persia, 41, 46.
Peter the Great, Emperor of Russia, 41, 125.
Peterborough, Lord, 47, 48.
Pett, family of, shipbuilders, 21.
Philip II., King of Spain, 10, 16, 44, 46, 52, 198, 238.
Philip V. of Spain, 34, 35, 45, 66, 67.
Picardy, 4.
Pilnitz, Treaty of, 136.
Pitt, William, the elder. See Chatham, Earl of.
Pitt, William, the younger, 123, 131, 134, 136–140, 157, 163, 170, 172–174, 185, 192, 204, 221, 287.
Pitt, William, the younger, his successful policy, 128—general view of his foreign policy, 129— unfair literary treatment of his war measures, 146—his India Bill, 123, 149—his alliances, 151 —his efforts to make peace, 155 —resumes office, 174—his earlier peace administration, 131, 195— his death (1806), 196—failure of

his successors, 199 — Canning's training under him, 202—foresaw the Peninsular war, 205 note—his spirit as seen in Canning, 218.
Pius IX. (Pio Nono), Pope, 271.
Pizarro, Francis, 53.
Plantagenets, the, 5, 20.
Plumer, Mr., 77.
Pocock, Admiral Sir George, 91, 94, 103.
Poerio, Carlo, 270.
Poland, 17, 41, 127, 136, 227, 249—partition of, 125—its oppression by Prussia, 256—British sympathy with, 280.
Pombal, Marquis de, 131.
Pomerania, exchange of, for Norway, 234.
Popes, the, 6, 16, 27, 42, 272, 273.
Porte, the, 125, 126, 261, 262, 282.
Portland, William, 3rd Duke of, 150, 202.
Port Mahon harbour, 48, 49, 111.
Porto Bello, harbour of, 80—blockade and capture of, 58, 69.
Portugal, 20, 46, 53, 104, 108, 123, 130, 151, 206, 217, 280 — its friendly relations with Great Britain, 130—is seized by the French, 210.
Portuguese colonies in America, 53.
Pragmatic Sanction, the, 112.
Press, the French charter providing for liberty of the, 240.
Pretender, the (James Edward Stuart), 36.
Pretender, the Young, 85, 100.
Protestantism, British defence of, 106.
"Protestant Ascendancy" in Ireland, 42.
Protestants of Europe, 11.
——, of Germany and France, 15.
Prussia, 17, 40, 43, 84, 103, 114, 123, 125, 151, 157, 159, 167, 191, 226, 227, 230, 233, 255, 256, 258, 263, 276.
Pulteney, William, Earl of Bath, 74, 77, 79.
Pyrenees, the, 203, 236.

Quadruple Alliance of 1718, the, 51.
——, 1834, the, 267.
Quiberon, battle of, 104, 177.

Radetzky, Marshal, 272, 278.
Rebellion, the Great, 14, 18, 31.
——, the Scottish, of 1745, 84, 98, 99, 100.
Reform Bill, the, a literary epoch, 134.
Reformation, the, 6, 10, 14, 38.
Renaissance, the, 9.
Restoration, the, 19, 22, 54.
Revolution, the English, 54, 89, 90, 264.
Revolution, French. See under France.
Rhenish Confederation, 40, 198, 233.
Rhine, the, 39, 157, 233, 234, 239, 243—the Allies cross it, 237.
Richard II., his reign, 4.
Richelieu, Cardinal, 17, 18, 39.
Right of Search, the British, 124, 144, 254—the Spanish exercise of, 56, 57, 64, 79.
Roberts, Lord, his estimate of Napoleon and Wellington, 247.
Rochefort, 102, 184.
Rochelle, 18.
Rodney, Admiral Lord, 103, 120, 143, 174.
Roman Catholic Emancipation, 170.
Roman Catholic Powers in the 18th century, the, 38.
Roman Empire, 2, 6, 39.
Romanism, 14.
Rome, 170, 273, 275.
Rooke, Admiral Sir George, 48.
Rosilly, Admiral, 187.
Rousseau, 127.
Rupert, Prince, 23.
Russell, Admiral, Lord Orford, 32.
Russia, 40, 138, 151, 162, 167, 191, 214, 231, 233, 235, 245, 255, 258, 259, 262, 263, 284.
——, becomes a great Power in the Baltic, 125 — protectorate over Christian provinces of Turkey abolished, 128—Convention between Russia and Great Britain (1801), 169 note—is defeated at Eylau and Friedland, 198—allies with Napoleon, 206—revolts from

INDEX. 301

the French alliance, 224—Napoleon's invasion of, 227—Russian strategy, 228—forward march of the Russians, 230—the Crimean war against, 274, 282.
Ryswick, Peace of, 33.

St. Helena, Napoleon at, 247.
St. Lawrence, the river, 108, 109.
St. Lucia, island of, 248.
St. Vincent, Cape, battle of, 158.
St. Vincent, Admiral Earl, 176, 178.
Salamanca, battle of, 228, 235.
Sal Tortugas, islands of, 72.
San Sebastian, storming of, 236.
Saragossa, siege of, 215.
Sardinia, kingdom of, 60, 151, 272-275, 278—coast of, 178, 188.
Sarpi, Fra, 38.
Saunders, Admiral Sir Charles, 91.
Savoy, Duchy of, 16—princes of, 270.
Savoy and Nice annexed by France, 275.
Saxe, Marshal, 85.
Saxons, the, 53.
Saxony, 230, 249.
Scharnhorst, 227.
Schwartzenberg, Prince, 233, 237—his army, 231.
Scotland, 13, 31, 43—its union with England, 31, 43, 98, 151.
"Sea-Power," doctrine of, 92.
"Seas, Sovereignty of the," an acknowledged English right, 20, 21, 63, 64.
Sebastiani, General, agent of Napoleon, 171.
Secret Societies of Italy, 270.
Sepoy mutiny, the, 285.
Seven Years' War, 91, 94, 104-106, 112, 126, 151, 180.
——, Treaty concluding the, 106—its effects, 114.
Seville, Treaty of, 74, 75
Shannon, the frigate, Broke's victory over the Chesapeake in, 254.
Ship-money of Charles I., 21.
Ships, colonies, and commerce, British policy with regard to, 89, 102, 140—the English ships superior to the Dutch, 21.

Sicily and the Sicilies, 6, 108, 122, 269, 272.
Sikh war, the, 285.
Slavery, responsibilities of the English for, 200-202.
Slave-trade, abolition of the, 200, 202, 207, 268—the Abolition Act, 202.
Smith, Sir Sidney, 161, 177.
Smolensk, storming of, 228, 242.
Smuggling of British goods into the ports of Europe, 54, 64, 65, 70—licensed by Napoleon, 213.
Society for the Propagation of the Gospel, 201.
Solferino, battle of, 275.
Soult, Marshal, 236, 237, 245.
South Sea Company, the English, 67.
Spain, 5-10, 12, 13, 15, 16, 18-22, 30, 33-35, 52, 53, 58, 59, 96, 105, 106, 108, 109, 130, 132, 148, 151, 158, 159, 171, 243.
——, Spaniards in Ireland, 13—failure of the Allies in, 47—capture of Gibraltar from, 47—attitude as to British commerce, 55—secret treaty between France and Spain, 60—Spanish insults to the English, 69—Napoleon attempts to conquer Spain, 203—the "Spanish ulcer," 204—later interference of France in, 256—invaded by the French, 259. See Peninsular War.
Spain, Queen of, wife of Philip V., 51.
Spanish Bourbons, the, 269.
Spanish colonies and colonists in America, 53, 57, 65, 68, 200.
Spanish treatment of British claims in West Indies, 52-86.
Spanish ships in Villeneuve's fleet, 180, 181.
Spanish Legion, the, 267.
Spanish peninsula, the, 205, 257, 259, 265.
Spanish prisons, 64.
Spanish Succession, the war of the, 45-50, 216, 217.
Spanish Treaties of 1667 and 1670, 65.
Spithead, Mutiny of, 157—the fleet at, described by Metternich, 193.

302 INDEX.

Stair, John, 2nd Earl of, 93, 95.
Stamp Act, the American, 118.
Stanhope, James, 1st Earl, 48, 51.
———, Philip Henry, 5th Earl, 134.
Stein, Baron von, 227, 235.
Steinkirk, battle of, 33.
"Storm of Nations," the (1813), 152.
Stuarts, the, 2, 6, 8, 14, 38, 87, 96 — pensioned by France after the Restoration, 22, 23.
Subsidies, discussion of the policy of, 152 — system of subsidies broken up, 198.
Suchet, Marshal, 237.
Suez Canal shares, bought up by Lord Beaconsfield, 285.
Sully, Duke of, 15, 16, 17, 129—his doctrine of the Balance of Power, 15, 129.
Sweden, 16, 123, 125, 167, 169 note, 209, 230.
Swiss and Lorrainers, the, conquer Charles the Bold, 40.
Switzerland, 16, 40, 162, 171, 237, 243, 280.
Syria, Egyptians driven out of, 281.

Tagus, the, 210, 211.
Talavera, battle of, 221.
Talleyrand, 205 note, 241, 265.
Tartars, the, 41, 126.
Tencin, Cardinal, Prime Minister of France, 85.
Teneriffe, Spanish commerce interrupted by Blake at, 55.
Thiers, Louis Adolphe, 281.
Thirty Years' War, the, 19.
Tilsit, Treaty of, 206, 207.
Tippoo Sultan, 160.
Tobago, island of, 248.
Töplitz, Treaty of, 233.
Torres Vedras, 222, 228.
Toulon, 49, 84, 104, 111, 174, 178-184—Mathews' battle off, 84, 94 —Nelson's fleet off, 178.
Toulouse, battle of, 237, 247.
Tourville, Admiral de, 32.
Townshend, Charles, Secretary of State, 116.
Trade, West Indian, 51—change from quasi-free to restricted British trade, 66—working of the new system, 67—hopelessness of its improvement, 69. See West Indies.
Trafalgar, battle of, 89, 175, 181, 182, 186, 188, 189, 191, 195, 209, 252.
Transylvania, 17.
Trent affair, the (United States), 284.
Tréville, Latouche, Admiral, 178, 179.
Trinidad, island of, 170, 185—acquired at the Peace of Amiens, 248.
Tripoli, 22.
Troppau, Congress of, 258.
Tudor foreign policy, the, 2, 9, 10, 13, 14, 23, 25, 42.
Tudors, the, 20, 23, 30, 87.
Tunis, 22.
Turin, Parliament at, 275 — Lord Minto at, 273.
Turkey, 46, 126, 128, 159, 171, 199, 263, 281—its relations with Great Britain, 125, 126—is saved by Pitt, 128—Greek insurrection against, 259—tyranny of, 260—Egyptian invasion of, 281—"Protectorship" of, 280.
Turkey merchants, 126.
Turkish fleets, destruction of, 126, 281.
Turks, the, 9, 38, 259-263.
Tuscany, 151—court of, 273.

United Provinces. See Holland.
United States, 121-123, 142, 194—establishment of their independence, 120, 122—causes of the war with, in 1812, 197—resent the British Orders in Council, 252—the war of 1812, 252-254—non-intervention in the, 283.
Utrecht, Peace of, 17, 41, 48, 66, 67, 85, 95, 110, 131, 200, 250.

Vendôme, Marshal, victory of, 48.
Venetia, 275, 276, 278.
Venice, 9, 16, 38.
Vernon, Admiral, 79, 84.
Verona, Congress of, 259, 266.
Versailles, Peace of, 120, 122, 123, 125.
Victor Emmanuel, King of Italy, 272, 274, 275.

INDEX.

Victoria, Queen, 281, 284.
Vienna, Congress of, 243, 247, 255 —Treaties of, 61, 96, 159, 164, 165, 238, 249, 278.
Villafranca, Peace of, 275.
Villeneuve, Admiral, 180-185 *et seq.*—escapes from Nelson, 179, 183—loses his opportunity, 186, 187.
Vittoria, battle of, 235.
Voltaire, 127.

Wager, Admiral Sir Charles, 90.
Wales, conquest of, 5.
Walmer Castle, Pitt at, 173, 174.
Walpole, Sir Robert, 57, 58, 60, 61, 74, 81, 82, 100, 102, 111.
——, his timid policy, 72—his conduct on the seizure of British ships by the Spaniards, 74-81—is attacked on all sides, 77—his final blunder, 79—resigns, 82—his fall, 97 — imbecility of his later foreign policy, 112.
War, Declaration of, issued by Walpole, 81.
War of Liberation, the (1813), 230.
Warbeck, Perkin, 29.
Warren, Admiral Sir Peter, 91, 94.
Washington, capture of, 254.
Washington, George, 95, 119.
Waterloo, battle of, 246, 247, 282.
Wellesley, Sir Arthur, afterwards Duke of Wellington, 95, 146, 155, 199, 220, 235, 236, 243-249, 260, 262, 265, 266.
——, Secretary for Ireland (1807), 202,—the "Iron Duke," 216—early training in India, 219—succeeds Canning as the national representative, 220—first victories in Spain, 220—bears the whole responsibility of the Peninsular War, 222—carries the war into France, 235-237—correspondence of his victories with the movements of the Allies, 235—at Vienna, 243—at Verona, 259, 266 —his opinion of Talleyrand, 264. See Waterloo.
Wellesley, the Marquess, 219, 205 note—his rule in India, 199—superior to Canning as to Spauish policy, 218.
Wellington, Duke of. See Wellesley, Sir Arthur.
Weser, the river, 195, 211.
West Indies, the, 19, 51-55, 61, 111, 117, 123, 124, 170, 171, 180, 184, 188, 193, 200, 201, 248.
——, Spain and Great Britain in, 52—trade of, 55, 62—settlement of English, French, and Dutch in, 63—British right of trade in, 72—petition from West India merchants, 73, 80.
Westphalia, Peace of, 17.
Wexford, rising in, 149. See Ireland.
Whigs, the, the service done by, 26 —their patriotism, 150, 202.
Whitworth, Lord, 171.
Wight, Isle of, 193.
Wilberforce, William, 157, 200, 203.
William III., King, 40, 42, 45, 46, 62, 83, 85, 87, 88, 95, 97, 100, 264.
——, "the Deliverer" of England, 26—restores English supremacy in Ireland, 30 — and practical unity with Scotland, 31—secures the Channel, 32 — his military headship of the Allies, 33—unpopularity of, 35.
William IV., King, 266.
Wolfe, General, 93, 102, 104, 114, 120, 122, 192.
Wolsey, Cardinal, 10.
Wyndham, Sir William, 74, 77, 80.

York, Frederick, Duke of, 95, 146, 219.
Yorktown, Lord Cornwallis' surrender at, 95.

www.ingramcontent.com/pod-product-compliance
Lightning Source LLC
Chambersburg PA
CBHW022045230426
43672CB00008B/1073